Understanding Intranets

Tyson Greer

PUBLISHED BY
Microsoft Press
A Division of Microsoft Corporation
One Microsoft Way
Redmond, Washington 98052-6399

Library of Congress Cataloging-in-Publication Data
Greer, Tyson, 1943-
    Understanding Intranets / Tyson Greer.
      p.   cm.
    Includes index.
    ISBN 1-57231-702-7
    1. Intranets (Computer networks)   I. Title.
  TK5105.875.I6G74   1998
  650'.0285'46--dc21   97-38785
                                                CIP

Printed and bound in the United States of America.

1 2 3 4 5 6 7 8 9 QMQM 3 2 1 0 9 8

Distributed to the book trade in Canada by Macmillan of Canada, a division of Canada Publishing
Corporation.

A CIP catalogue record for this book is available from the British Library.

Microsoft Press books are available through booksellers and distributors worldwide. For further
information about international editions, contact your local Microsoft Corporation office. Or contact
Microsoft Press International directly at fax (425) 936-7329. Visit our Web site at mspress.microsoft.com.

FoxPro, FrontPage, Microsoft, PowerPoint, Visual Basic, Visual FoxPro, Windows, and Windows NT
are registered trademarks and ActiveX, Authenticode, NetMeeting, NetShow, Outlook, Visual
InterDev, Visual J++, and Visual SourceSafe are trademarks of Microsoft Corporation.

Other product and company names mentioned herein may be the trademarks of their respective owners.

Acquisitions Editor: Eric Stroo
Project Editor: Saul Candib

*I would like to dedicate this book to my delightful
Dad who, at the age of 88, allowed me to bully him
into getting an e-mail account.*

Table of Contents

Acknowledgments   xiii

Chapter One

Intranet Basics 1

Intranet Defined   2
A Network by Any Other Name   10
Productivity   14
Four Major Productivity Applications   17
Benefits from Multiple Points of View   19
Push and Pull Concepts   27
What Are the Most Compelling
  Reasons to Shift to an Intranet?   29
Conclusion   32

Chapter Two

From Mainframe Culture to Internet Technologies 35

Hosts and Hierarchies—Command
  and Control   37
Network Computing—Economics
  of Sharing   45
The Network Solution   48
Network Communications   51
Network Functionality   54

Network System Management   56

A Bouillabaisse of
   Computing Technologies   60

Internet-Intranet Technology Basics   61

Conclusion   66

Looking Ahead   67

Chapter Three

The Extranet Option 69

Defining an Extranet   70

Overview of Extranet Issues   73

Anatomy of an Extranet   74

Software and Server Compatibility 74

Security Measures   77

IP-Based Network Connections   77

Performance and Support—The
   Main Reasons to Outsource
   an Extranet   82

Are You Ready For An Extranet?   84

How Could You Use An Extranet?   84

Technical Restraints to Extranet
   Development   90

Extranet Planning Overview   90

Looking Ahead   91

Chapter Four

Risks and Mitigation Strategies 93

A Goal-Oriented Approach
   to Intranet Security   94

Overview—Avenues of Risk   96

The Changing Hacker Community   101

Protection Basics   102

Setting up Structural Safeguards
    with Firewall Systems   106

User and Data Authentication   110

Protecting Data with Encryption   116

Designing a Strategy   120

Evaluating the Costs and Risks   125

Official Assistance   126

Looking Ahead   128

Chapter Five

Using an Intranet for Quick Publishing 131

Quick Publishing Defined   132

Advantages   134

The Process of Quick Publishing   148

Static and Dynamic Pages   157

Looking Ahead   161

Chapter Six

Using an Intranet for Information Management 163

Who Needs What Information?   164

Acquiring Types of Data   169

Organizing and Integrating the Data   182

Easy Access to Information   194

Looking Ahead   209

Chapter Seven

Knowledge-Working 211

Definition	212
Before Intranets	213
Intranet Opportunities for Knowledge-Working	214
Conferencing	216
Virtual Meetings	222
Workflow	225
For Managers—Program Management and Decision Support	228
What Are the Challenges?	230
Solving the Downside of Collaborating	232
Looking Ahead	233

Chapter Eight

Distance Learning Systems on an Intranet 235

Definitions	238
Foundations for Web-based Distance Learning	238
Web-based Distance Learning Environment	242
Learning Models for Teams or Individuals	247
Modular Courseware—Learning Objects	249
Cost Effectiveness—What Can You Save?	249

Adapting to a Virtual Teaching
    Environment   251

Looking Ahead   252

Chapter Nine

Planning 253

Overview   254

Determine the Purpose   255

Define the Audience   257

Design the Look and Feel   263

Apply User-Centered Design
    Principles   266

Looking Ahead   268

Chapter Ten

Launching a Pilot Project 269

Addressing the
    Return on Investment Dilemma   270

Focusing on Functional
    Business Requirements   271

Choosing the Project and
    Developing a Marketing Plan   275

Measuring for Success   279

Assembling the Resources   280

Developing a Usability Analysis   283

Identifying Lessons Learned   285

Selling the Intranet—Steering
    the Change   285

Looking Ahead   286

Chapter Eleven

Building a Business Case 287

Handling Resistance   288

Identifying Assumptions   292

Examining the Cost   293

Reducing Total Cost of Ownership   295

Measuring Intranet Productivity   299

Saving Paper and Gaining
   Efficiencies   300

Questioning the Cost of Not
   Adopting   302

Looking Ahead   303

Chapter Twelve

Implementing Your Intranet 305

Decide Who Is In Charge   306

Create the Team   307

Set Technology Standards   312

Set Policies and Procedures   321

Move from "Nice to Have" to
   "Business-Critical"   326

Consider the Costs   327

Address Performance Issues   327

Looking Ahead   329

Chapter Thirteen

Maintenance and Evaluation 331

Outsourcing and Out-tasking   332

Updating Web Pages and
   Controlling Change   337

Monitoring Performance   342

Maintaining Security   349

Looking Ahead   352

Chapter Fourteen

Looking Further Ahead 353

New E-Business Applications   354

Enhanced Data Displays   356

Convergence: More Data,
  More Access   357

Sophisticated Access Control   360

Sensory Enhancements   361

Dealing with Evolving Standards   363

Going Forward   364

Index   367

Acknowledgments

Thanks to the kindness of Microsoft's Sam Adkins, Acquisiton Editor Eric Stroo gave me the opportunity to write a Strategic Series book. I thank Eric and Project Editor Stuart Stuple for their guidance in shaping it. My thanks also to Steve Sagman, compositor extraordinaire for his sense of page and visual display, and to Travis Beaven, graphic artist, and Gail Taylor copy editor, and Jill McManus proofreader. I worked closely with Devra Hall, a project coordinator and technical editor who made my life a little more bearable for her ability to maintain good humor while inflicting deadlines. The book is better for her hand in it. If I have committed any technical misstatements on her watch, the mis-step is mine.

I am also indebted to two friends at Microsoft, Brad Hamilton and Donna Conner, for their loyal willingness to share their knowledge, comment chapters, and point me to numerous online and people resources. Such resources include Peter Wise, a valued presenter with the Microsoft Executive Briefing Center, who agreed to co-write Chapter 11, "Building a Business Case;" and Mark Spilde, who drew on his experience to co-write Chapter 12, "Implementing an Intranet." The support of two (non-Microsoft) writer friends—Luanne Brown and Phil Jennings, who connected me with Kirby Leeper—made this book easier to write. Kirby provided me with an excellent grounding in networks and intranet management. I also wish to acknowledge Richard Atkinson, Steve Cameron, and Ken Fenwick for their willingness to discuss their applications of intranet technologies in detail to further my understanding and to provide rich examples for others to learn from.

Writing this book led me to some wonderful people. Including them in the following list does not do justice to their generosity in sharing their knowledge: Air Products and Chemicals, Inc., Steve Cameron and Bob Majowicz; AltaVista, Ilene Lang and Brad Nelson; ARAMARK, Brian Gale, John Kallelis, and Ted Wagner; Amkor, Rob Bilson; Bank of Hawaii, Mark Williams and Derek Baughman; Baltimore Gas and Electric, Kim Ethridge; BC Hydro, Bill Fernihough and Steve Whan; Boeing, Chris Esposito; City of Vancouver, Scott Macrae; DataChannel, Jim Lyle; Data-Tronics, Diana Jones; Dixon Mastercare, Keith Martin-Smith; Georgia-Pacific West Inc., Aaron Bathum, Ryan Christian, and Mark Polhamus; Harris Corporation, Bill Monroe, Phil Blatchley, and Sheryl Olguin; Lakewood Community College, Bill Ryan; London Underground, Alec Bruty; North Slope School District, John Ringland; Northrop-Grumman, Richard Atkinson and Natalie Stone; Norwich-Union, Sue Winston; SAFECO, Ken Fenwick; Seattle Times, Tom Boyer; Warner Bros, Wendy Aylsworth; Weyerhaeuser, David Coburn and Earnest Phillips. I also wish to thank Derek Barron, Beth Beatty, Cindy Layner, Bob Metcalf, and T.V. Raman.

Three others deserve a special spotlight: My sons, Captain Erik for his habit of phoning in encouragement from base locations stateside and abroad, and Aaron for sharing his grasp of "things technical" even when fully immersed in his projects at Disney. And Jim, my husband, who surprised me repeatedly with my favorite maple Starbucks scones, and kept generating support as warmly as the sun and unfailingly as the Seattle rain.

Chapter One

Intranet Basics

Whoever it was who coined the term intranet should have his mechanical pencils taken away and his license to speak withdrawn for a month. If I had a dollar for every time someone has had to enunciate as precisely as Eliza Doolittle, "No, an inTRAnet—I'm not saying 'InTERnet'—we've got an inTRAnet…," I'd be writing this book on a laptop that even a Disney VR designer would admire. Legend has it that an unnamed person at Amdahl Corporation[1] coined this term referring to the company's internal network and, like an unfortunate childhood nickname, the word stuck.

In spite of the elocution challenge, many organizations are embracing intranets with an enthusiasm usually reserved for good news from Wall Street. By 1998, whether or not an organization has an intranet will be a determining factor in judging it as an old-world or a New Millennium organization. Actually, the *intra* and *inter* distinction is not unique to the world of computing. The Latin prefix *intra* means "within" and the prefix *inter* means "between," so it was always clear on the Star Trek series that an *inter*galactic voyage (one to other galaxies) was a longer journey than an *intra*galactic jaunt (one within the galaxy).

The words inTRAnet and InTERnet sound too much alike

---

1. Mellanie Hills relates this origin of the word "intranet" in her book *Intranet as Groupware*. Amdahl Corporation, based in Sunnyvale, California, provides hardware, middleware, and consulting services for computing-intensive environments.

Intranet Defined

An intranet uses Internet standards and protocols to foster efficient communication and collaboration

An intranet is a private computer network that uses Internet standards and protocols to enable members of an organization to communicate and collaborate more efficiently with one another, thereby increasing productivity.

Another name for an intranet is the corporate-wide Web— the corporate cybersite where business and communication take place. The nice thing is, you don't have to have a yard sale and get rid of all your existing network computing equipment in order to convert your local area network (LAN) or wide area network (WAN) to an intranet. Although intranets and traditional corporate networks are related, comparing them is like comparing apples and oranges. Unlike traditional networks, intranets rely on special open standard technologies and protocols (see "A Network by Any Other Name," page 10). Standards and protocols raise complex issues, and this subject will be addressed throughout this book.

Purpose

Intranets can save time and cut costs

An intranet is like a multi-purpose appliance: it can chop, slice, and dice the costs of communicating, sharing content, managing information, delivering training, and collaborating, both within an organization and with trusted external partners. However, it will not make good coffee or balance your budget!

Intranets can provide up-to-date information

With proper permission, individuals can retrieve up-to-date information about diverse topics and can collaborate with colleagues around the globe. Some of the activities and information that you might find on an intranet include:

- Company news
- Corporate policy
- Project management
- Workflow management

- Knowledge repositories
- Regulatory compliance status
- Just-in-time training
- Product and pricing information
- Shipping and inventory data
- Sales reports
- Claims processing
- Employee locator and skills directories
- Job postings
- Benefits enrollment
- Stock prices

Besides being a place to post information, an intranet can be a vehicle for hosting discussion groups or employee surveys (offering the added advantage of results posted immediately), scheduling meetings in a real conference room, ordering materials, and collaborating on designs or documents in a shared virtual space.

Intranets eliminate the distance barrier and speed up tasks

InTRAnet and InTERnet: Similarities and Differences

While the Internet and intranets share the same technologies, the biggest differences between the two are ownership and access.

The Internet is like a public park, while an intranet resembles a private club.

- The Internet is not owned by any one person or entity; anyone in the world with access to a computer, a modem, and a connection to either the Internet or an Internet service provider can join in and *surf the Net*. (If you want to host your own site, you also need to register a domain name.)
- An intranet is a private network, owned by the organization that it serves; access is by invitation only.

Depending on its design, an intranet can be a powerful enclave or it can be outfitted with connections to the wider world of information. You can create what is known as an extranet by extending specified intranet privileges to trusted external partners or clients, either through direct connections over private lines or through the Internet (see Figure 1-1). Chapter 3, "The Extranet Option," explains network connections and shows how you can use an extranet to share information and collaborate with customers, vendors, subsidiaries, and joint venture partners.

Figure 1-1   *An intranet that extends outside the company to customers, vendors, or other partners is called an extranet.*

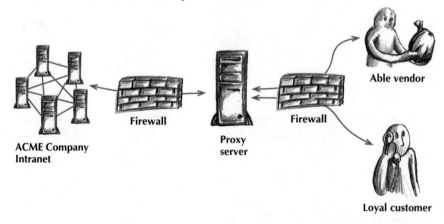

Within the context of this book, an extranet does not include all instances of communication with vendors and customers via an organization's Internet Web site; it includes only communication among those who have been granted *favored partner status*.

Comparison of Internet, Intranets, and Extranets

	Access	*Ownership*	*Tools*
Internet	open to everyone	no owner	computer, browser, and modem or network connection
Intranet	organization members, by permission	organization	computer, browser, and modem or network connection
Extranet	customers, vendors, partners, by permission	organization	computer, browser, and modem

Five Core Functions

Five core functions form the foundation of a full service intranet. With them, an organization can publish information; store, retrieve, and manage its information; and facilitate collaboration across the organization—whether users are working on different floors of a building, within a region, or anywhere in the world. These functions are:

Intranet functions fall into five categories

- E-mail: person-to-person or person-to-group communication
- File sharing: sharing knowledge, information, and ideas
- Directories: management of information and user access
- Searches: finding what you need, when you need it
- Network management: maintenance and intranet modifications

Your current network probably provides each of these functions, but it might provide them on different platforms and interfaces. On an intranet, these functions can run across platforms using open standard Internet-based technologies.

Intranets support cross-platform functionality

Hardware

Intranets are built with technology borrowed from client/server computing environments and Internet technologies. Figure 1-2, on the next page, shows the basic client/server network architecture.

An intranet runs on the same hardware as other client/server networks. Networks need routers, switches, wires, and cables, as well as client and server computers. Client machines (front-end devices) make requests of the network resources through servers (back-end machines). Servers store, manage, and serve information for the private network. Typically servers have robust processors (Pentium 166, at a minimum), and large mass storage devices.

Figure 1-2   *Basic client/server network architecture.*

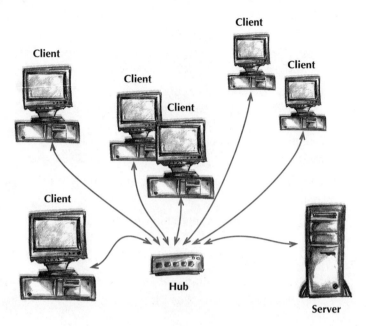

Almost any powerful computer can be used as a server

The computer acting as a server can be any type of machine (personal computer or mainframe), running any operating system (such as Microsoft Windows, UNIX, or the Macintosh Operating System). A simple intranet might have one server to handle all intranet services. A large-scale intranet might employ ten, twenty, or hundreds of servers to host and replicate information. Servers can be dedicated to a specific use, such as a *mail server*, or can be partitioned for several uses according to the types of server software installed and data they manage. Figure 1-3 shows an example of how a mail server and a file server might send and receive information on an intranet.

The type of client depends on the type of work to be done

Any type of computer or workstation (such as an IBM compatible, Macintosh, or Sun) can act as a client computer. Some client machines are actually dumb terminals. Also known as *thin clients,* these machines depend on the servers

Server hardware on an intranet.   *Figure 1-3*

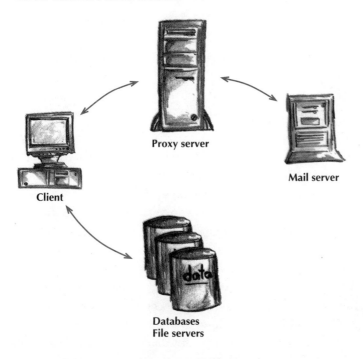

Proxy server

Mail server

Client

Databases
File servers

to store applications as well as all data; with a thin client, you can practice *lite* computing. A thin client cannot operate without the network: when the network goes down, everyone can go to lunch.

A smart client is equipped with its own operating system and software programs, such as spreadsheet, word processing, scheduling, and HTML authoring tools. Data can be stored locally on its disk drive(s). Smart clients can be anything from lean and mean machines for task-working (with minimal memory and processing power) to high-powered workstations for knowledge-working. Task-working is employment that requires attention to specific tasks, such as telephone sales or updating customer records. Knowledge-working implies collaborating as part of an active, cross-functional group, either in design, development, or problem-solving. Because of the complexity of knowledge-working, or collaborating on problems such as analysis or

Smart clients have processing and storage capabilities

engineering development, the workstation requirements for memory and computing capacity can be far greater than for task working. Throughout this book, we'll assume that the clients are smart clients, rather than dumb terminals.

Software

Both servers and clients have specific software needs

There are software needs on both the client and the server sides. The server has software to manage its functions and to perform specialty services. The client software varies according to the needs of the user—the software needs of a person making telemarketing calls differ from those of a tax analyst or a network systems administrator. Some programs come off-the-shelf and perform complex services, such as mail programs. Others are small, customized applications—scripts, applets, controls,[2] and libraries[3]—that developers can use to perform specific tasks within a browser. While this chapter highlights the basic types of software, Chapter 2, "From Mainframe Culture to Internet Technologies," gives more details about intranet software.

Server software handles administrative tasks

Server applications Server application programs reside on the server and manage the business and administrative functions. Such functions include mail processing, storing files, searching, and handling financial transactions. Server software is platform-specific: Windows NT has its own server software, as do UNIX, IBM, Macintosh, and others. As long as the server is running TCP/IP (Transmission Control Protocol/Internet Protocol), it can communicate with other devices on the intranet. (See Chapter 2, "From Mainframe Culture to Internet Technologies.") There are some basic, generic Web server software programs, written in Perl, available at no cost (freeware) for some platforms.

---

2. Scripts, applets, and controls are very small software applications (or subroutines) that perform specific functions.

3. If a function is used repeatedly, it is often put in a library for easy reuse. For instance, a control that searched for a "new hire start date" might be included in a library of controls.

Chapter One

Browsers Browsers are Internet or intranet client programs that communicate requests from the client to the server and display the retrieved information for the user. A browser is the interface between a user and the content stored on the network. It's the universal front end for client machines and many types of server software.

Internet browsers work on intranets as well

Search engines Programs that retrieve data by keyword or other search parameters are usually referred to as search engines. Operating systems and other applications have some search functions built in that can find files on a hard drive by name, date or content. There are also some off-the-shelf search programs available, such as AltaVista Personal Extensions (see "Easy Access to Information," page 194). Developers use applets or scripts to create highly specific search routines, usually as part of a larger intranet application.

Specialty software A variety of controls, scripts, plug-ins, and other small programs or applets fall under the heading of specialty software. Some specialty programs are available as freeware, while others can be obtained at very low cost (shareware). In addition, specialty software can be programmed (with relative ease) through modular component technology. (See the "Examples of Specialty Software" sidebar.)

Speciality programs often use modular components

HyperText Markup Language HTML is not software per se, it is the document format that organizes and codes content in such a way that a browser can display it. Basic HTML authoring is simple, and there are numerous HTML conversion programs that make it easy for anyone to use. Programs such as Microsoft Word, Microsoft PowerPoint, and Microsoft Publisher all have a file conversion option that allows you to save a file as an HTML file. There are also separate authoring programs such as HomeSite, WebEdit, and Microsoft FrontPage that allow you to create an HTML file from the ground up. Not all the information shared across an intranet is in HTML format, but all Web pages, whether on the Internet or an intranet, are written in HTML. Like any

HTML is the "language" of a Web page

language, HTML continues to evolve, with new versions of the language emphasizing display and interactivity (see "Intranet Software," page 64).

Examples of Specialty Software

Here are some examples of specialty software components:

ActiveX Controls are reusable software components that add specific functionality quickly, such as a stock ticker control.

Java scripts are used to link and automate a wide variety of objects in Web pages, including ActiveX Controls and applets created with the Java language from Sun Microsystems, Inc.

Agents are helpful drones that can be employed to find material on the internal Web and send a notice when specific new information is available.

Plug-ins are small programs that plug into your browser. When a file requires some special functionality (such as video, audio, and graphics animation), the browser invokes the plug-in program to handle the action.

A Network by Any Other Name

Organizations have been sharing information and computing resources over networks for decades. Computing networks are a group of computers and associated devices configured to share computing resources with the aid of special interfaces, protocols (rules), and hardware devices. The purpose of a network is to conserve resources and to enable communication and the electronic distribution of data.

Intranets use TCP/IP and HTTP protocols

The distinction between an intranet and any other network is that an intranet runs on Internet protocols, such as TCP/IP and HTTP (HyperText Transfer Protocol). Internet protocols are a common language that can bridge proprietary differences in various operating systems across different types of computing devices. (See "Network Communications," page 51). An intranet can run on a LAN or any other network; the presence of one type of network does not exclude the presence of another type.

Types of Computer Networks

The five basic network types are: sneaker networks, peer networks, LANs, metropolitan area networks (MANs), and WANs. On a sneaker network, computer users literally *walk* data diskettes back and forth between computers. Peer networks link up two or more computers and peripheral devices like printers on an unregulated sharing basis. On a LAN, the sharing activities between server(s), computers, and peripherals within a group are orchestrated for efficiency. A MAN is a campus-wide or citywide sharing group. WANs, which can share information worldwide, are networks of LANs.

Features Comparison:
Traditional Networks and Intranets

If an intranet were a vehicle, it would be a HMMWV (Highly Mobile, Multi-Purpose, Wheeled Vehicle, pronounced hum-vee), a ruggedly powerful, infinitely adaptive *all terrain vehicle* (which would also look way cool parked in front of your organization).

Compare the features of an intranet with those of a traditional client/server network system, and you'll probably want to get in and drive the intranet off the lot—not only because it's newer or because it has a lot of horsepower under the hood, but also because it's so easy to drive. In the next chapter, you'll find more detail about network basics, but here, just take a moment to do a walk-around and kick the tires.

Intranets are conducive to speed and flexibility

What features are you looking for in a network? If it's going to be a productivity tool, it had better be easy to use—easy for administrators, easy for programmers, and easy for the end users. Ease of use helps to control the total cost of owning computing resources. The next section details the

Ease of use is a crucial factor

limitations of traditional network systems, as compared to intranets. The table on the opposite page, "Comparing Features of Network Systems and Intranets," summarizes how well intranets and traditional network systems handle five critical features: ease of use, cost to build and deploy, cost to maintain, scalability, and interoperability.

Limitations of Traditional Networks and Proprietary Systems

Interoperability is a problem with traditional LANs and WANs

Traditional LANs and WANs[4] have built-in limitations both for information technology administrators and for users. The main difficulty for administrators is in making different computers and different operating systems talk to each other.

Traffic between computing islands is difficult

Because traditional LANs run on proprietary software and use different protocols, there is always the problem of inter-operability between different systems. For instance, file sharing might use NetWare with IPX protocol.[5] Databases could be running on UNIX systems using TCP/IP. A mainframe would probably use SNA protocol.[6] Without either running some sort of translating software on a connectivity point or having a *common denominator protocol* like TCP/IP on all systems, you will have difficulty making one system talk to another.

Maintaining separate directory systems and software systems adds expense

Traditional networks require users to master the software on each different system. Network administrators have to manage several separate directory systems, for example, one for e-mail, one for Lotus Notes, and one for the corporate scheduling package. Besides being time-consuming to manage, this type of cumbersome network architecture is prone to failure and downtime.

---

4. LANs and WANs operate on client/server architecture.

5. IPX stands for Internet Packet Exchange.

6. SNA stands for Sequenced Packet Exchange.

The architecture of traditional networks is made up of islands of legacy systems, as shown in Figure 1-4. In addition, proprietary systems deployed across the LANs are often designed to handle only a certain number of desktops; scaling up is difficult and expensive.

Scalability is difficult with many legacy systems

Islands of legacy systems.

Figure 1-4

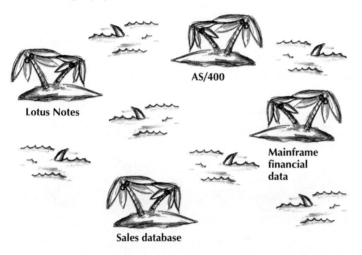

AS/400

Lotus Notes

Mainframe financial data

Sales database

The solution is an intranet. Built on a foundation of open standard Internet technologies, intranets unleash the real power of the client/server structure in LANs and WANs by sharing information—from a job announcement posting to a whiteboard image—in HTML format, employing HTTP,[7] the only protocol designed for handling HTML documents.

Intranets are easy to use, scalable, and interoperable

Comparing Features of Network Systems and Intranets

Feature	Network system	Intranet
ease of use	poor	excellent
cost to build and deploy	high	low
cost to maintain	moderate to high	moderate
scalability	limited	excellent
interoperability	difficult	excellent

7.   HTTP stands for HyperText Transfer Protocol.

Productivity

Early productivity tools, geared for individuals, took a lot of time to learn, and to relearn

The advent of the client/server environment brought electronic productivity tools to the desktop. Proprietary software gave users tools to manage personal contacts, maintain their calendars, schedule activities within a group, and keep in touch quickly through e-mail. However, many of those programs were designed for individual productivity (single-user application), not for sharing information across a group. In addition, many of the tools were difficult to master, and that meant more user support from the information technology people.

Bill Gates Speaking at Comdex, 1996:

"… [An] intranet is more than read-only. It's not just looking at pages and reading them, it's also creating pages. It's annotating pages. It's editing what other people have done. And the top problems that productivity software has been addressing, letting people view data in different ways, letting them coordinate their activities, all of those things play very well for the intranet. We basically moved from a file sharing world, where information is just too hard to find, into a world of pages."

The Quest for Productivity Tools

Information can be structured or unstructured

Individuals, groups, and organizations use both structured and unstructured processes to get their jobs done. Intranets can accommodate both types of process environments. (See "Structured and Unstructured Data," page 169.)

Intranet technology is a Swiss Army knife of productivity tools

Intranet technologies, in the right hands, are the raw materials for building a powerful assortment of individual, group, and business productivity tools for converting both structured and unstructured communication into useful knowledge.

A browser provides a uniform interface

Individual productivity With browser-based software (applications that developers create to run in a browser), it's easier and quicker to update customer profiles, manage a "to do"

list, or schedule time to work on a task for a specific project. Every time you have to learn new software, your real work gets put on hold. However, if your main avenue to computing resources—information and collaboration—is through the *Front, Back, Search,* and *Favorites* buttons on your browser in a Web environment of familiar icons, getting to where you want to be and doing what you need to do is simpler than loading (and learning) separate programs. Moreover, you'll be able to spend more time working and less time wondering about how to use the software.

Group productivity In addition to benefiting from maintaining group schedules and communicating by e-mail, groups can gain productivity by sharing information and ideas using newsgroups, discussion forums, and online chat technologies. A casual note posted on an electronic whiteboard might contain the idea that sparks a solution or sets in motion a chain of ideas for the next project. An electronic whiteboard program is just one feature of intranet groupware products. Some products, for example, NetMeeting, include audio and video conferencing capabilities. Some group conferencing programs also include voting mechanisms for anonymous or user-identified ballots. For users, the difference between traditional client/server tools and intranet groupware tools is a steep learning curve versus the ease of using a browser.

The new intranet tools can document the flow of ideas

Group productivity tools fall into three basic categories: knowledge-ware programs and libraries, document-sharing and editing tools, and workflow (or project management) tools.

- Knowledge libraries store documents such as white papers, trip reports, memos, customer profiles, safety data, calendars, and software utilities. Knowledge-ware programs make those documents available in public folders on internal Web sites and make catalog information retrievable through search tools.

- Document-sharing programs enable teams to write and revise the same material—either separately or simultaneously—whether they are in the same city or spread out around the world (see Figure 1-5). Such tools are ideal for collaboration on design specifications or product descriptions, in an orderly fashion.

- Workflow programs automate and track business processes. Task management, timelines, and dependencies can be managed with greater ease than ever before with intranet productivity tools.

Figure 1-5   *Intranets provide many opportunities to enhance group productivity without geographic limitations.*

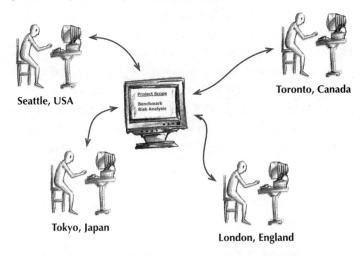

Seattle, USA

Toronto, Canada

Tokyo, Japan

London, England

The addition of Internet-technology multimedia tools, such as audio and video streaming and embedded graphics, can increase the effectiveness of group productivity tools, as described in Chapter 7 (see "Virtual Meetings," page 222).

Intranets can elevate productivity across the organization

Organization productivity Depending on the configuration of an organization, some of the same productivity tools that benefit groups can also serve the whole organization. For instance, public folders containing discussion threads and project files can be made available to all employees. Knowledge repositories can house corporate-wide communication, including the templates and graphics for building internal Web pages. Information resources are instantly available to any field representative, branch office, subsidiary, or partner, practically anywhere around the world.

Four Major Productivity Applications

Although it's correct to say *an intranet can boost productivity*, an intranet is more than a turbo-charge. Certainly an intranet can shorten the time it takes for routine activities and cut a quicker path to decisions. But it's not just an attractive add-on: it can transform the way you do business.

Intranets transform business processes

Each organization defines the scope of its own intranet services. The main opportunities for an intranet are in quick publishing, information management, knowledge-working, and distance learning. These areas of opportunity do not make up *stages* of intranet maturation; they represent the activities that an organization can engage in using its intranet. Each is an opportunity to increase productivity.

Quick Publishing

Imagine shortening the time-intensive process of publishing (and updating) all the procedural, safety, environmental, and policy manuals in your organization. Imagine if you could reclaim the time that people spend distributing, filing, and reissuing pages that get stuffed into notebooks that sit on dusty shelves. Intranets offer the opportunity to eliminate those processes, save the paper, and put the same information on line in an easily accessible format that's always just a few keystrokes away. Anything now on paper can be rendered electronically and displayed through a browser on a desktop, a laptop, or a kiosk computer. And, perhaps more importantly, it can be updated quickly and easily.

Publishing on an intranet is faster

Quick publishing offers more than paper savings: it presents the opportunity to empower employees by encouraging them to at least make the first try at finding information for themselves. When they do this, they save more than paper. They save their time and the time of the people they used to call, and call back. And, employees become more productive as they grow more confident and self-sufficient.

Employees become more self-sufficient

Information Management

Information resources are growing exponentially, and intranets provide a more efficient way of *managing* these vital resources. With an intranet, you can structure the way information is acquired, the way it is organized, and the way it is distributed and accessed.

Intranets offer a unified strategy for handling information assets

Information that is not accessible within a useful time frame degrades in value. Intranet tools can bridge legacy databases and make the data more easily accessible. New dynamic data tools can deliver information just in time. The art of information retrieval is racing to meet the new demands for accessing filtered information. Webcasting (or push) technologies offer new means for distributing information on a timely basis. (See "Easy Access to Information," page 194.) All in all, new tools and Web-based technologies are changing our relationship with data.

Knowledge-Working

For team-based cultures, an intranet provides a welcome vehicle for expanding opportunities for collaboration, and for making it easier to collaborate. At the heart of the shift from the industrial to the digital age that Don Tapscott discusses in his book, *Digital Economy*, is the shift in the value of assets.[8] He seconds Peter Drucker's opinion that the traditional resource values of land, capital, and labor have

Knowledge-working turns information into knowledge

---

8. Don Tapscott, Digital Economy, p. 46.

been supplanted by the value of its *knowledge assets*—the only meaningful assets today.

Organizations that have decided their future success (and perhaps survival) lies in leveraging the *intelligence* or knowledge of their workers view intranets as a means to fuel their efforts with lightning-fast access to data and ideas. With new products and technologies, organizations can provide teams with the Web-based tools they need to turn information into knowledge and to arrive at decisions most quickly and confidently. The knowledge-working opportunities on an intranet will reshape the way organizations develop products and deliver services. (See Chapter 7, "Knowledge-Working.")

Intranets help leverage your knowledge assets

Distance Learning

As the implications of conducting business on a *just-in-time* basis filter through an organization, training opportunities are a natural productivity application. Distance learning slashes the cost of delivering training and expands the options for timing and scope: learners can acquire the specific knowledge and skills they need, when they need them. As with other intranet activities, online learning will change some roles. It can shift the responsibility for learning to employees, alter the approach of instructors, and still afford administrators tight control of curriculum planning and learning assessments.

Putting learning on line makes it more accessible

Benefits from Multiple Points of View

Users, managers, information technology professionals, communicators, external partners—everyone looks through a slightly different lens and sees the benefits of an intranet from a slightly different point of view (POV). Some features, like ease of use and speed, are appreciated by all. The "Benefits Summary By User Population" table on page 27 summarizes the benefits from these various points of view.

Benefits vary with your point of view

POV: The User

From the user's perspective, intranet benefits include:

- Ease of use (uniformity, simplicity of navigation)
- Ease of publishing and retrieving data
- Sense of empowerment
- Reduction in time-wasting activities

A universal front end makes an intranet easy to use

Whether end users are knowledge-workers or information-providers, they will find many tasks easier to accomplish with an intranet than with a standard LAN or WAN. It's easy to learn how to use a browser—click buttons for *Back, Next,* and *Search,* or use *Favorites* to bookmark a site. Furthermore, they can use the same interface to get to the information they want, wherever it's located.

Information can easily be published and retrieved

Imagine the executives speeding around their intranet with no fear. Imagine work teams putting meeting agendas (and changes) on their site and resolving work-slowing dependencies on line. Imagine anyone who needs to find something quickly and then get on to something else. (See "The Intranet and the Eye Appointment," below.)

The Intranet and the Eye Appointment

It's 5:08 p.m. on a Thursday, and a lab technician has just remembered that she wanted to check human resources benefits before scheduling an eye appointment for her daughter. Because her company has invested in intranet technology, the lab technician can use her browser to go to the human resources Web site, click on the Vision Benefits area, read about coverage and procedures, and select an ophthalmologist from the list of preferred providers. If the lab technician has any further questions, she can read the FAQs (frequently asked questions) or click the *Got a Question?* button to send an e-mail message to someone in the human resources department Then, using a scheduling calendar or project management program, the lab technician can check her schedule and her team's workflow. She can also send e-mail to advise her manager she's taking time off and then get back to work quickly. Her e-mail will probably generate an immediate response.

Using an intranet can be more productive than phones and file directories. As you can see in Figure 1-6, the cycle of actions is simple and straightforward. Compared with the process described in "The Lab Tech Does It the Traditional Way," the intranet scenario (see the sidebar on the following page) wins hands down in time savings (5–10 minutes vs. 2–8 days), fewer working interruptions (1–2 vs. 4–7), and less support time required (3–5 minutes vs. 20–40 minutes).

A visual depiction of the activities described in "The Intranet and the Eye Appointment" sidebar.

Figure 1-6

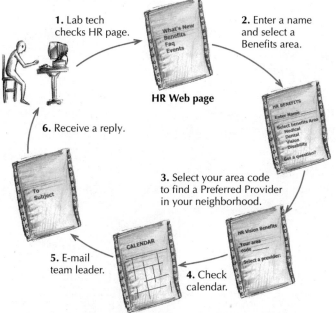

Furthermore, the other intranet benefits listed at the beginning of this section, though somewhat intangible, have also come into play, increasing the lab technician's productivity and therefore the productivity of the organization as a whole.

The Lab Tech Does It the Traditional Way

It's 5:08 p.m. on a Thursday, and a lab technician has just remembered that he wanted to check his company's human resources benefits before scheduling an eye appointment for his son. Because the company has not invested in intranet technology, he has to do things the traditional way, and it takes much longer to complete his task. First, he has to locate the personnel brochure with the information on vision benefits. Is it here in his desk, or must he call home and ask someone to look for it? Of course he could just wait until the next morning, and then call human resources, and ask to speak to the person who handles vision benefits coverage. But if the HR person is unavailable when the lab technician calls, a round robin of telephone tag will follow.

If the lab technician finds his brochure, so much the better. But chances are he'll have to talk to someone, and that someone will explain the benefits and offer to send over a list of preferred providers (and a copy of the Vision Benefits brochure) by company mail. It will take one to five days to arrive, assuming the lab technician and the HR person are in the same building, campus, or city. Once the list and the benefits package arrive in the mail, the lab technician can begin checking schedules (his own, those of his team members) and project workflow reports. If he does not have e-mail, he will have to call or write a memo to advise his manager about taking time off.

Information is easy to access, publish, and retrieve

First is the ease of use, applying not only to the use of the browser, but also to the ease with which the human resources department is able to publish the information, and the ease in retrieving or viewing that same information.

Users feel a sense of accomplishment and independence

Next is empowerment or the sense of accomplishment—for both the lab technician and the HR person. Each faced a task, did it with minimal, if any, assistance, marked it off the list, and moved on to the next order of business.

Less time is wasted

Last is the reduction of time-wasting activities, thereby enabling employees adequate time to perform their highest level of work. Phone tag was eliminated, and the HR person, not having to respond repeatedly to routine questions, was free to use his or her time more productively in solving real problems.

The growth of intranets mirrors the trend toward shifting greater responsibility to employees. Using a well-designed and well-functioning Web site, you can find up-to-date information quickly, whenever you need it.

POV: Information Technology Personnel

From the information technologist's perspective, intranet benefits include:

- Ease of network administration and management
- Ease of modification
- Decreased requirement for user support

As managers of the computing environment for the organization, information technology professionals orchestrate network load,[9] provide user support, and assure security. All these functions are easier on a cross-platform, integrated, browser-based system.

Intranets simplify system management and reduce support needs

An intranet offers a simple interface for integrating and managing disparate computers and software applications across the organization's network. Every organization laden with legacy systems knows it's unreasonable to abandon a large investment in hardware or software systems. It's also very expensive (and somewhat risky) to convert data from legacy software; it's difficult to assure that the data can be accurately translated into new databases. With Internet-based technology, that is rarely necessary. Beyond the system management tools that come with the new platforms, there are browser-based monitoring and tracking tools that aid administrators in managing their network.

Integrating hardware, software, and legacy systems is easy

---

9. An important part of an administrator's job is to balance user demand on the system. This is done both in advance, to schedule maintenance downtime or large projects (such as the running of a major accounting program).

In addition, the scalability of intranet designs makes it easier for administrators to balance the load. Many legacy systems have built-in limits to the number of users the system can support (sometimes as a means of memory management). A system that's easier to maintain means less downtime, too. Equipment downtime is always expensive, whether it's a broken winder on a paper machine or a downed server on the network.

Intranets support
solutions that free
technical personnel
to work on tool
development rather
than just solve crises

With a network system that is easier for users to operate, one of the side benefits is that the network administrators and programmers can shift their focus (and time) from providing a high level of ongoing user support to devising productivity tools. This benefit is aptly described by Kirby Leeper, Chief Technology Officer for Teleres:[10] "Developing an intranet application, programmers get to concentrate on the core business rule that they are trying to develop, rather than looking for printers and modems. We can focus on the real work of the application—say it's a program to manage the company's inventory—and stay within that core competence area. End users will see a deliverable that is more sympathetic to their needs, because we're putting 100% of our effort [into developing an inventory management program], instead of 60% to the core, and 40% to making it work with all the variables."

POV: The Communications Department

From the perspective of the communications department, intranet benefits include:

- The ability to reach target audiences
- Up-to-date information
- Speedier communication
- One-source credibility

---

10. Teleres is the joint venture of Dow Jones & Co. and AEGON USA that created the first online service of news, information, and analytical software for the commercial real estate industry.

The communications department releases messages inside and outside the organization and sets the standards for the *look* of the organization. Whether the topic is the announcement of a new chief financial officer, a new policy on Internet surfing, new training offerings, or the annual report, its mission is to assure that accurate, up-to-date information is distributed.

Intranets enable the communicators' creed: publish early, publish often

An intranet makes it infinitely easier to accomplish this mission. Publishing and maintaining internal Web pages involves far fewer resources than printing and handing out pamphlets that are all too quickly out of date or putting up posters in the cafeteria that someone has to put up and take down.

Fewer resources are required

Push and pull technologies (see "Easy Access to Information," page 194) make it even easier to reach target audiences. Using these tools, a communications department can lead the way in delivering information to members of the organization.

POV: External Partners

From the perspective of an external partner, intranet benefits include:

- Sense of community
- Up-to-date information
- Speedier communication
- Reduction in time-wasting activities

By extending the organization's intranet to select vendors and clients, you can build better partnerships. When you provide an extranet and invite partners to access the information they need, when *they* need it, you demonstrate to them that you respect their time, as well as their business, and that they are valued (and trusted) members of your trading community. Feedback forms from before and after an

An extranet can solidify partner relationships

extranet implementation show increased satisfaction: every type of partner—vendor, customer, subsidiary, distributor—appreciates being able to access information quickly on an as-needed basis. Vendors value the time they save when they can review and submit bids on line. As illustrated in Figure 1-7, customers especially appreciate the convenience of having catalogs, order forms, and shipping status available on line so that they can find what they need to serve *their* customers, whether they are across town or in another time zone. (See Chapter 3, "The Extranet Option.")

POV: The Managers

From the perspective of managers, intranet benefits include:

- Low development costs
- Materials cost savings
- Enhanced productivity

"Will it make the organization more competitive?" "More productive?" "What will it cost?" These are some of the questions good managers will ask.

Figure 1-7　*Giving your customers a view to information they need for their customers helps them succeed in their business.*

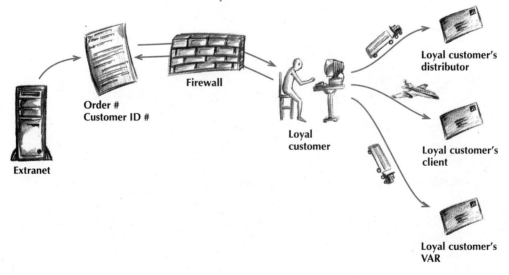

Extranet

Order #
Customer ID #

Firewall

Loyal
customer

Loyal customer's
distributor

Loyal customer's
client

Loyal customer's
VAR

Having a system that is easier to use will reduce the cost of support, which in turn will reduce the total cost of ownership. After all, the cost of the cables and the keyboards is only part of the cost of maintaining an organization's network resources. As you will see in Chapters 5 through 8, when users can get what they need and do their work with fewer calls for intervention, everyone reaps the benefits.

Intranets reduce the total cost of computer ownership

As described in the above sections and summarized in the table below, the benefits will accrue to all parties through reducing direct costs, reducing total cost of ownership (computing resources), improving workplace morale, spurring creativity, building strong partnership ties, and reducing product cycle time.

Benefits Summary by User Population

User	IT Staff	Communications	Managers	Partners
easy to use	easy to administer	reaches target audiences	low cost to develop	better connectivity
easy to publish	easy to modify	up-to-date information	many cost savings	up-to-date information
empowerment	reduces need to support users	speeds communication	empowers employees	speeds communication
reduces time-wasting activities	easy to manage network	one-source credibility	enhances productivity	reduces time-wasting activities

Push and Pull Concepts

When most people first searched or surfed the Internet, they pulled down information from this Web site and then that one. Used in this way, *pull down* means accessing data on remote machines (servers) and downloading or copying files to a user's machine, if desired. Internet users quickly discovered two problems. First, having available a ton of information was a mixed blessing. A simple search could set off an avalanche of potentially useful citations. Second, it took too

Timely access to specific information helps prevent an information avalanche much time and attention to continually revisit favorite sites to see if new information had appeared since the last visit. To make the available pool of information more useful, what they needed was more orderly access to new information.

Push technology delivers timely information as requested

When the opportunity arose to have data *pushed* onto their desktops—delivered like a daily newspaper without requiring any action on their part—people jumped at the chance. The solution was push technology, pioneered on the World Wide Web by PointCast, to deliver timely information as requested. Of course, if you *over-requested*, you could still be avalanched, but at least you could save time by being more selective about choosing the information you requested.

Browsers come equipped with multicasting

Responding to their customers' needs, Microsoft Internet Explorer 4.0 and Netscape's Netcaster 4.0 have taken slightly different approaches to push technology. However, both programs allow you to schedule the time and amount of content delivered to your computer's hard disk, where it can be viewed off line at your convenience. Both allow the *locking* of a full-screen image of the push browser (called *Webtop* by Netscape) on the desktop, as a main interface at start-up and always running *under* any application.

Microsoft and 30 industry partners have introduced a new open standard, Channel Definition Format (CDF), which is a boon to Web sites and their administrators. Microsoft's *Webcast* approach extends push technology (with new XML tags) to scheduling, event-logging, authentication, and options for current display. These capabilities will benefit site administrators: it will allow them to manage traffic and track usage and cost assignment.

Netscape has partnered with a number of channel providers, such as Marimba and CNNfn (CNN Financial Network) to offer content to subscribers. Netcaster is capable of using HTML, Java, and Javascript, but not Microsoft's ActiveX controls or emerging CDF or XML standards.

What Are the Most Compelling Reasons to Shift to an Intranet?

What's the one thing you can't buy more of? Time. You can hire more employees, but doubling the number of human assets on a task seldom gets it done in half the time. You can invest in more equipment, but more isn't always better. Whatever business you're in, you probably feel the pressure of time more than ever before. You probably have less time to research, less time to make decisions, less time to get to market, less time to waste. Time is still money.

You cannot make, buy, or borrow more time

And knowledge is still power. On the surface, by making knowledge available, you are giving away power. Actually, you're transferring power to work groups. Intranets fuel the change from the static, hierarchical organizational structure to a team-based, highly productive, learning organization. Picture a collaboration of information technologists and communicators and knowledge-workers—all empowered to work more productively. Those are the people who are more apt to take a new idea and run with it—all the way to the bank.

Leveraging intellectual assets increases productivity

Setting up an intranet sends a message to employees: if you need something, go and find it. It sets new expectations for a more direct way of doing business. Pack your own parachute and take off.

Intranets foster empowerment

When you implement an intranet, look for these three primary benefits among the changes that will occur:

- Empowered employees who take the initiative and become more productive
- A stronger sense of unity within the organization and an appreciation for the parts of the whole
- Enhanced partnerships, not only between workers in a group and between different groups in the company, but also between the company and external partners, vendors, and customers

Divisions and Islands

Building a
collaborative
enterprise has its
challenges

An intranet doesn't make for instant harmony. Internal quarrels and long-standing competition or outright indifference between divisions or departments can sabotage the effective use of an intranet, or even completely derail efforts to build one. (See "Handling Resistance," page 288.)

Information is
perishable and
no longer worth
hoarding

Many organizations still operate on the knowledge-hoard-as-power principle. People will quite naturally protect their turf. They might find a change toward information-sharing very threatening—especially when layoffs loom and people feel the need to prove their value. A private knowledge store has always been the way to demonstrate value, so one way that islands of power fight hard to protect their turf is to avoid building bridges and to maintain the status quo of the company's intelligence. That strategy won't win in the long run: information has become a perishable commodity.

It is perhaps ironic that while information technology departments, once *outsiders* in their own companies, are now the ones achieving a more visible role in leading organizations toward greater productivity, other forces may undermine their attempts at unifying the corporate intelligence asset.

Building More Than Bridges with an Intranet

An intranet delivers
unity and spreads
understanding

When walls are torn down, contact increases. Knowing more about other operations within the organization helps the members operate for the good of the larger organization, rather than for just the survival of the group. A good example is provided by the Baltimore Gas and Electric intranet, which played an important role in keeping employees informed of progress toward their merger with Potomac Electric. News and job openings were regularly posted on the intranet. Departments within the utility also posted reports and information about projects and safety.

Kim Ethridge, a member of the Corporate Communications department, is an involved member of the Baltimore Gas and Electric intranet team. "More and more departments are putting up home pages. They're showing the work that's done in all these different departments—making it more real for others in the company. Cruising through Route 96, (that's the *BGE intranet*), you get a better picture, better insight as to what we do here, what people's jobs are, and what they bring to the company. The company ceases to be *My Accounting Department*."

In some instances, people in one department might think that the problems and activities of another department are beyond the scope of their interest. Why would a sales department need to know or care about how the billing department took care of business? Because they are both part of one company with the same customers, there may be opportunities to share data that can simplify work for both departments.

Sharing information can improve business processes

By exploring how to move processes to an intranet (see Chapter 9, "Planning"), they might find new ways to streamline processes and improve productivity. Instead of routing paperwork through interoffice mail, what if the sales department filled in an online form on their Web site whenever they initiated an order? And what if that triggered an automatic account status check (for flags) in the billing department that same day? *What if* is the start of improved productivity.

Always ask "what if..."

In addition, an organization will need to build incentives and new ways to reward employees for sharing knowledge. Otherwise, access to knowledge can backfire: being part of the great collective can work against individual initiative. Progressive companies recognize that the value is in the sum of the team and they restructure their rewards based on an employee's performance as a team contributor.

The rewards system must change to promote knowledge sharing

Conclusion

Intranets are
time-saving,
strategic tools

In today's market place, information is a rapidly depreciating asset and product cycles are shrinking. To stay in the game, you need to make decisions more quickly. There's a sea of information available, but unless you have a way to manage the flow, it can immobilize your organization.

Tools are needed
for rapid decision
making

Old information—whether it's last year's shipping charges or last month's stock price—wastes time and can cause bad decisions. The fact that information needs to be reliably fresh and focused is changing the way business is conducted. Employees don't have time to run something up the chain of command. More and more, employees need to make front line decisions. They need immediate access to current information and knowledge to make the right decision. Intranets can be a strategic tool for getting up-to-date, useful information into the hands of the right people, right when they need it.

The evolution of
intranets mirrors
the growth of
work teams

Intranets are not just the *technology du jour*—a fad that keeps journalists and information technologists employed (and thrilled). Intranets are the next evolutionary stage in the natural confluence of computing, communication, and content. The rise of intranets is a natural fit with the evolution of the culture of work teams.

Chapter 2 provides
more technical
information

The next chapter explores the transition from the Industrial Age to the Digital Age, skims the surface of the shift from command and control computing to client/server computing, and covers the basics of Internet technologies.

Chapters 3 and 4
discuss extranets
and security risks

Chapters 3 and 4 complete this first section on the basics of intranet technologies and applications. Chapter 3, "The Extranet Option," examines how and why organizations are extending certain intranet privileges to selected external partners or clients. Chapter 4, "Risks and Mitigation Strategies," addresses the security risks that accompany an intranet and offers solutions.

Chapters 5 through 8 explore the main ways to use an intranet to reduce cycle time and increase productivity. Chapter 5, "Using an Intranet for Quick Publishing," looks at how to get information up where people can get at it. Chapter 6, "Using an Intranet for Information Management," deals with the basics of acquiring, organizing, and setting up fast access to information on the internal Web. Chapter 7, "Knowledge-Working," explores using an intranet for collaborative computing, to get the most out of a team-based environment. Chapter 8 examines "Distance Learning Systems on an Intranet," the fastest growing use of intranets.

Chapters 5 through 8 examine intranet solutions

The last group of chapters, Chapters 9 through 13, covers the full scope of building and maintaining an intranet. These chapters include planning, building a pilot project, building a business case, implementing the intranet, and after the launch, maintaining and evaluating its performance.

Chapters 9-13 cover the intranet life cycle

Chapter 14 looks at horizon technologies and opportunities that may (or may not) come to pass—because *book time* takes longer than *Internet time.*

Looking way, way ahead

Chapter Two

From Mainframe Culture to Internet Technologies

The way an organization identifies and manages its resources—and that includes its intellectual capital assets—will define the organization. An intranet will change not only your computing activities, but also the way people relate to each other and to the organization.

To understand the value of an intranet and how your organization can take full advantage of one, you will find it useful to have an overview of the evolution and fundamentals of network computing and the basics of Internet technologies.

Intranets represent a stage in the Darwinian progression of computing that began when the mainframes first crawled onto dry land and then changed direction when the first personal computers began walking upright. Intranets were an outgrowth of the same fundamental elements that govern

Intranets evolved from network computing

other forms of network computing—the *need* for communication protocols, the *physics* of data transmission, and, as you will see in this chapter, the *reasons* why computing networks evolved in the first place.

Networks help conserve resources

The driving force behind network computing is the economic advantage of sharing resources, and resources include both tools and data. In the past, organizations divided some of their computing power into networks in order to distribute the organization's computing intelligence.

Collaboration Begins at Home

Interdisciplinary collaboration enriches a working environment

During the interval between the concept and the launch of an intranet, diverse groups within an organization must collaborate. These groups, such as business specialists, network specialists, and communication specialists, may not be used to communicating with one another very often (much less collaborating). That's the first change that will flow from an intranet, even before you've chosen a platform or a browser.

In some organizations, the first challenge for a manager trying to understand the world of intranets is to understand the folks from *IT*—IT being the information technology department—or information systems, or whatever other name (other than *nerds*) your organization uses to refer to the computer folks.

Information technologists were walled off in glass houses

Besides affording protection for the machines, the glass walls of the early computing environments sealed a culture of initiates from the organization they served. Walls of language, values, assumptions, and habits divided the information specialists from the business specialists, and they drifted apart. To outsiders, information technology professionals have appeared more profoundly interested in the world of information bits than in the larger world of the organization or the still-larger world of market forces.

Business executives have had their eyes focused on the bottom line. Experience, training, and probably temperament separated them. As Charles Wang points out in his book, *Techno Vision*, "The executives were talking about customers, world-class service, global competition, and return on investments. The information people seem fixated on platforms, client/server computing, and object orientation."

Only twenty years after the birth of the microprocessor, business has been turned inside out and, in many cases, upside down. It is now clearer than ever that information technology can be a powerful force in reshaping the way an organization does business. Investments in computing and communication technologies can promote keener use of knowledge assets, create competitive advantages, build esprit de corps, enhance partner relations, and offer other strategic benefits. If this change fills you with trepidation, you should quietly bury this book. Intranets will continue this trajectory and change the way we can access, disseminate, and use information.

Use information technology to build intellectual capital assets

There is much to understand about the economic, computing, and cultural histories that have led us to this *moment* and this *configuration* of players. By taking the time to understand the context of today's technologies, you will find it easier to avoid misunderstandings that could undermine your success.

Understanding the context of intranet technology

Hosts and Hierarchies— Command and Control

The story begins in the latter half of the 19th century with an organizational style we're only recently moving beyond. The agricultural economy gave way to the industrial economy. The factories of the 1870s offered a steady paycheck to the farmers who relinquished their life on the land. They lined up at factories ruled by command and control hierarchies.

Farmers became factory workers

Industrial economy relied on paper

As Don Tapscott points out in his book, *Digital Economy*, throughout the industrial economy, information flow was physical. People sat down at face-to-face meetings, issued stacks of papers, catalogued reams of files, handled bills of lading, drafted blueprints, printed maps and, more recently, sent entirely too much direct mail (see Figure 2-1).

The Digital Economy substitutes virtual for physical

But in today's emerging economy, Tapscott's *new media* or *interactive media* economy, information is no longer physical, it is digital—and you can't see it, smell it, or taste it until it's *media-ized*.[1] This simple fact has far-reaching ramifications for the way we perceive, store, access, value, and share information. In fact, around the world, people are in the process of revising their relationship to information and knowledge.

Figure 2-1   *In the industrial economy, people relied on paper for communication and transactions.*

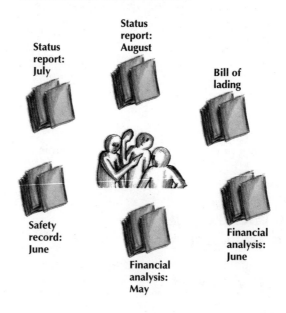

Status report: July

Status report: August

Bill of lading

Safety record: June

Financial analysis: May

Financial analysis: June

1.   Tapscott, *Digital Economy*, p. 6.

Until the dawn of the Internet, however, the *command and control* organizational model had persisted for more than 100 years—through the assembly line, two World Wars, one Cold War, and on through the development of computers.

The old model persists

Mainframes and the Glass House Culture

In the beginning, there were mainframes—the Tyrannosaurs of computing. They ate all the information in sight. They were big as the mountains of Nepal and about as easy to access.

In the 1950s, programmers and information managers (not called that then) worked in *glass houses*. There the ordained trod the static-free floors of the climate-controlled *clean rooms* and ministered to the insistent flashing lights of the monstrous mainframes. Inside the monoliths, the invisible records of thoughts and deeds were maintained—your company's third quarter results, your allotment of sick days, the identities of operatives, and that sort of thing (see Figure 2-2 on the next page).

Only specialists could access information on mainframes

ENIAC Computer, Very Big But Not Very Bright

In 1946, when the two guys at the University of Pennsylvania turned on the 30-ton ENIAC[2] computer with its 18,000 vacuum tubes, all the lights in the city dimmed. Fifty years later, the same year we celebrated the birthday of HAL[3] (January 12, 1997), every kid with a Sega machine in his or her hands held more power under one twitching thumb.

2. The ENIAC, Electronic Numerical Integrator And Calculator, was an 1800 square-foot computer. It was considered the first truly electronic computer. ENIAC was operational from 1946 to 1955.

3. HAL, Heuristically Programmed Algorithmic, the not-so genial computer imagined by Arthur C. Clark in *2001, A Space Odyssey*.

Figure 2-2   *Mainframes housed organizations' intelligence.*

Mainframes
reflected top down
organizations

Mainframes were the electronic embodiment of the *command and control* organizations. All intelligence resided in the host computer. It was the knowledge repository for the organization. However—and here's the part that most needed to be changed—only a select few could retrieve information locked within the mainframe.

Information was
processed in batches

When someone wanted information, such as a projection of the cost and availability of energy supplies for the company's operating areas throughout the globe, the supplicant passed the request to the mainframe priests. Processing was usually done in large batches, rather than in a flurry of individual requests. The Wizard of Oz delivered responses in a timelier manner. After many days, an accordion stack of green-edged tractor-feed paper would be delivered to answer the question. If, after the data was pored through, the answer remained elusive, the supplicant would reframe the question and try again.

Command and
control suited the
military-industrial
complex

Through the fifties and sixties, organizations functioned with a fear-based, Cold War mentality. In that environment, the leaders—the ones with sunlight glinting on their brass buttons—rallied the troops and, if the leaders were charismatic, the minions followed. That's what they were paid to do. Not unlike 1950s school children sitting in neat rows with their hands folded, 1950s workers waited for instructions and did as they were told (see Figure 2-3). Nobody colored outside the lines.

Command and control culture in the workplace.

Figure 2-3

The glass house phenomenon was simultaneous with IBM's domination of the information technology hardware market: one vendor, one solution—one glass house, one source for company secrets. In those days, upgrades were scheduled at the behest of the vendor, not the customer. *Account control* became control of the entire information system. Changes to the software were served to a captive audience.

Proprietary systems were tied to a vendor

The 1950s were also the days of Ma Bell, another queen of command and control. Not a lot of other choices out there, so what were you to do? Go out and install an abacus on each desktop? Hand out a tin can and a string to each employee?

Lots of Standards

For a long while, mainframe hardware vendors enjoyed assured sales of their software, virtually unimpeded by

Vendors controlled customers

competitors. They controlled their markets by cautioning their customers that they would not and could not support another vendor's software. And further, if their customers did install other software, the hardware vendors declared they would not and could not be responsible for problems in the system. That kept competition in its place—in other businesses besides command and control computing.

Miniaturization began the shift in computing

Advances in miniaturization technology slimmed the mainframe host computers down from city block-size to just very large machines, about the size of a large dog, but still commanding a prominent position in a big room. Minicomputers, although smaller in capacity, performed the same functions as their mainframe elders did—they held gigabytes of disk storage capacity and large, whirring tape drives.

Proprietary systems created islands of information

Most organizations had several mainframes or minicomputers connected to each other, handling different processing requirements or processing in different locations. However, each machine had to belong to the same family—IBM, Hewlett Packard, DEC, or Univac—to talk amongst themselves. Isolated by their own software dialect, they were not on speaking terms with hardware from the other vendors. As illustrated in Figure 2-4, technology isolated information.

UNIX was the first common API

UNIX - A Solution Found and Lost Then came UNIX. UNIX was heralded as a solution—a universal operating system. The goal of UNIX was to have a common application programming interface (API[4]), so that developers could write a software application and move it across all UNIX environments. Ironically, competition among the vendors worked against the IT people trying to build, maintain, and grow computing systems.

---

4. API is an acronym for a set of routines that enables an application program to request or carry out low level tasks performed by a computer's operating system.

Islands of information separated by software.   ***Figure 2-4***

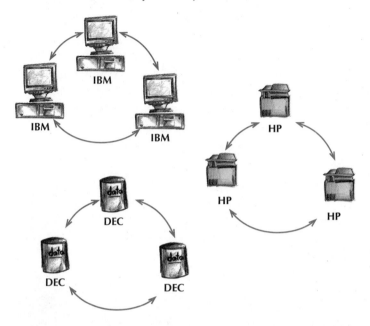

An Interest in Computer Games Led to UNIX

UNIX came to life in the same manner that many good computing ideas have come into being. Two members of a joint AT&T Bell Labs/MIT team (Ken Thompson and Dennis Ritchie) liked playing the computer game *Space Travel*, but it didn't play well on the MULTICS (MULTIplexed Information and Computing System) they were testing on the General Electric's GE645 mainframe. So, Thompson borrowed a little PDP-7 minicomputer from another Bell group, wrote a little operating system for it, and the game resumed. The new operating system was dubbed UNIC (UNIplexed Information and Computing System), which later became UNIX. Since AT&T was forbidden by antitrust decree to profit from UNIX or UNIX-based products, they shared the source code with others within AT&T and universities. Versions proliferated.

UNIX environments multiplied, and incompatibilities between the systems grew with each new version. Soon there was the UCSD (University of California, San Diego) UNIX,

UNIX flavors
soured the hope
of standardization

and the SCO UNIX, and the 4.BSD (Berkeley System UNIX), and IBM's AIX version of UNIX, A/UX for the Apple Macintosh, and the Linux that traces its lineage to UNIX. UNIX manufacturers fell into a *my UNIX is better than your UNIX* spitting match by touting their differing capabilities, and the hope of standardization dissolved. Eight different *standard* kinds of UNIX emerged (see Figure 2-5), all with slightly different operating systems, and all with slightly different hardware requirements. Some of them got along better with others; for instance, IBM's AIX shared more defaults with the Berkeley UNIX than with SCO UNIX. Today the quest for standards continues to walk a thin line between technological improvement and technological chaos.

Figure 2-5   *Flavors of UNIX.*

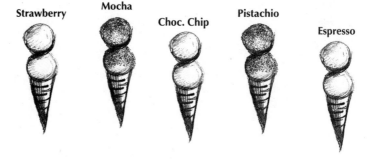

Primitive Networks

Dumb terminals had
no local processing
capabilities

When the mainframe host culture expanded to primitive *interactive computing*, it was still just a variation on the main theme. As illustrated in Figure 2-6, instead of a stand-alone computer (with printers), a number of *dumb* computer terminals were tied to the intelligence of the mainframe like cows at a trough. While dumb terminals had no local processing capabilities, individuals with access to the terminals could use them to make their requests directly to the mainframe, without intercession by IT people. The relationship between a host computer and a terminal was similar to that between a speaker delivering a keynote address to a conference and the audience. The speaker talked; the audience listened. They could pass questions written on note cards to an usher, who would hand them to the expert.

Early network computing – mainframes and dumb terminals.

Figure 2-6

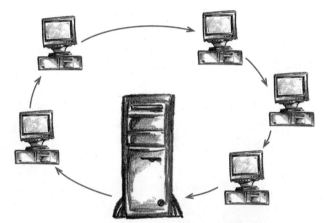

Of course, there was a down side: the heavier the traffic from the terminals, the slower the processing of the mainframe. In addition, as before, if the mainframe choked, the entire computing (and information) function of the organization was brought to its knees.[5]

Heavy traffic meant slow processing

Network Computing— Economics of Sharing

People were being inundated with information, and often there was more coming at them than they could handle. The deluge of information—more magazines to read, more trade publications to keep up on, more advertisements, more telephone calls, more meetings—became an endless stream of information bits.

Information overload triggered business changes

---

5. Scott Fuller & Kevin Pagan, *Intranet Firewalls*, p. 16.

Middle managers
handled the
information load

Businesses reacted by expanding. They added staff to keep
up and added managers to keep everyone on track (see
Figure 2-7). In an expanding economy, they could afford it.
The middle managers acted as traffic cops, funneling and
channeling the information load. As Tapscott expresses it,
middle managers kept themselves busy "boosting the faint
signals that passed for communication in the pre-digital
economy."[6]

Figure 2-7   *The pyramid of information processing.*

The influx of *how to manage your time* books that burdened
bookshelves in the late 1970s were symptomatic of the
problem. *Work smarter*, they implored. Everyone was trying
to cope with the new quantities of information using the
old methods.

The 1980s recession
forced a change;
downsize and
streamline

The recession of the early 1980s was a signal of the belt
tightening that was to come. By then, most organizations
had amassed infrastructures that were overwhelming the
enterprises. As the flow of information increased, it became
clear that the chain of command was too long; it took too

---

6.   Tapscott, *The Digital Economy*, p. 56.

much time to respond within the centralized command and control model of business. The hierarchical structure began to implode. The message was clear to all middle managers: *add value, or you'll be subtracted*. Waves of downsizing rippled across the land and flattened corporate America. Inevitably, the downsizing, right-sizing, smart-sizing, re-focusing, and re-engineering prophets *down-*, *right-*, and *re-organized* businesses into leaner, more streamlined machines.

A distributed model of business was proving more effective. The economics of information management followed suit and began to change too. While the jump was perhaps kick-started by the introduction of the personal computer, with-out the middlemen, the relationship between people and their information had to change. The size of organizations alone was not the problem; rather, it was the architecture of intelligence. Vital knowledge had been locked in little islands of power, a mirror of the calcified hierarchical struc-tures of the organizations. Organizations shifted more deci-sion power to the local units of business, and the information managers put the tools on the desktop.

Individuals were given information and management tools

However, distributing tools did not result in shared informa-tion. Information was still power, and everyone wanted to keep control. The 1980s culture self-expressed itself with personal computers. We all could keep our information at our fingertips. We all also needed to have our own printer, our own disk drives, our own software, our own upgrades, and lots of technical support. We used a word processing program to process words. We used a spreadsheet to ar-range numerical data. Each of us did one task at a time. With all of us maintaining our own data sets, it was very difficult to share information, unless it was done the old way, by physically printing and distributing it. Instead of unlocked information, islands proliferated.

Each person became an information island

The Network Solution

Client/server
environments
introduce
distributed
intelligence

When client/server networks moved into the workplace in
the 1980s, they provided a more nimble means of distributing information than the massive mainframes did. Both the
client and the server act as intelligent, programmable devices by dividing processing responsibilities between the
front-end client[7] and the back-end server.[8] The client, or
user's machine, issues requests to the server, which serves
and manages the information. A group of clients and one or
more servers can be linked together in a local area network
(LAN).

Obsolescence means
redeployment

The evolution of network computing did not render obsolete
all that equipment—the mainframes and minicomputers that
starred in the command and control era. Network computing is a new configuration of the intelligence within an
organization. Mainframes and minicomputers could be re-
deployed as high capacity servers on a network.

Local Area Networks (LANs)

Networks can
share computing
equipment
managed by
the network
operating system

As illustrated in Figure 2-8, a LAN is a work group of computing equipment—intelligent workstations (the clients) and
computing peripherals (such as printers) connected to server
computers. A network can be as simple as two computer
workstations sharing a printer. *Or* it can be a peer network,
a group of computers linked to each other by communication devices to share data. *Or* it could be hundreds of workstations connected to an array of minicomputers, mainframes,
file servers, print servers, mapping devices, and more.
Cables or wireless connections link the various devices.
Network operating system (NOS) software handles the
communication between the machines.

---

7. Unlike the dumb terminals associated with mainframes, the front-end
client uses its own computing power to run applications.

8. The back-end handles data management, multi-user functionality, and
security.

Local Area Networks (LANs) connect computing equipment.   ***Figure 2-8***

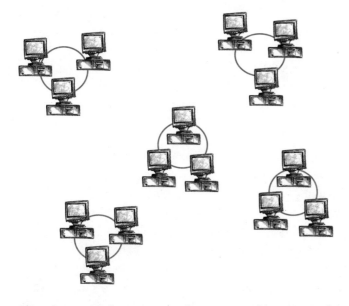

Client/server architecture can be supported by a typical LAN configuration. The server computers store, protect, manage, and serve up the information from the network that its clients (the users' computers) request. A server computer can be any computer—a mainframe, a minicomputer, or even a powerful desktop computer. Servers must have a high input and output rate (I/O rate), so that they can handle hundreds of requests at a time. Some servers are dedicated, such as mail servers, and others are partitioned to handle several functions. The *central file server* on the LAN stores the network operating system, system buffers, and cache.[9]

Intelligent client/ server environments are more flexible

Client machines request data from the server and use their own computing power and applications, such as Microsoft Word or Adobe Photoshop, to process it locally. Compared to the mainframe/dumb terminal configuration, this intelligent client/server environment has several advantages: a

Client/server environment shares intelligence and processing

---

9. Cache memory improves performance by storing data for quick access.

smaller footprint,[10] lower cost, and greater flexibility. Both the individual client and server machines, as well as various other devices on the network, can be reconfigured to suit changing needs. With the evolution of network computing, departments within an organization could get much of their work done in their own LAN neighborhood, without the traffic delays often associated with the mainframe environment.

Other network architectures include the Token Ring and Ethernet configurations. In a Token Ring setup, each computer in the ring takes its turn to transmit data over coaxial or twisted pair wires as a token passes from one computer to the next. Fiber Distributed Data Interface (FDDI) is an example of a token ring using fiber-optic cable. ARCnet and IBM Token Ring use the token signal mechanism. An Ethernet comprises coaxial cables or standard telephone wires (twisted-pair) connected to a hub that directs traffic for the network.

Wide Area Networks (WANs)

WANs extend the reach of the organization

Two or more LANs linked together form a WAN (Wide Area Network), as shown in Figure 2-9. An organization with numerous LANs can link them together with fiber-optic cables and high-speed telephone lines to form WANs. A WAN can link two departments down the hall from one another, or it can reach across a continent or around the world.

Proprietary problems compound across a WAN

Because LANs often operate with different proprietary software, interconnectivity problems persist. For instance, finding information across a WAN involves searching numerous network segments,[11] rather than initiating just one network-wide search.

---

10. A footprint is the area occupied by any equipment.

11. A network segment is a physical section of the network, usually divided by location and separated by gateway equipment.

Two or more LANs can form a WAN.

Figure 2-9

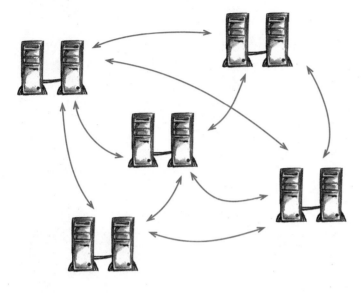

Network Communications

Specialized network equipment, such as routers, bridges, brouters, and gateways, enable messages to travel across networks:

Standard protocols enable communications

- Routers are small traffic-directing computers that transmit (or *ricochet)* data packets between networks from point to point until the messages reach their final destination. Routers also can evaluate the most efficient route.

- Bridges handle addressing and can manage security between the LANs by isolating one network from another. Bridges can also divide networks into small areas for automation.

- Brouters are a combination of a bridge and a router, with programs that can run routing instructions and move packets between networks of unsupported protocols.

- Gateways act as translators between the dissimilar network protocols.

TCP/IP is the primary Internet protocol

Communication protocols are the operating rules that govern communication between networks. Although hardware from different manufacturers may use different protocols, the protocols themselves are standardized. Unless networks share the same communication protocols, connections between them are either difficult or impossible. TCP/IP is the primary Internet protocol.

TCP/IP Stack

TCP/IP is a stack of internetworking protocols

TCP/IP (Transmission Control Protocol/Internet Protocol) is actually a group of protocols (see Figure 2-10) that form the foundation for internetworking and are therefore the basis for Internet communications. These protocols are not laws, like the law of gravity; they are part of the evolving Internet technologies.

Figure 2-10   *TCP/IP stack of protocols.*

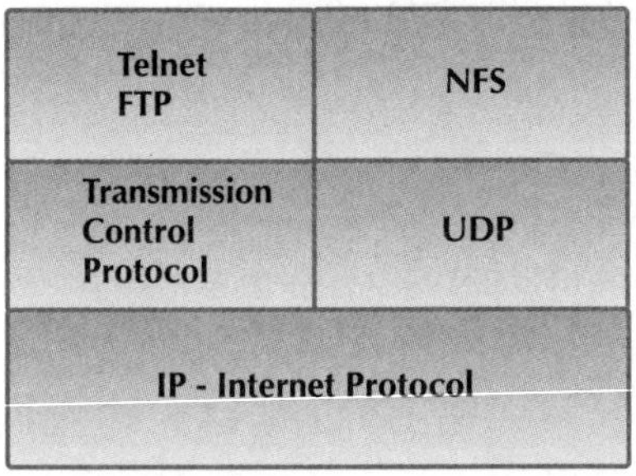

We tend to equate TCP/IP with Internet technology, and this is correct. However, the TCP/IP stack of protocols had been in use for mainframes that were never connected to the Internet. TCP/IP[12] and FTP (File Transfer Protocol) are the best known, but there are other important protocols in the stack.

---

12. TCP/IP governs addressing and sending messages across networks.

- Internet Protocol (IP) is a connectionless protocol that breaks messages into data packets and assigns numeric addresses. It delivers messages between systems, but does not guarantee delivery or receipt.
- Transmission Control Protocol (TCP) is a connection-oriented protocol that places the data packets into secure envelopes and ensures delivery.
- User Datagram Protocol (UDP) provides the basis for remote file systems and management protocols.
- Remote Call Procedures (RCP) enable an application to call and run routines on remote computers.
- Network File System (NFS) is a means of using remote files and disks from a user's computer.
- Simple Network Management Protocol (SNMP) manages network devices and diagnostics.
- File Transfer Protocol (FTP) provides bi-directional transfer of binary and ASCII files between local and remote computers.

IPX and SPX Data Packets

IPX (Internetwork Packet eXchange) and SPX (Sequenced Packet eXchange) make up another stack of communication protocols. They are usually used in tandem. These protocols, which are based on TCP/IP protocols, belong to Novell's NetWare, a suite of client/server networking software. IPX and SPX are used for packet forwarding and routing. They are connection-oriented protocols that guarantee delivery of data. Both these protocols have very good packet filtering capabilities, and so they are frequently used in tight-security firewalls.

Network Functionality

Networks can reduce
costs and increase
productivity

The basic advantages in network computing are reduced
costs and increased productivity through sharing—sharing
physical resources, data, and ideas. Users across a network
can share expensive printers, plotters, image scanners, or
other hardware devices. They can also share the same
software license (the price goes down in an inverse ratio to
the number of desktops that may use the program). Workgroup
or collaborative computing products may include document
sharing, calendar and task-keeping, and public folders, as
well as e-mail.

E-mail

E-mail is an
essential business
communications tool

E-mail has been regarded as one of the *killer apps*[13] of
network computing. The full value of this method of communication wasn't appreciated at first, but then neither was
the telephone.

Early e-mail was limited to text-only messages. Collaborative computing programs like Microsoft Exchange and Lotus
Notes provided the ability to attach files: document files,
spreadsheets, graphics, audio files, and even executable
software programs (see Figure 2-11). For IT people, managers, and communicators, e-mail has become business-
critical. However, unless the people sending and receiving
e-mail are using the same protocol, the mail may not go
through.

Document-sharing

To avoid proliferation of many versions of the same document, administrators set document locking rules (or file

---

13. Killer app is a phrase used to describe an application that will radi-
cally change how we use computers. For example, Mosaic was a *killer
app* because it changed how people used the Internet.

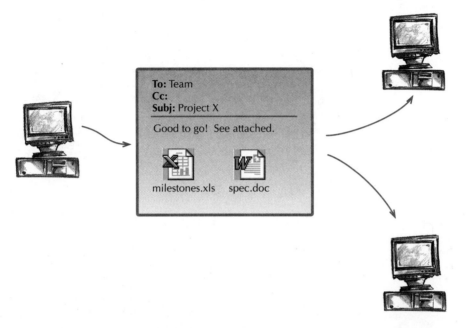

To: Team
Cc:
Subj: Project X

Good to go! See attached.

milestones.xls   spec.doc

sharing rules) about who may actually modify a file as opposed to who may access a file in a *read only* mode. As a way of managing network load, the rules can also set limits as to the number of people who can access a file. A shared file can be a word processing document, a PowerPoint presentation, or a database file. Ideally, there is one *true* or master document. Depending on the permissions, an individual can have privileges to read, update, or delete the document (see Figure 2-12 on the next page).

You must have version control to update a shared document

With some database applications, the master file remains on the server and users with read/write privileges actually make changes on that document. For other applications like Word, the server downloads a temporary file (usually a file named with a .tmp extension) to the client machine. When the modified file is returned to the server, it replaces the file on the server.

Some programs download temporary file copies

Figure 2-12   *Users have different privileges for document-sharing.*

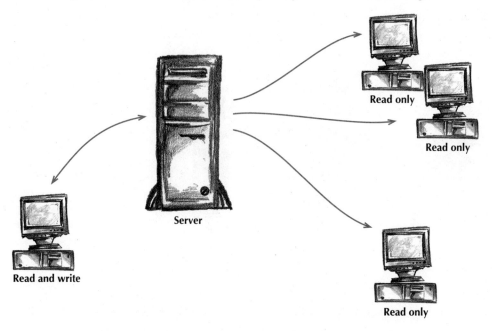

Read only

Read only

Server

Read and write

Read only

Network System Management

Information technology specialists have evolved industrial strength procedures and tools to manage access to and to protect data on their networks. To define user privileges for network resources, an administrator can use security services and directory services on the operating system. Those resources might include disk space, print servers, and e-mail services. Administrators also have tools like performance monitors to track network load, as well as tools to update access lists and to add new members to domains. (See Chapter 4, "Risks and Mitigation Strategies.")

Network Operating Systems (NOS)

The tasks of overseeing and managing the activities of the network machines are the province of the network operating system (NOS). The NOS manages multitasking by organizing the sharing of computing resources (multiple devices) among all the users across the network. In this context, sharing includes enabling as well as restricting, deciding who may have access to what information and which resources.

The network operating system is the central nervous system of a network

Directory Services

Directory Services are a means of managing the complexity of a living network, a network that is growing and changing. As illustrated in Figure 2-13 on the next page, a network structure resembles the hierarchy of a tree. System managers use Directory Services to store information about components on each *branch,* such as the individual users, file servers, applications, printers, and print queues. With the tree structure, it's easier to add or remove network components.

Networks tend to grow like extended families

Login

Before a remote server and a computer can begin to work together, the user must *log in* to the network. This process involves more than a handshake.[14] By entering a pre-determined *user name* (also called an *alias*) and password combination, the user requests permission to enter the network. When the server recognizes the password, it verifies exactly which areas of the network the user may access. The system administrator may change permissions and passwords. Once the user is *on* the network, distances disappear and all the remote drives and services are available (and appear to be resident) on the user's computer.

The login process verifies permissions

Unbeknown to users, when they power down their computers, the remote server manages a *logout* process. By electronically disconnecting each user's machine from the shared resources, the remote server can conserve network resources.

The logout process is automatic

---

14. In computer terminology, a handshake is the process of two machines' recognizing each other's existence. .

Figure 2-13 *The Directory Services tree structure shows the relationship of users on a network.*

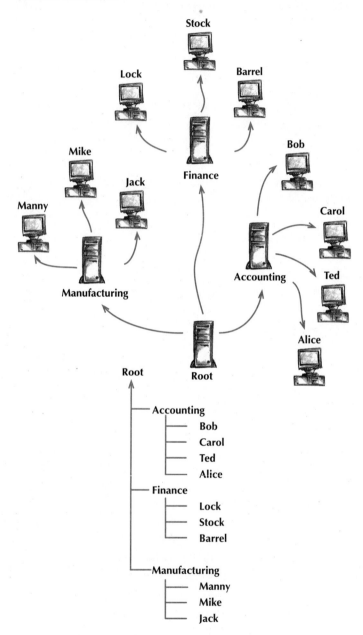

Data Transmission

A good network, like a good edit of a film, should stay beneath the threshold of your attention. Users don't usually care a whit about whether they're using a broadband[15] or a baseband[16] network. They are indifferent as to whether they get the files they want over a Token Ring network or over an Ethernet network; just as long as they don't have to use a decoder ring to make the thing work. Most people don't notice their network until it's not working at all or it's so slow that they have to wait and wait for it to work.

Nowadays, network operating systems can operate on many different types of hardware. Intel's iNDX and Novell's Sharenet were two early NOS products. The Microsoft Windows for Workgroups (WFW) NOS enabled any manufacturer's personal computer—Gateway, IBM, Toshiba, NEC, you name it—to communicate with another manufacturer's and to signal peripheral devices, too. The Windows NT network operating system can also link a mix of computer types— IBM compatible machines, UNIX stations, DEC, Sun, ASA240s, and others—into one cooperative network.

Network Limitations

The main frustrations of collaborative computing across traditional networks are tied to the limitations of networks running proprietary software systems. These frustrations include:

- lack of uniform search capability
- lack of interoperability
- lack of scalability
- expense of proprietary networking software

Network functionality should be invisible

The NOS handles communications between brands and types of computers

Proprietary systems cause frustration

---

15. Broadband communications are modulated signals; they can handle multiple channels of video, audio, and data.

16. Baseband communications present one unmodulated message at a time. They do not have capacity for real-time video.

A Bouillabaisse of Computing Technologies

An eclectic mix of technology

Whoever coined the phrase *everything but the kitchen sink* might as well have been speaking of a contemporary computing environment, which, in many ways, may resemble the kitchen of the house you've lived in for 25 years. There's the three-speed blender you got as a student, a microwave, a bread-making machine, a glass orange juice squeezer, and an electric juicer.

Old hardware is put to new uses

Many computing environments today are living museums of computing technologies. Dowager mainframes sit beside sleek young servers. IBM's AS400s are in the traces with Microsoft NT 5.0. Old-style computers aren't abandoned when the technology faithful flock to Comdex each year to admire (and plan how to acquire) the new toys. The old war-horses get repositioned on the network. "People have been saying that the mainframe has been dead for about 10 years," said Anthony Brown, Manager for Object Technology, IBM, at the 1997 Comdex PacRim, "But each year we've sold more than the year before. In 1996 we sold more than ever in the history of IBM. So there's a lot of money in dead products."

Many mainframes have joined the client/server world as powerful servers on a network. Some measure their memory in terabytes (not to be confused with *pterodactyls)* and one large corporation even leases out its spare capacity to local municipalities.

The role of information technologists is changing

IT professionals are also experiencing a change in their role within their organizations. Because of the growth of the team culture in organizations today, and because of the growing recognition of the value of knowledge sharing, IT departments are moving more into the mainstream of their organizations. Some organizations have even created a new slot: Vice President of Knowledge.

Often it's someone within the IT group that starts pushing for an intranet, as a better way of networking. For them, it solves the scalability and interoperability problems that have plagued networks for years.

Intranets overcome network limitations

Internet-Intranet Technology Basics

The originating purpose of the Internet was to link disparate types of computers and file formats into a high-speed, flexible, bullet-proof network. Data exchange protocols accomplished this purpose, by enabling vastly different computers with different operating systems to speak a common language to each other.

Use of Internet protocols solves interoperability problems

An intranet offers the opportunity to achieve full integration across an organization's network because it uses:

- Internet-based browsers
- Internet-based communication protocols
- Internet-based server software
- Internet-based development tools

There is a growing number of tools that developers have at their disposal to build Web applications. Some are comprehensive kits. For instance, Visual InterDev is a Web application development system. It contains a suite of tools to create HTML pages, Active Server pages, and database schema. Microsoft FrontPage is a Web content-management tool that can also be used to build small Web sites. Other tools are more specific, like the Microsoft ActiveX controls and Java scripts mentioned in Chapter 1.

As discussed earlier in this chapter ("Network Communications," page 51), the TCP/IP suite of protocols is fundamental to the working of the Internet and company intranets.

Primary Internet protocols of use on an intranet include:

- TCP/IP, the underlying stack of communication protocols, which includes FTP, SNMP, Telnet, and others
- FTP, File Transfer Protocol for copying large files from archives
- HTTP, the HyperText Transfer Protocol to move text and graphics.
- SMTP, Simple Mail Transfer Protocol
- IRC, Internet Relay Chat for interactive real-time conversations on line
- Usenet, protocol for bulletin-board type messaging
- NNTP, News Network Transfer Protocol for handling newsgroup communications

Any product that is built to use these protocols can interact with other products built to the same standards.

Intranets also use
the URL and
HTML standards

In addition to these Internet protocols, two additional standards are required for Web-based communications. In fact it was the development of these two standards that facilitated the existence of the World Wide Web (WWW) and led to a communication revolution. They are:

- URL (Uniform Resource Locator)—a uniform addressing system
- HTML (HyperText Markup Language)[17]—an Internet-based language that provides a method for displaying text, images, sound, and video (see "HyperText Markup Language," page 9.)

In addition, these new standards greatly expanded the user-friendliness of the Internet by enabling the transfer and display of information in forms other than plain text.

---

17. The HTML standard provides interoperability between numerous formats, such as word processing, database publishing, and interactive applications.

Together, these open standards and protocols form the foundation for intranet technologies. Because the standards and protocols are the same on an intranet as on the WWW, users of the internal network who have permission can move unimpeded across the Internet and the WWW. New products like Internet Explorer 4.0 make it easier than ever to move seamlessly from an intranet to the Internet.

Users with access can move easily between their intranet and the Internet

Open Systems and Standards

In a perfect world, all computers would play well with others. As in any rapidly developing arena, compatibility is a problem. The aim of *open systems*[18] is to give customers choices and provide developers with some direction in a multi-vendor world that is in a state of constant change.

Compatibility is always an issue

There are two types of industry standards:

- De jure standards are formal standards that have been approved by official, academic standards-setting bodies, such as IEEE (Institute of Electrical and Electronic Engineers) and ISO (International Standards Organization).
- De facto standards are widely adopted, reality-based industry standards, not *officially* sanctioned by any particular body, but in general use.

It takes time for an official standards body to meet, debate, and decide. It cannot keep pace with the rate of technological change driven by the rush of market forces. Internet standards are largely de facto because by the time the academic bodies come out with the standard, it's old technology.

Developing formal standards is time-consuming

The World Wide Web Consortium (W3C) is the de facto standards-making group for the World Wide Web. W3C was formed in 1994 and is jointly managed by MIT and CERN. Anyone at all can propose a new standard to W3C. As with

Anyone can propose a new standard

---

18. Open systems are systems designed according to accepted standards.

all Web technology, HTML standards continue to evolve. As of this writing, HTML 4.0 has been approved. It incorporates some of the proposals made by Microsoft and Netscape for improving the display functionality of Web pages.

Intranet Software

Faster software development using component technology

An intranet can use of a mix of shrink-wrapped products like Microsoft Internet Explorer, Microsoft Exchange Server, and Microsoft Office 97 (which has built-in HTML publishing capabilities), along with specialty software created for specific tasks, such as ordering materials or reviewing and updating customer records from a database. Building software products with *component object technology* speeds development because components are reused and repackaged to form new solutions quickly.

At this stage in the evolution of intranets, most organizations custom-build software solutions to reap productivity benefits from their intranets. In the four chapters that focus on ways to use an intranet (Chapters 5 through 8), different software solutions are highlighted.

HTML and VRML are used to display objects

While HTML is still the basic language of Web-based applications, VRML (Virtual Reality Markup Language) is an offshoot language for displaying objects in three-dimensional space. VRML is also an evolving language. Besides its obvious applications, showing products or architectural spaces, VRML is also being used to show complex relationships between data.

XML may replace HTML

XML is another emerging language that has been proposed to W3C. XML has many advantages over HTML, and many experts foresee that it will replace HTML. XML offers more flexibility because tags can be described in the document, thus ending the problem of proprietary tags that only certain browsers can read and display. This will make it easier for developers to build distributed applications.

Developing in a Standardized Environment - ActiveX Platform

In order to avoid the complexities of traditional LAN network programming, developers need a standardized environment in which to build an intranet. The Microsoft Active Platform is a construction set of client and server technologies that developers can use to build intranet solutions. The platform includes ActiveX technologies, server technologies, and client technologies.

ActiveX technologies enable component applications to work seamlessly across client and server components of the network. The server technologies run on the Windows NT Server network operating system and Microsoft Internet Information Server (IIS). The client technologies run in an Active Client browser.

Browser software On the user's workstation, a GUI (graphical user interface) browser communicates with the server. Browsers are free (Microsoft Internet Explorer, Mosaic, Midas, or Emacs) or available for a very small fee (Netscape Communicator). The word *browser* under-represents its function, because it does more than browse.

The browser is the window to the Web

A browser is a powerful device that contacts servers, requests data, receives the requested data, and then interprets the retrieved HTML files for on-screen display. The browser must also be able to invoke additional applets as needed to play any attached non-HTML files (such as audio or video clips) or to execute other programs.

Browsers request, receive, and interpret data, and they host applets

As browsers evolve to include more and more features, their developers frequently push the standards by incorporating new capabilities that are not universally supported. While departing from standards drives more innovative browser products to market, it also means that people using one browser may not see or experience features on a Web site geared to another browser. The solution for an organization building an intranet is to specify a company-wide browser. Then Web site builders can make full use of the features of the browser they have chosen.

Stick to standards for universal support

Internet Explorer 4.0 has taken a giant step beyond the original function of a browser to organize and display Web-based content. It incorporates integrated tools for retrieving, receiving, and sharing information using one familiar interface.

Internet Explorer 4.0's new search features can make searching less time-consuming and more productive. For instance, by right-clicking the browser's Back button, you can view a history of sites you've visited and by highlighting one, you can jump right to it.

Internet Explorer 4.0 push (or Webcasting) technology allows you to subscribe to sites that will deliver information to your desktop, where you may view it off line at your convenience. (See "Webcasting—Push Technology," in Chapter 6.)

Internet Explorer 4.0 employs Dynamic HTML (DHTML), a standard under review by W3C that enhances the multimedia capabilities of Web sites. In addition to providing improved display functionality, DHTML conserves network resources and improves browser speed by minimizing round-trips to the server. It is also very easy to update and modify pages authored in DHTML. Internet Explorer 4.0 also supports Java and ActiveX.

The new browser is really a suite of Web tools and applications. It includes NetMeeting, audio and video conferencing software; NetShow broadcasting software; FrontPad, a simplified Web authoring tool; Web Publishing Wizard; and Personal Web Server. It also offers basic services like e-mail, newsgroup readers, and chat.

Conclusion

Intellectual capital thrives on intranets

What a long strange trip it's been from ponderous command and control mainframes to distributed networks of quick-acting computing. The underlying need for intranets comes from the shift in the nature of capital. In the industrial economy, assets were measured in steel, bricks, and machinery. The most valuable assets in the digital economy are intellectual. Ideas can speed across intranets, unhindered by the barriers of traditional network computing.

The early adopter organizations didn't build their intranets by executive order. In many cases, some of the information technologists got to tinkering with the tools, but others quickly joined in and put the tools to use. Generally, intranet development is an iterative process of continuous improvement characterized by enthusiasm and discovery.

Intranets grow organically

Looking Ahead

Many organizations found that once they had a useful intranet up and running, the next logical step was to build an *extended* intranet or extranet for select external partners. The next chapter, "The Extranet Option," continues the broad overview of intranets in light of networking and Internet technologies. That chapter explores the benefits to your organization from extending specific intranet privileges to certain external customers and suppliers and suggests some mutually beneficial activities and resources you might offer them to carry out your mission.

An extranet extends intranet benefits to partners

Chapter Three

The Extranet Option

As recently as 1996, when the word *extranet* started showing up in newsgroups and other online sources,[1] some people rolled their eyes—*oh no, not another Net buzzword!* However, by mid-1997, it was clear that extranets would take their place in the evolution of business-to-business communications.

The same advantages that organizations were seeking with intranets for their internal customers and suppliers—quick dissemination of information, access to the knowledge base, collaboration—could be realized with their *external* partners through an *extension* to their intranet. Ford Motor Company has an extranet, called FocalPt, that connects 15,000 dealers worldwide. It provides the sales force with promotional and financial information, and automates information exchange between Ford and the service centers. And it's open twenty-four hours a day, 365 days a year.

Extranets extend the benefits of intranets

---

1. According to Bob Metcalfe, who invented Ethernet in 1973 and founded 3Com Corp. in 1979, he is the word-smith who coined the term "extranet," in his *From the Ether* column, "Summer Olympics to use IBM's 'extranet' 390s, but beware the Ides of July," April 8, 1996, p. 43, available on the InfoWorld WWW site.

Defining an Extranet

An extranet bridges the business interests of trading partners

An extranet is a bridge between organizations that is built with the same Internet-based open standard protocols that form the basis of an intranet. Using an extranet, organizations can share private and timely information secured on their intra-nets with their trading partners. It may be a mutual extranet, with two or more organizations granting access to specific areas on their respective intranets, or, as illustrated in Figure 3-1, a hub extranet, with one organization inviting one or more partners to engage in activities on its intranet. The focus of an extranet is towards the needs of an organization's supply-chain community, whereas the focus of an intranet or a WWW site is directed towards its own objectives.

Figure 3-1   *A hub extranet.*

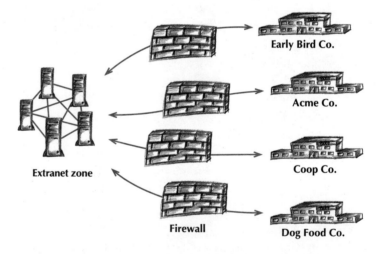

The benefits of extranets extend beyond efficiency and speed. Sending out pre-release copies of a national advertising campaign to vendors or letting dealers check inventory on their own time schedule fosters enthusiasm and a sense of alliance with trading partners.

Extranets can build a sense of community with your trading partners

Where exactly is the extranet located? The *shared space* can exist either on actual portions of the organization's intranet or on separate servers in a secure zone. The space an extranet occupies is sometimes referred to as a DMZ, a demilitarized zone between two networks (see Figure 3-2).[2] It could be a firewalled area between two trusted networks (parts of the intranet) or, if partners use an Internet connection to access the extranet, between the intranet and the Internet (between trusted and untrusted networks).

The location of an extranet depends in part on the access connections

Network DMZ.

Figure 3-2

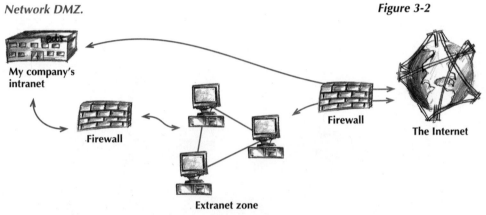

My company's intranet

Firewall

Firewall

The Internet

Extranet zone

For the purposes of this book, the term *extranet* excludes a generic customer area, which is really a marketing area in disguise, on an organization's World Wide Web site. The defining difference is that an extranet offers access to *data that enables business,* rather than simply providing consumer product information.

A WWW marketing site is not an extranet

Also considered as extranets are virtual communities and vertical industry networks for collaboration and sharing between registered industry members across a private IP network. This type of extranet can be realized in two ways. Teleres Corporation provides an example of the first way.

The term *extranet* includes vertical industry networks

---

2. Then again, some IT people refer to their entire intranet as a DMZ, a safe zone that is very separate from the Internet.

They have an extranet into information services on their intranet for members of the commercial real estate industry (see "Connecting over the Internet," page 79). The second way (see Figure 3-3) is for industries to form their own proprietary extranets, such as those formed by chemical and auto industries. The number of vertical market extranets will increase as more organizations experience success with their intranets and when more extranet-oriented software applications become available.

Figure 3-3   *A vertical industry network.*

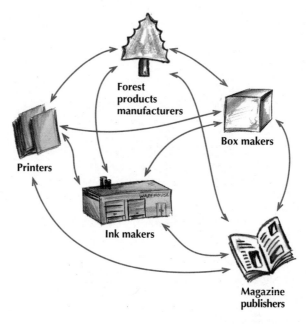

Before Extranets

Before extranets, most organizations depended on telephone, fax, overnight, snail-mail, e-mail, newsletters, bulletins, and face-to face contact at trade association gatherings to connect with their customers and suppliers. They *faxed* the latest price lists and *e-mailed* shipping schedules. They *mailed* product documentation. They *fielded* support telephone calls. They *extended* their hours. They *asked* for feedback. Their partners waited to be fed the information they needed.

Going Beyond the Limits of Value-Added Networks (VANs)

Many large organizations have used high-cost value-added networks (VANs) to engage in traditional EDI (electronic data interchange).[3] Using proprietary software, the VAN providers assumed the responsibility of transmitting, managing, logging, and archiving all messages through an electronic central clearinghouse. The length of time it took to negotiate trading partner agreements and the high cost of the service (transmission charges plus set-up fees) have been barriers for companies not large enough to reach the Fortune 500 list; this barrier has prevented them from taking part in electronic commerce.

Value-added networks linked partners through proprietary systems

While large organizations were able to conduct electronic commerce using VANs, those networks did not provide a place, open twenty-four hours a day, seven days a week, where their trusted partners were welcome to avail themselves of the data they needed. The driving forces behind extranets are the larger trends to automate business processes, tighten time frames, and to maintain closer, more productive alliances with business partners at a lower cost.

Unlike VANs, extranets provide direct access to information through a browser

Overview of Extranet Issues

Extranet challenges are similar to those of remote intranet access: security, performance, and user support (see "Reaching—Remote Access and Productivity," page 206). While the main concern with intranets is ease of deployment, extranet development requires walking the fine line between granting easy access (to trusted partners) and keeping the organ-

Security, performance, and user support are important extranet issues

---

3. EDI is a set of specifications for ordering, invoicing, and payment over a private electronic network.

izization's core data secure. When it comes to performance, software product availability is of concern. Until the vendor community builds open standard and turnkey extranet software applications, organizations will have to fight their way through mix-and-match compatibility issues themselves.

Business goals and technical standards must be clear among all partners

Building an extranet also requires attention to the human interface side of development. The various players within the host organization must define extranet business goals, standards, and metrics among themselves, then repeat the process with external partners. The scope of this task is more complex than that of planning an intranet.

Anatomy of an Extranet

Building an extranet takes hardware, software, and a network connection. Both the primary organization and the trusted partners' intranets need:

- Open standards business application software that can function through both host and partners' firewalls
- Server hardware and software
- Defined and documented security measures
- IP-based network connections

Software and Server Compatibility

Most extranet applications are custom-tailored

Extranets are going through that awkward stage between a promising concept and the bandwagon. To avoid being blocked by the compatibility issues between software vendors, early adopters have had to create custom applications to run on their extranets. (These organizations probably had to overcome compatibility issues with proprietary groupware and messaging software when they built their intranets.) Extranet developers need an open standards environment for the same reason intranet developers needed it: to cure interoperability problems.

Custom extranet software also needs to be flexible enough to handle large numbers of concurrent users and to work compatibly across firewall borders *without breaking*. Performance and reliability are crucial. After all, what's at stake is a partner relationship.

Maintaining up-time is crucial for business relationships

To share applications across the extranet, partners will need to use mutually compatible software. Netscape and about forty partners are supporting the Crossware initiative, a core set of open standards for extranets. These standards include directory, security, and software distribution standards. However, a host organization and its partners will also have to agree on the technologies that provide specific functionality for Web pages, such as Microsoft ActiveX controls or Java applets. Participating partners will have to use browsers that are ActiveX-compliant or Java applet-compliant.[4] In addition, they will have to use the recommended version of a browser, in order to support browser functionality. For instance, if you build Web pages with dynamic HTML and Channel Definition Format (CDF) push technology (features that Microsoft Internet Explorer 4.0 supports), then all participating partners also need to install Internet Explorer 4.0.

All partners must be able to meet the same minimum technical standards

The host organization will have to decide on the lowest common denominator approach to software (and other technology as well) and publish minimum standards for partners. Some partners may not be able to participate (at least not fully) on the extranet until they can meet those standards.

---

4. ActiveX controls and Java applets are fundamentally different in the way they interface with a client machine, but can co-exist within an application. A Java applet runs on a "virtual machine," which means it emulates an operating system and compiles the code in a virtual environment, not on the client machine. ActiveX controls operate directly on the client machine. Different versions of browsers support different functionalities. Internet Explorer 3.0, 4.0, or Netscape Navigator 3.0 with an ActiveX plug-in can support ActiveX controls.

Vendors are working overtime to bring extranet products to market. PFN (Publishing for Networks) introduced its Continuum software server product to create business-to-business connections. Their first product runs on UNIX, but a second release will run on the Windows NT operating system. Novell offers Border Services technology, with VPN support, security services, and proxy caching.

Extranet server software handles the running of extranet operations. Some are management functions, such as access control, security, transaction management, and site management. Every request to a server is a *transaction*—a request for a report, or a product order, or check on order status. Extranet servers must be able to fulfill the requests quickly and to the satisfaction of site managers. A larger issue is multi-platform compatibility. Partners who operate on proprietary systems could be excluded from participating in the extranet.

When an extranet
exists on a separate
server, duplicate
data must be
carefully managed

If the extranet runs on a server that is separate from the intranet (where the host data lies), security issues are reduced. However, this configuration can cause headaches in keeping information current. When data on the extranet is updated through batch downloads, there can be problems in keeping the data synchronized with the core data on the intranet. Add a Web site to the mix, and the complexity of content management increases. It requires more effort to assure that updates are sent to the right receiving entity (intranet, extranet, or Internet Web site), and not posted where they should not be seen. One solution is a database that authorizes requests to an NT file system where master copies are stored. Then when an item such as a sales report is updated, it will be posted to the receiver servers (intranet, extranet, or Web site) that are authorized to post it.

Security Measures

The basic security methods include firewalls, encryption, and data and user authentication. (See Chapter 4, "Risk and Mitigation Strategies.") Your security design will depend on the size and number of high security areas you need and the type of network connection you use. For example, if you only need browser-based encryption, then one of the easier ways to build an extranet is to follow the electronic commerce model: use a commerce server that supports Secure Sockets Layer (SSL) protocol for sensitive pages only or for your entire extranet. However, to give partners access to software applications, you need to build either a virtual private network or a tunnel (to encrypt all data end-to-end at the IP level).[5]

The type of network connection determines security solutions

IP-Based Network Connections

There are three options for an extranet connection: a dial-up connection, private (leased) lines, and a secure tunnel on the Internet.[6]

Dial-up

Dial-up connections (see Figure 3-4, on the next page) are private links over standard or ISDN lines, similar to the RAS (Remote Access Server) connections to an intranet, LAN, or WAN. However, many area telephone company central switching offices, which were designed early in the twentieth century to handle voice telephony, are already overloaded and have difficulty supporting packet access by modems over their analog networks. Although relatively slow, this connection has high potential for security.

A dial-up connection is very secure, but can be slow

---

5. In this context IP refers to one of the levels within the TCP/IP stack of protocols.

6. A secure tunnel on the Internet is a connection, sometimes provided by an Internet service provider, with end-to-end encryption.

Figure 3-4   *Dial-up connections.*

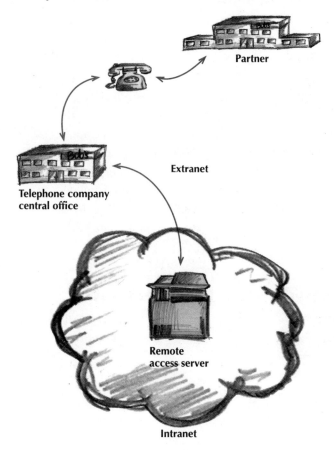

Partner

Extranet

Telephone company
central office

Remote
access server

Intranet

Private Lines

Extranets connected via private lines (see Figure 3-5) have
high capacity, speeding data at 56 Kbps to 45 Mbps. They
can be point-to-point lines owned by the organization, but
they are more likely to be leased lines over a public packet
network provided by one of the long distance carriers such
as AT&T, Sprint, or MCI. The extranet partners that connect
this way can get a direct permanent virtual circuit connection (PVC) protected by the carrier; they are thus freed from
the risks and vagaries of an Internet connection. Like a dial-
up connection, this option is considerably more secure than

sending data coursing across the Internet, where it may be easily intercepted.

Private lines are owned by the organization or leased from long distance carriers.

Figure 3-5

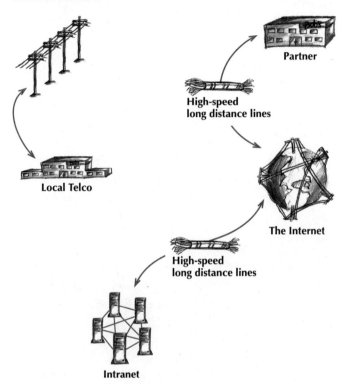

Partner

High-speed long distance lines

Local Telco

The Internet

High-speed long distance lines

Intranet

Connecting over the Internet

A third option for an extranet connection is a tunnel into an intranet from a URL on the Internet, the public network. By using encryption at both ends of the tunnel, you can be assured of a relatively safe passage of data and messages. Many organizations do not trust their proprietary data to travel over the Internet, even to their own facilities or outposts on their intranet, much less over an extranet. Wendy Aylsworth, Vice President of Technology and Facilities at Warner Bros. Animation Studio, agrees that they could

Relative safety may not be enough

benefit from being able to transmit art and ideas between various studios. However, concerns about their proprietary materials' getting sidetracked to the wrong people (who could be holding hands with a pirate merchandiser or a competitor) have kept the studio cautious about trusting transmissions over public networks.

Making a Decision

Access type and speed effects data availability

The advantages and disadvantages of each option will change as technology evolves. The type and speed of network access relate directly to the traffic (number of partners and frequency of use) and types of data available from the extranet. For instance, if you're an auto manufacturer offering clips of an advertising campaign and video walk-arounds to all your dealers in North America, you could require a lot of bandwidth. Nevertheless, this type of application extends value and builds community.

Some companies provide multiple options

Teleres, headquartered in Dayton, Ohio, is an interactive information service for the commercial real estate industry. They provide real estate news, as well as filterable market, demographic, and financial data. They give their subscribers several connection options.

Teleres' customers make their own choice

"We do not depend exclusively on the Internet to connect to our customers," wrote Kirby Leeper, Chief Technology Officer, by e-mail. "We offer them a choice. If a customer has a good connection to the Internet and is happy with service levels and performance, etc. we are available there with all our products… However, we have classes of customers that absolutely do not have or want the Internet in their shop attached to work stations which are also attached to their backoffice LAN/Intranet/Extranet…"

"For all our dial and dedicated circuit connections," Leeper's e-mail continued, "we also have direct connections into our data centers and special routing classes set up with our network providers. Therefore, a customer may be provided a physical private connection to Teleres, not just a virtual private connection over the Internet."

A separate issue for the private and dial-up connections is *who hosts the connection?* Is it the organization offering the extranet or a network ISP? (See "Performance and Support - The Main Reasons to Outsource an Extranet," page 82) Other crucial issues include speed, reliability, and security.

Issues include the host, speed, reliability, and security

According to an e-mail message from Bob Metcalfe, founder of 3Com Corporation, many organizations currently use private networks for their intranets, because they find the Internet too insecure, too slow, and too unreliable to meet their performance needs. For their extranets, most are using Internet connections, "… but that will change as applications become more important and if THE Internet does not grow in security, speed, and reliability."

3Com uses both private networks and Internet connections

Northrop Grumman Corporation, which began as a little airplane company in California, is now an international aerospace and electronics entity. They have had internal networks for quite some time, and following the Sun Microsystems model of phases towards intranet maturity, they consider that they are entering the fourth stage,[7] coordinating large activities. As the company has grown quickly through various mergers, they have wrestled with ways to simplify and consolidate growth capacity at the WAN level. To do this, and to partner with outside vendors via an extranet, they have to choose between running their WAN over the Internet (and using the commercial wire network) or staying within their own private leased lines.

According to Richard Atkinson, Chief Communications Technologist at Northrop Grumman, the company is trying to decide the economic feasibility of operating its WAN on

For Northrop Grumman, the issue is economic feasibility

---

7. The four phases of the Sun Microsystem model are: grassroots activity, managed chaos, managed services, and organized structure and strategy.

public or private lines. When they are not moving a lot of information, or when they are moving information that is not mission critical, running across the Internet lines is fine. "But," says Atkinson, "once we reach a certain level, such as a major teaming arrangement on a program, then it's time to get a leased line." For their Joint Strike Fighter (JSF) program in 1996, with partners McDonnell Douglas and British Aero Space, they began collaborating over the Internet (see "Serving Joint Venture Partners, page 89). But as needs for greater capacity, tighter encryption, and security grew, they went to leased lines.

Liability plays a role, too

"Security?" says Atkinson, "For us, it is a concern. Our secrets—if they find out you leaked it, you go to jail. Warner Bros. or Walt Disney, there's no prosecution. You might be fired or you might be sued, but there's no threat of jail time."

Performance and Support—The Main Reasons to Outsource an Extranet

Using outside hosts helps organizations to focus on their core business functions

After making a promise to a partner about the smorgasbord of data and value waiting on the extranet, you had better deliver. Your problems with understaffing in the IT department may not appease a partner frustrated by an extranet application that stalls or whose calls for help (from another time zone) go unanswered. As networks become increasingly complex, organizations are looking at outsourcing the hosting responsibilities. (Let *them* take the calls in the middle of the night.) In exchange, organizations are asking for performance guarantees, like the ones the telephone companies routinely provide. If a partner encounters a busy signal on either the access line or the help line, your extranet isn't working for you, it's working against you.

Many organizations are actually considering handing management of their WANs *back* to public network operators, whose core business *is* network services.

Some Internet service providers, such as UUNet and Concentric Network Corporation, manage virtual private networks (VPNs) for organizations with intranets and extranets. They lease long-distance lines and manage networks isolated from the Internet. Intranet or extranet users dial into the ISP for their connection. UUNet was the first, with Extra-Link, to offer an extranet service over T1 lines priced competitively with frame relay services.

Some Internet Service Providers will manage your virtual private network (VPN)

The Trend to Outsourcing WANs

After the divestiture of AT&T, many organizations installed and maintained WAN equipment themselves as private networks, so they could make changes on their own without waiting for service from the public service providers. Changing the time-division multiplexing equipment connections was tedious; the connections (and changes) had to be made manually, one by one. The changes within the telephone industry added to the delays.

Then in the early 1990s, frame relay technology drastically cut the time it took to install new communication lines, and public network service started to look more appealing. It also seemed that outsourcing could be the key to resolving the growing disparity between rising network traffic and shrinking in-house technical network staff numbers.

Client/server computing, increasingly powerful desktop computers, and Internet use have quickly driven up demands for network bandwidth. In addition, networks are becoming increasingly complex, with WANs encompassing a mix of leased lines, remote access, ISDN, frame relay, Asynchronous Transfer Mode (ATM), and Asymmetrical Digital Subscriber Line (ADSL). Often, due to mergers or acquisitions, numerous organizations own hybrid networks with both public and private network services. In spite of increases in complexity and service demands, budget restraints have kept network technical staffs from increasing.

For smaller companies, handing over network management chores to one of the public network managers such as AT&T, MCI, or Sprint can solve many day-to-day headaches and free network staff for long-range planning tasks. Many larger organizations are more cautious about giving up the control over transmitting mission-critical data.

Are You Ready For An Extranet?

Do not undertake an extranet until your intranet is running smoothly

Before sharpening those mechanical pencils to design your extranet, make sure your organization is ready for the extranet option. An extranet should be undertaken only when you have a well-functioning intranet in place. This means you've resolved questions about bandwidth, remote access, and reliability. You should also be able to answer *Yes* to the following questions:

- Do you have a robust plan for maintaining and extending your network security?
- Do you know exactly what information or services need to be shared?
- Do you know whether that information is static or subject to change? If it's changeable, at what intervals?
- Do you know which of your trusted partners you want to invite to participate?

How Could You Use An Extranet?

Think about what activities and information belong on your extranet

Look to your supply chain to see the benefits of building an extranet. How could you increase productivity if you had a private communications link with customers, dealers, distributors, resellers, suppliers, contractors, and joint venture partners?

Share test results and sales leads

What could you exchange in a secure environment? You might wish to share test results or lists of sales leads. Perhaps you could publish and receive responses to requests for proposals?

Provide parts lists and host sales contests

Which self-service activities or information could you offer on your extranet that would make it easier for your partners to do business with you? Product updates, parts lists, and sales contests come to mind.

Then consider how you could work with partners in a shared space to achieve your business goals more quickly and efficiently. Perhaps you could collaborate on regulatory change or new product development.

Online collaboration becomes an option

Think also in terms of being on the receiving end of an extranet. How could different departments in your organization benefit by gaining access to one of their business partners? For instance, links to your health plan provider can keep the inevitable changes in the health care plan flowing to the HR department without delay. Or a link to a 401k provider can be augmented with other investment services for your employees. These links can perhaps bridge the gaps caused by staff reductions and provide value-added services to employees.

Consider the potential benefits of access to other companies' extranets

Serving Business Partners

Business partners can include dealers, distributors, support personnel, contractors, suppliers, subsidiaries, and key customers. The types of information and activities that organizations share with their partners over an extranet include database access, messaging and groupware applications, parts and materials requisitions, and workflow systems. From video conferencing to posting new software releases, almost every business activity can be adapted to an extranet. The following four sub-headings provide examples of more specific types of information and activities for specific populations on an extranet.

Partners can access parts and materials lists or shipping status data

Key customers Some customers deserve special consideration. You can use an extranet to *park* product updates, upgrade options, warranty information, and even marketing presentations or promotions that your key customers or clients can view at their convenience. If you employ push technology, you could notify them when new information is available. You may wish to allow a key customer to look up order status and account balances, and to do database

Share research data with selected customers

transactions. You can also share knowledge-base articles to help them understand issues or to present research findings. An extranet is also an excellent place for soliciting feedback and for encouraging customers to send questions, for your immediate attention.

Air Products and Chemicals, Inc. has two extranet applications under development that will make vital information available to key customers. They manufacture the cabinets that their customers in the semiconductor industry use for their products. According to Bob Majowicz, Manager of Electronic Commerce for Air Products, "We guarantee the purity of the gas at the point of use in the semiconductor fabrication facility, and we'd better be right sure that anything in our system—pipe, valve, regulator—that product will not contaminate the gas. They [customers] say, 'How do I know it will not contaminate the gas?' We show them the test results of every part of the system."

Another customer segment makes large purchases of polymers, ordering multiple products from many locations. Air Products and Chemicals, Inc. allows them access to their own sales data, by location or by product. According to Majowicz, half of APCI's business comes from 50 of their 3,500 polymer customers. "We're giving them *extranet*," said Majowicz.

With the right hardware you can provide discussion forums and online training

Sales representatives, dealers, distributors, and subsidiaries Sales representatives, value-added resellers, and subsidiaries can use the same types of data and activities listed above for clients. In addition, you can offer these partners sales leads, customer records, market surveys, and data about the competition. You may also want to give them access to wholesale pricing figures and inventory status. And you can set up discussion forums and make sure your experts respond quickly to questions and escalate any important issues to someone who can make decisions and respond. Depending on whether or not you have specified hardware standards for your extranet that will support multi-media, you can give them access to ad campaigns and sales training on the extranet. Using software such as NetShow, you can broadcast special programs or events to your partners.

Data-Tronics Serves Subsidiaries

Arkansas Best Corporation, a holding company, offers their subsidiaries the opportunity to do business on an extranet. Among the ways the subsidiaries use the extranet is to offer *their* customers up-to-date information about orders and accounts or to offer their sales force instant access to customer information stored in a datamart. The extranet functions over a combination of leased lines and dedicated lines, depending on the size and needs of the subsidiary.

One of the subsidiaries of Arkansas Best Corporation is ABF Freight Systems, Inc., the fourth largest LTL (less than truckload) carrier in the United States. ABF offers their shipping customers, large and small, Web-based access to *track and trace* information maintained in ABF's databases. To take advantage of this extranet offering, customers use a dial-up connection through an Internet Web site, and enter their customer identification information and password to gain secure access to their records. Using their Web browser, customers can filter data and create reports detailing the status of individual shipments; send inbound and outbound shipments to a certain location within a specific time frame, by dates and by direction; or check what a certain shipping arrangement would cost. The availability of this information through a Web page allows ABF to pass on to their customers the advantage of instant and easy access to the data they need, when they need it. "We are expanding the Web interface," said Diana Jones, Data-Tronics Manager of Systems Analysis Programming, "so that anything the customers can pick up the phone to do, they can do with their Web browser." The extranet is managed by Data-Tronics Corporation, another subsidiary of the Arkansas Best Corporation.

Data-Tronics Corporation provides information technology services for the various members of the holding company. Arkansas Best Corporation's core data is locked up in IBM mainframes. Data-Tronics staff use the REXX programming language to write the server-based applications that retrieve and format mainframe data into HTML.

Dixons Mastercare Technicians Use Extranets for Support

Dixons is Britain's largest consumer electronics retailer of brand goods and business products. The technical bench-jockeys at Dixons Mastercare, in Nottingham, England, are on the telephone twenty-four hours a day solving their customers' technical computer problems. A normal day brings in 2,700 calls. Using their intranet, support personnel can quickly find a customer's warranty status and then use hyperlinks to jump to manufacturers' technical support sites to troubleshoot a problem quickly. Once on the partner's extranet, they can check to see if the software upgrades that their customer needs have been issued. Or they can check a parts list.

"An extranet is important for customer relations," said Keith Martin-Smith, PC Services Director for Dixons. "For instance, Apricot—a brand name for a Mitsubishi PC [a personal computer available in Britain]—they have one of the best manufacturer's support sites. You dial into the Apricot web site—if you know the address—and on one of the pages, type in the APC serial number, and download a parts list from the Apricot manufacturing system. And what we see are the parts and part numbers. It's accurate and up-to-date, and has in-depth technical data." The name of the game in customer satisfaction—for both Apricot, and their partner Dixons—is speed. Dixons technicians let their fingers do their (electronic) running; they don't have time to thumb through a manual.

Provide up-to-date information to those in the field

Repair and support personnel Extranets are ideal for providing repair and help desk personnel with the information they need to do their jobs. A repair person needs the latest information about product updates, release notes for new software products, or specifications. They look to you for parts descriptions and availability and troubleshooting tips; priority response to e-mail acknowledges that you value their business. You can offer discussion forums for reporting known problem and solutions. Granting access to knowledge-base articles and skills-upgrade opportunities reflects your commitment to them.

Suppliers and contractors Your key suppliers and contractors will also appreciate access to topical discussion forums, knowledge-base articles, product updates, and opportunities to upgrade their skills. They may benefit from being able to check project development status and materials requisitions. Contractors and suppliers will value the convenience of having new project or product specifications on line and submitting their bid in a secure environment.

Check on project status and requisitions

Serving Joint Venture Partners

Another category of extranet user is the joint venture partner. The activities of such partners could include any of those listed for the other extranet user populations, plus more closely held financial, research, project-development, and regulatory compliance data.

For example, working on the Joint Strike Fighter (JSF) program with their joint venture partners British Aero Space and McDonnell Douglas, Northrop Grumman engaged in many types of data collaboration over their extranet. Besides using e-mail, they shared project reports and other program information, primarily from personal computers, and used Net-Meeting. They exchanged engineering/design information, mostly from UNIX workstations, and Unigraphics CAD design data.

Collect and exchange data online

The JSF program was the first extranet endeavor for Northrop Grumman. Several other applications followed. Now most business units have requirements for national and international extranet solutions.

Serving Vertical Industry Communities

A newer variation on the theme of extranets is as a service for a specific vertical market. Each industry has its own regulatory, financial, materials, supply, technical, and market focus. Industry-specific trade associations and vendors aim to meet the common needs of organizations that oper-

Extranets can serve vertical markets

ate within their industry. An extranet can provide a meeting place, enabling registered members to exchange ideas and broker resource information, or to access data they need to make decisions. Power companies, chemical companies, and automobile manufacturers have formed closed networks for collaboration and EDI.

Technical Restraints to Extranet Development

Extranets should use standards-based technology

Extranets need the same interoperability and open standards environments that intranets need. It seems that the constant evolution of Internet-based technologies and standards is the only *steady state*. Partners and the host organization must clear these hurdles before engaging in barrier-free exchanges of information.

Watch for limitations of current network products

Limits in the technology of individual network components that plague remote access also crimp development of extranets. For instance, routers can make frame relay connections, but cannot authenticate or manage large numbers of sessions. Firewalls and encryption boxes can build in safety, but not routing. RAS servers support dial-ups, but route poorly. Until a new device or a new generation of products has been invented and has proven able to handle all these functions cohesively, systems will have to be built with multiple component complexity.

Extranet Planning Overview

Planning process is similar to planning an intranet

The first place to begin is at home with the same players who worked together to develop your intranet. The extranet planning group should include the extranet Webmaster and representatives from IT, communications, finance, and all relevant operations, as well as public relations.

Together they must *define* the business goals of the extranet. Each group, of course, will see the goal (and ways to measure its success) from its own perspective. For IT, security and reliability rule; for finance, cost containment is paramount; departments want to increase customer satisfaction; and Webmasters want to satisfy the department heads.

All internal departments must agree on common business goals for the extranet

The team then needs to *inventory* existing computer and communications platforms and *review* existing computing security (and contingency) plans.

Review existing platforms and security

Communicating with selected business partners about business goals of the extranet is crucial. *Partnership* is the over-arching goal. The team will need to identify and resolve platform and software incompatibility issues between your organization and partners. Finally, it will be time to develop the pilot, launch it, monitor it, review lessons learned, and...redesign it.

Build consensus for mutual goals and set minimum technical standards

Looking Ahead

The next chapter, "Risk and Mitigation Strategies," explores some of the known risks and ways to mitigate them in building intranets and extranets. It may seem that as soon as someone develops a new lock, ten people are busy day and night hunting for the key. But the biggest risks may not be from people in electronic ski masks trying to hack their way inside to get at your data, but from people already inside the palace walls. Just like safeguarding a home, setting up structural safeguards and eliminating careless behavior are important steps in securing your valuables.

Chapter Four

Risks and Mitigation Strategies

Perhaps no event strikes more fear in a manager's heart than a breach of information security—whether the data is sensitive employee information, a proprietary formula, or a customer's transaction. Whether the damage comes from sabotage or carelessness, from an internal employee or outside hacker, from a trusted contractor or from a valued client, a security lapse that results in the escape of business data is serious business.

Bernard Mayles created his own retirement plan, feathered with the information he had gained from his employment with both Merck & Company and Schering-Plough in the drug manufacturing industry. The government is now managing his retirement. He was convicted of trying to sell company secrets for $1.5 million. The White House Office of Science and Technology estimates that lost sales from business espionage cost companies $100 billion a year.

With the advent of network computing, the risks of theft, unauthorized changes, and flagrant damage to data have increased. In the olden days, mainframes and minicomput-

Security risks are serious business

Information theft is big business

Network computing has increased risks

ers were constructed like the doors of a vault—they could be opened up or locked down. They were very secure. The personal computer changed everything: it opened the door to risk. A solo machine left unattended is vulnerable. A computer connected to a network is a potential highway to trouble. According to International Data Corporation, in 1990, only 15 percent of the personal computers in the United States were tied to networks; by 1996, the percentage had jumped to 50 percent. And it's rising. Unprotected, a document-sharing, multi-user system is an accident waiting to happen. Because these are the days of intellectual capital, the risk strikes deep into the core of the organization.

While intranets bring ease of access, you must guard against added risks

The very things that users love about intranets are the very things that keep network administrators awake at night. Because intranets make it easy to publish and easy to access information, they compound the level of risks. Add to the intranet scene Internet access or partner access through an extranet, and you've added a lot more doors through which spurious data can enter and confidential data can exit. Not only must organizations protect their own data from unauthorized changes, they must also ensure that their employees do not put them at legal risk by compromising laws on intellectual property rights when they publish. (See Chapter 5, "Using an Intranet for Quick Publishing.")

This chapter explores the types of risks intranets introduce and presents some solutions to mitigate those risks. It is hoped that this information will not only keep you from leaving your house keys in the front door overnight, but will also help you identify proactive steps you can take that will help you get a good night's sleep.

A Goal-Oriented Approach to Intranet Security

The goals of any network security system are to control access to the network and to protect the confidentiality and integrity of the data. When sitting on the network, as well as when in transit, data is vulnerable to attack and theft. One type of attack on your information assets is introducing a virus. It's like planting a bomb on your property. Copying and redirecting confidential data are two forms of computer theft. Computer fraud and computer crime are on the increase.

Goals include controlling access confidentiality, and integrity

The main defensive weapons are firewalls, authentication, and encryption. No one is betting their business that the *killer app* in network security will be *Keep the Bad Guys Out version 1.0*. There is no silver bullet, and no amount of shouting *Shields up!* will protect you. The best security is a combination of hardware, software, and administrative strategies. Policies and procedures that are realistic are a crucial component of ongoing security. Procedures that are sound but cumbersome will backfire and leave an even wider hole in the wall and a great gap in your intelligence.

The best solution is a combination of security measures

Although the risks are rising (see "The Changing Hacker Community," page 101), the situation is far from bleak. Hardware and software vendors are devising solutions to keep the intranet safe for business (and electronic commerce). In addition to specific security products, security features are being built into browsers, servers, and networking equipment.

Vendors are contributing security solutions

A full-fledged security strategy should include *deterrence, protection, detection,* and *response* measures. Implementing a strategy is a continuous process, because threats to your security will only escalate in ingenuity and severity. Risk management tends to fall into two categories:

An effective security system must be dynamic

- People and procedures
- Hardware and software

A strong security strategy is an ongoing process that weaves both elements into a flexible structure that is proactive.

Overview—Avenues of Risk

The first step to safety is to recognize the types of damage and the avenues of risk. You may sustain deliberate attacks on confidential business data or on the productivity of your employees. Downtime spent repairing a damaged network and restoring destroyed data can amount to a crippling blow to a development or production cycle. Security risks can originate from inside the organization or from the outside.

Virus Attacks and Bug Damage

Downloaded files can bring unwelcome viruses and with them bugs

This era of *try it, then buy it* software on the Internet threatens the composure of IT managers and the security of networks. Downloaded programs from the Web can contain viruses or bugs that can bring down a system. It's like taking candy from strangers.

Virus protection requires ongoing vigilance

A virus is a small program that can cause great and irreversible harm to a computer or network. An activated virus can annoy, disable, or destroy a computer workstation and its network. Viruses have two access routes: in the front door on a floppy disk and through a firewall with downloaded software. The only defense is the rigorous application of virus detection and cleansing software (updated frequently) that sniffs out the intruders like a troop of rottweilers that will do bad things to a virus when they find it. Some types of virus detection software stand guard on a server or client and isolate incoming viruses before they can do damage.[1] They scan for and capture viruses from disk insertion, copying files, renaming files, executing a program, and system startup and shutdown, as well as viruses in memory. Other types perform regular sweeps, like a security guard, to see if a virus has entered the premises. Of course, this software protection does no good in the drawer. It must be used on a

---

1. Virus scanning software can be implemented as Terminate and Stay Resident (TSR) programs or Virtual Device Driver (VdX).

frequent and regularly scheduled basis, for example auto-matically at 1 a.m. each morning.

Virus-detection software, such as McAfee's VirusScan, searches for code fragments known to be common in virus programs (such as the *put* command). Most anti-virus programs offer protection against hundreds of viruses and derivatives, but when a new viruses breaks out, a new and specific antidote may need to be administered. Because viruses are a growth industry and new versions are constantly being released that can escape your detection mechanisms, it's essential to remain closely connected to organizations that monitor and develop antidotes to mutants or new releases. A study released by the National Computer Security Association found that in February 1997 alone, nine out of

Keep up with new antidotes; most anti-virus programs offer upgrades

Categories of Viruses

It's beyond the scope of this book to detail the numerous viruses that may infect your network. But the following are some of the major categories.

A *Trojan Horse*, like its mythological predecessor, catches a ride on a benign file or software application. Once inside, the virus goes to work.

A *logic bomb*, such as the Michelangelo virus, sits dormant until a certain event (such as a date) triggers it to become active.

A *mutant virus* enters a computer in one form, then mutates and replicates. For instance, one virus spreads by attaching itself to all outgoing mail from an infected host computer.

A *prank virus* is not inherently destructive, but has been used by some to point out vulnerabilities in software. The *Word Macro* virus changes a Word document into an unopenable template file by changing the extension from *.doc* to *.dot*. It caused lost productivity in many offices, although its effects were reversible—there is an antidote program.

Buggy software can
chew up your
network

ten large companies in the United States reported having been infected by a virus. Web-available software, besides exposing you to the risk of viruses, might be unstable Beta releases rushed out too soon, or unproven code from The Fly-By-Night Developers Company, or even software components from reliable software designers unaware of potentially dangerous flaws. Early versions of both Java applets[2] and ActiveX controls created vulnerabilities that malevolent software designers could have exploited to insert invasive programs on the host computers.

Internal Risks

Primary cause of
risk is careless
employees

Studies have shown that the greatest risk to your data security—sources estimate between 50 and 80 percent—comes from your own organization. Access is astonishingly easy. Browser security set to low when someone is downloading from the Internet, a password pinned to the wall of an office cubicle, or an unattended computer that is not equipped with a screen-saver lockout utility are all open invitations. (Computer equipment left on at night without this protection is especially vulnerable.)

The heart of the problem is a careless attitude. Until employees realize the consequences of practicing unsafe computing, they cannot join the battle to protect their company assets. In fact, they probably don't even realize there is a war going on. Security begins at home. Risk awareness is the first step in putting security measures into practice. Education (and re-education) is the solution. Managers, of course, must walk the walk.

---

2. Researchers at Princeton University found a flaw in Netscape Navigator 2.0 that lets users execute Java applets on their computers, and from there make contact with other computers on an internal network and access off-limits data. Sun Microsystems, originator of the Java language, plugged the leak immediately.

While employees constitute the largest risk pool, a second group is the army of contractors and other partners who have access to network resources over the intranet or extranet. The same cautionary education about security procedures should apply to them as well. While contractors may operate under a non-disclosure agreement, it's up to managers to make that a *living* agreement, rather than a paper that's signed, put away in a drawer, and forgotten.

Contractors and other partners extend the risk

The third risk group is disgruntled employees (or former employees) who may commit acts of sabotage. These are people who have the knowledge and the motivation to do harm. When employees are terminated or transferred, they take with them the knowledge of passwords and locations of sensitive data. They may go into business for themselves, using your data. Or they may destroy your data files before leaving. Employee profile data and access lists must be updated promptly to reflect changes in status. Otherwise, you're leaving the door open.

Terminated or transferred employees can carry vital data out the door

One final type of inside security risk, quite different from the others, is the risk of intentional sabotage caused by excessive competitiveness, either from an individual or a group. Outright data destruction—or an action as insidious as surreptitiously changing the sales representatives' calendars so they look bad when they repeatedly show up late to customer meetings—obviously undermines the success of the organization. Computer cut-throat methods, perhaps undertaken to look good to a boss, are sometimes difficult to prove, but leave a residue of mistrust in their wake.

Excessive competitiveness can lead to destroyed data and careers

External Intruders

A new breed of external intruders are robots. However, robots do have a beneficial purpose as they go about their business of indexing Web servers on the Internet, as you'll see in "Searching for Data," page 196. If your intranet is accessible from the Internet, it's a good idea to evaluate

Robotic intrusions can be controlled

whether you want to lock robots out of your Web site entirely, or just some areas of it. Your administrator can block the robot's access by adding a /robots.txt file using the Standard for Robot Exclusion (see the "To Block Access to a Site," sidebar, page 200).

Some hackers can be
extremely destructive

Human-type external intruders range from curious, to malicious, to profit-motivated individuals. For the most part, hackers used to be benign explorers and experimenters. Early hackers viewed cyberspace as a giant electronic public playground—actually, more like an absorbing and challenging puzzle. Trying to break into a system (and get out without being caught) was a competitive sport. Ironically, early hackers received more credit for acts of electronic terrorism, such as the AT&T rippling crash of January 15, 1990 that silenced seven northeastern states in the U.S.,[3] than they deserved at the time. Unfortunately, curious hackers are not the only hackers anymore.

An intruder can plant a virus or hack in and intercept, change, or steal data. And they do. Corporate espionage is on the rise and computer crime is one avenue of attack.

Attempted break-ins
are reminders of
your vulnerability

There are still many thrill-seeking hackers, who lurk and look but do no actual damage. While their intrusion is unnerving, their main motivation is a sense of achievement and power (without invoking it to do harm). In a way, their *attention* to your network can be positive—let it serve to remind you that you are always vulnerable and to point to some specific deficiencies in your shields.

---

3. The real culprit was a couple of lines in AT&T software, written in C language. The "do...while" construct contained a "break" clause within an "if" statement. The "break" clause was intended to break the "if," clause, but instead broke the "switch" clause, and telephones in seven states (and three airports) broke down.

The Changing Hacker Community

However, according to an official from Britain's Defense Evaluation and Research Agency (DERA),[4] new types of hackers are emerging that have abandoned the hacker *code* and willfully cross the line into crime and destruction. Information brokers are doing a brisk business by contracting hackers to steal specific business or military information, and then reselling it to competing rivals. So-called *dark-siders* use their hacking talents for financial gain or the joy of doing damage. Even long-time members of the hacking community have expressed grave concern over the chaos and new breeds within their milieu.

Hacking is now a military and economic threat

While some hackers excel at code breaking (they're known as *crackers)*, and others are expert at breaking and entering, some are surprisingly adept at *social engineering.* This is the term that describes talking their way smoothly (by lying) into your system. Stories abound about how an intruder impersonated a vice-president who'd lost a password, and then conned a network administrator into revealing it; or how easily one discovered the dial-up access phone number for a modem line and then got a Help desk person to hand over the password. What's particularly astonishing is how quickly they can *engineer* their way into your system. A good security system test will include frequent tests of social engineering.

Hackers have professional specialties

In the United States, law enforcement has been trying to get its arms around the new issues of computer crime since the 1980s. Law enforcement communities (federal, state, and local), already stretched to the limit with *real* crimes in the streets, find it hard to allocate enough funds and find enough expertise to go after the bad guys in cyberspace. There are only about 200 professional cyber-sleuths in law enforce-

Cyberspace is on a par with Tombstone, circa 1879

---

4. The DERA is the agency that develops security systems for the British military.

ment offices across the United States. They are outnumbered. They are outgunned. The new laws and court decisions are not yet reassuring. Neither the Computer Fraud and Abuse Act nor the Electronic Communications and Privacy Act (both passed in 1986) have made significant dents in malicious hacker activities or computer-assisted theft.[5]

Jurisdiction is problematic

This new frontier has experienced confusing jurisdictional problems. Did the crime take place on the thief's computer in one state or on your server in a different state? When prosecution does get hold of a good case, the wheels of justice may move more slowly than the useful life of the stolen data. In addition, some decisions already on the books have actually hurt more than helped. The 10th District Court of Appeals' (Denver, Colorado)[6] narrow interpretation of data is a case in point. The court ruled that copying data and transporting it across state lines was not theft. In this decision, a computer, but not its data, was defined as a personal item.

Protection Basics

A secure, collaborative environment is not an oxymoron

The problem is, how do you exchange information, conduct transactions, collaborate, and control access on an intranet at the same time? You can devise a military-compliant security system[7] that would make the CIA proud, but if it's too complex and cumbersome for your users to live with,

---

5. The Electronic Communications Privacy Act of 1986 criminalizes unauthorized electronic break-ins. As the equivalent of telephone anti-bugging and anti-tapping legislation, it limits law enforcement activities as much as hacking. It also contains provisions regarding e-mail privacy.

6. The 10th U.S. Circuit Court of Appeals handles appellate cases for Colorado, Kansas, New Mexico, Oklahoma, Utah, and Wyoming.

7. The Department of Defense issued the Trusted Computer Standards Evaluation Criteria (a.k.a. the "Orange Book"), which details classification levels of computer security. It ranges from D1, a completely untrusted system through six more levels to the maximum Level A.

they'll find ways to work around it. Then your security people will have wasted their time and built only a false sense of security for their efforts.

The solution is to select the appropriate methods and levels of protection for each area of your intranet. You won't need to position a ring of Dobermans around the plans for the company picnic, but you will want to secure financial information and new product designs deep within a bunker. A good security system is a *relative* system, custom-tailored with appropriate technology. There is no one size that fits all. Different areas on your intranet require different levels of protection. Some extremely sensitive data should perhaps not be put on your intranet at all, at least until you are sure you have all the security you can afford.

Secure systems are flexible and tailor-made

Problems and Solutions Overview

More specifically, the problems are how to block unauthorized access to areas on your intranet, how to detect falsified identities and assure data integrity, and how to protect the confidentiality of the data. The following table lists these needs and their solutions.

Strong security protects data and blocks unauthorized access

Security Needs and Solutions

Need	Solution	Technology	What it does
block unauthorized access	firewall system	firewalls, VPN, passwords	filters (rejects or accepts)
detect false identity	authentication	digital certificate	verifies identity
assure data integrity	authentication	digital certificate	verifies identity
protect data confidentiality	encryption	symmetric encryption (includes authentication), asymmetric encryption	encodes data

Each of these technologies has a place in a well-designed security system. It's hard to overemphasize that it's the combination of these technologies that makes a system strong. It's the same as planning a menu using the U.S. Department of Agriculture's food groups. Some grains for B vitamins and fiber. Some fruits and vegetables for A vitamins and antioxidants. You need a healthy mix.

- Firewall systems work on the network or application level to filter incoming and outgoing traffic from one server or network to another. An intranet may have many firewall systems protecting sub-networks, as well as a DMZ (demilitarized zone) for the extranet, and another firewall system at the gateway to the Internet.
- Authentication technology guards against falsified identities by assuring both senders and receivers that each is who they claim to be. It is also used to assure data integrity—that the data has not been altered. (It does not protect confidentiality.)
- Encryption technologies ensure that data cannot be read other than through the secure server. It uses key systems to encode and decode data, so users can trust that the confidentiality of their data will be protected from view if it is intercepted. (To protect the integrity of the data, authentication technologies are used with encryption.)

These technical solutions depend on a growing number of security protocols that can be employed to help guard the intranet from intruders. The next section provides a brief description of some of these protocols, followed by sections (on firewalls, authentication, and encryption) that explore some of the ways these three technologies are being applied.

Internet Security Protocols

There are several Internet security standards for networks, Web applications, and e-mail. Standards continue to evolve

Internet Security Standards

SSL—Secure Sockets Layer

S-HTTP—Secure HTTP

S/WAN—Secure Wide Area Network

S/MIME—Secure MIME

PGP—Pretty Good Privacy

SET—Secure Electronics Transactions

SSN—Secure Server Network (can be a daemon internal to firewall or an external machine)

IPSec—encryption standard application and proxy gateway capabilities added to SSN

DES—Data Encryption Standard

RSA—public key encryption developed by Drs. Ron Rivest, Adi Shamir, and Len Adleman

to meet increasing needs for assuring confidentiality, authentication, and data integrity.

Secure Sockets Layer Secure Sockets Layer is a protocol layer between the TCP/IP layer and the application layer (HTTP). It enables secure data communication (server authentication, encryption, and data integrity) from an SSL-enabled server to an SSL-enabled browser. Microsoft Internet Information Server has support for SSL and the Microsoft Internet Explorer browser (since version 2.0) supports SSL on the client side. A working group of the Internet Engineering Task Force (IETF) is reviewing Transport Layer Security (TLS), a new protocol that uses SSL 3.0 as a base.

SSL is an Internet protocol employed in servers and clients

S-HTTP for user
authentication and
document secruity

S-HTTP Like SSL, Secure HyperText Transfer Protocol (S-HTTP) also ensures data confidentiality and data integrity across a Web environment. Specifically, S-HTTP supports user authorization and document security.

S/WAN for en-
crypting IP packets

Secure Wide Area Networks (S/WAN) The S/WAN protocols being tested by firewall and router vendors include standardized methods for authenticating and encrypting IP packets and for managing the keys.

S/MIME and
PGP for e-mail

S/MIME and PGP There have been numerous proposals to handle encryption of e-mail across the Internet. The most widely used is Pretty Good Privacy, which became a de facto standard for e-mail (see "Pretty Good Privacy," page 119). S/MIME (Secure MIME) uses digital certificates to secure mail, and must be used in conjunction with a certifying authority. Both PGP and S/MIME rely on algorithms from RSA Data Security, Inc.

Setting up Structural Safeguards with Firewall Systems

A firewall is a
system of
protection
between two
networks

A firewall is a barrier system that controls access between two networks. The barrier could be between an intranet and the Internet, or between sub-networks of an intranet. It's really more like a border crossing between two countries than a physical firewall between a car's engine and passenger compartments. If there were building codes for intranets, a firewall would be required. Most consultants and IT specialists agree that the biggest problem with firewalls is not that they are hard to build, but that they are hard to manage well. The term firewall system includes network-level protection as well as protection for specific applications such as mail or file servers. If your intranet is connected to the Internet, the first line of defense against intrusion is at the network level.

Microsoft Internet Security Framework

Microsoft developed the Internet Security Framework as a comprehensive set of cross-platform, inter-operable security technologies for use with Microsoft Windows 95 and Microsoft Windows NT. The technologies support Internet security standards for online communication and electronic commerce.

The set of technologies includes Microsoft Authenticode technology, Microsoft CryptoAPI, Microsoft Certificate Server, and the Microsoft Wallet, as well as support for client authentication, Personal Information Exchange (PFX), and secure channel services.

Secure channel services provide a private and authenticated point-to-point communications channel between a sender and a receiver, such as the connection between a browser and a Microsoft Internet Information Server (IIS 3.0) Web server. Secure Sockets Layer (SSL) and Personal Communications Technology (PCT) are two protocols that can be used to establish secure channel services. Secure channel services are also used to perform authentication of a client and server using digital certificate technology.

Packet Filtering

A device called a screening router sits between the network it is protecting and the outside world. A router filters packets from the Internet and grants or denies access to the intranet by comparing information in the packet's header[8] with the rules the network administrator has set up (See Figure 4-1 on the next page). For the administrator, new router products make it easier to write rules than before, because smarter screening routers can look at a table of rules and figure out which ones to apply first.[9]

The router acts like a bouncer

---

8. A packet header contains the IP address.

9. Until recently, administrators had to be extremely careful of the order in which they listed the rules. If one rule said *Sally can receive any packets* and the next one said, *Do not accept any packets from Harry the Hacker*, the cautionary rule about Harry had better be listed before the rule about Sally.

On the downside, rules for large networks can become very complex; the complexity can lead to vulnerability even for *smart* routers. Also, a screening router does not possess logging capabilities, so it can't help an administrator spot patterns of access attempts.

Figure 4-1   *Routers can screen messages.*

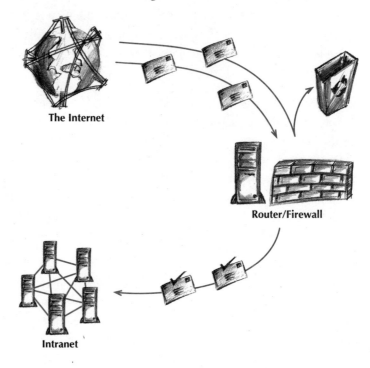

The Internet

Router/Firewall

Intranet

Proxy Servers

Server software has some built-in security features

A proxy server is a gatekeeper between the intranet and the Internet, or between certain file servers and the intranet, (see Figure 4-2). When a client machine is prohibited from making a request directly to servers in the outside world, a proxy server can makes requests to other servers on behalf of the client machine. Proxy servers can also check incoming traffic. Like a router, a proxy server checks the rules the administrator has listed (to see if the contact is authorized) before letting traffic pass. Proxy servers are specific to

A proxy server.

Figure 4-2

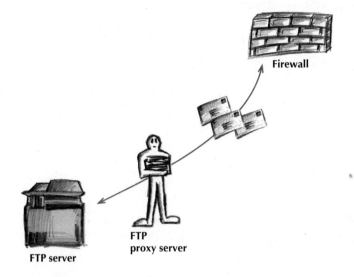

Firewall

**FTP
proxy server**

FTP server

applications. For instance, a mail proxy server protects the mail server, an FTP proxy server guards the FTP server.

Proxy servers can also inspect the contents of a packet and accept or reject them according to the administrator's rules. So, if an FTP proxy server spotted the *put* command in an incoming request and had a rule that read *do not admit any files with the put command*, the proxy server would reject the file. (The *put* command is used to write to a file and could be used maliciously to infect a site with a virus.)

Proxy servers have two other features that make them especially useful. Unlike routers, proxy servers can keep logs of traffic. So, if the server log shows an unauthorized site sending repeated requests for entry, this might indicate an attack. The cache feature on a proxy server helps it avoid becoming a giant bottleneck. A proxy server may cache some information, such as pages on the Internet that users request frequently or pages that are routinely pushed to intranet users.

Proxy servers can examine more than just the address

Proxy servers can log requests and cache data

Sacrificial Lamb

A *sacrificial lamb* is a server deliberately exposed to the Internet to attract attackers. It can be either isolated from your network entirely or stationed just outside a very robust firewall. The lamb should contain only non-confidential *disposable* information. The amount of attention the lamb (or victim) receives is an indication of the wrong sort of attention your network could receive.

Sub-networks

One way to control access is to set up sub-networks

A sub-network is a restricted area within a protected area. Setting up a sub-network involves some additional expense because of the extra hardware and software to run it. As shown in Figure 4-3, a sub-network is usually secured by firewall technology, such as a router and a proxy server. This type of demilitarized zone is often set up to house an extranet (to keep extranet visitors away from the rest of the intranet) or highly confidential sales data (to keep other denizens of the intranet away from it).

For instance, on the sales department's internal Web site, sales representatives in the field might have routine access to customer data, but will not have access to the sub-net that stores the details of the division's sales figures. Only manager-level individuals would have authorization to access the sales division's financial sub-net.

User and Data Authentication

The term authentication covers both user recognition and data validation. This next section addresses the use of authentication in controlling user access.

Controlling Access

Controlling access to information on a network is quite similar to controlling access in a hospital. You don't want to

A secure sub-network.

Figure 4-3

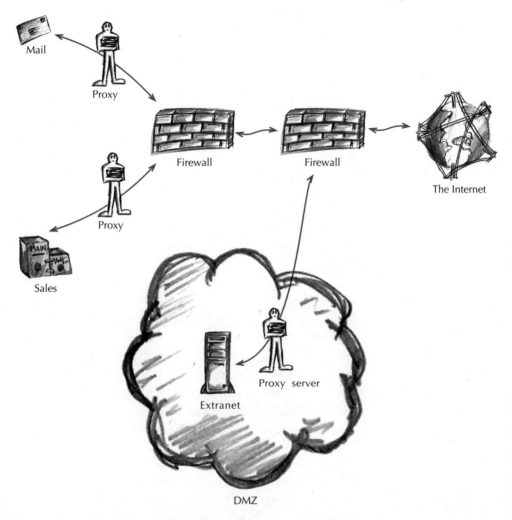

let everyTom, Dick, and Mary stroll into an operating room without their blue booties or have a nurse hand out medicine to the *visitor* in room #244-E instead of the *patient*. (That's one reason for the plastic ID bracelet: inventory control.) At the same time, you need to ensure that people get the access they need to be able to do their jobs. Better not lock the doctor out of the emergency room. In order to

Controlling access means controlling who does not get in, as well as who does

preserve privacy and prevent wrongdoing, there need to be different rules of access for patients, visitors, vendors, doctors, electricians, nurses, nutritionists, social workers, and lab technicians—different rules for trusted users and untrusted ones, and a way to tell the difference.

Access can be blocked at the NOS level, or at the directory, server, or file level

On a network, access to files, to entire drives, to servers, to directories, to individual files, or even to parts of a file can be granted or restricted. Files can also be locked at the Network Operating System (NOS) level. There are three types of access:

- Read Only—anyone can read but not change a file
- Read and Write—anyone can read from and write to a file
- Exclusive Write—only one person has permission to write to the file

Login procedures initiate a request for access

The first stage of security begins when the user logs in to the network. After users enter a user name (usually an *alias* of an acceptable character length) and password, the server checks to see what *permissions* they have—which servers, directories, and files they have permission to access. When users disconnect from the network, a transparent logoff procedure creates an orderly retreat and relocks the castle gates.

Administrators set access levels by setting ACD properties

Another means to control access is an Access Control Database (ACD). An ACD controls network *objects*[10] and their respective properties. Properties determine how an object behaves and who has access to it. For example, users' properties could include their real names, login histories, passwords, and the date their passwords expire. A printer object's properties could include what type of form it can print, such as a requisition order or a check. ACD is a powerful tool in anyone's hands. Security information cuts both ways.

---

10. A user, a printer, disk drive, or software application on a network can be an object.

Remote access presents extra challenges in authenticating users. IP spoofing is one technique that hackers use to impersonate a legitimate caller. In some cases simple procedures such as *challenge and response* or *call back procedures* can provide an extra level of security. Challenge and response directs questions to an incoming caller that he alone should be able to answer. With the call back system, a remote user dials in and then hangs up, and the system dials back to make the connection to a predetermined phone number.

There are ways to add security to remote access

Authentication – The Password

The password is the most basic form of user authentication. It is something that is known, theoretically, by one individual only. The longer a password goes unchanged, the more likely someone else will use it to compromise the security system. Designing a good password *should* be a challenge. Network administrators repeatedly advise users to avoid the obvious, such as a spouse or pet's name; but people do it anyway. Passwords that are easy to remember are easier to uncover. A password that is hard to remember, like a random string of letters and numbers, is harder to uncover.

Passwords should not be familiar words

Among hackers, there are more password-divining programs than you can shake a stick at. One type is a *password trap*. In one case a hacker got hold of a login sequence and modified it to trap passwords. So what had been intended as a login device, in the wrong hands, was transformed into a break-in device. There are other popular ways to capture a server's password file. The most common method of divining a password (besides asking for it) is a *war dialer* that barrages a system with renditions of possible passwords, hoping to get lucky.

Hackers have sophisticated password-cracking programs

How Not to Create a Password

The greatest area of vulnerability in any security system is the human mouth. The World War II adage *loose lips sink ships* applies to organizational security.

Do not use passwords with fewer than six characters. Automated password generation programs can discover them too quickly.

Do not use words found in a dictionary, even foreign words. Cracker programs can run a dictionary loop.

Do not use words from your surroundings, like *Great-View* or *Rover'sPhoto*. Break-ins often occur at the site and they will see what you see.

Do not use the name of a person or pet, either forwards or backwards. Backwards is not difficult.

Do not use dates that can be looked up, like birthdays or anniversaries.

Do not reuse a password, even if you like it.

Do not write it down, particularly anywhere near the computer or file it in a Rolodex under "P" on a card marked *Password.*

Do not use words signifying favorite things in your life, like *MyBigBoat* or *GoMariners!*

Do not use passwords found in a computer security book. Crackers read books, too.

Never, EVER, give out your password, even for a very good reason. Out of your hands, out of your control.

Temporary Authentication Server In some instances, you will wish to permit an individual to temporarily access areas on your intranet or extranet. For instance, if you are hosting a training session for a vendor's sales representatives, and wish to keep their course material and assessments confidential but not necessarily to retain individual scores on your records, you may use an authentication

Do's for Creating Passwords

Use a mix of numbers, symbols, and upper and lower case letters. Because passwords are case sensitive, this increases the complexity.

Make up a compound word, and eliminate the vowels or consonants. GiganticBeets could be *GgntcBts!*

Pick an expression or phrase and reduce it. *The quick brown fox jumped over the lazy dog* could be *TqbfjotlD.*

Create your own cryptographic sequence, such as the last letter of six streets in your neighborhood that lead to your home. (Oak Street, Elm, Spruce, Maple, Juniper, Cottonwood would turn into *KmEeRd.*)

Change your password every six weeks.

server to furnish them with short-term, one-time passwords. The Authentication Server issues a random alphanumeric password when a participant registers.

Digital Certificates

How do you know that people are who they say they are? At a gas station in Liberal, Kansas, when you hand over your credit card, they may ask to see some verification that it's your card (and not mine). You show them your driver's license with the photo-ID. The Department of Motor Vehicles has acted as a *certifying authority*, which we've all agreed to trust, and has issued you a *certificate of authenticity*, that you carry in your wallet in the form of a laminated driver's license. A passport office is another certifying authority (or trusted third party).

A driver's license is an authenticating certificate

How do you know that the software you are downloading actually came from a trusted source? A digital certificate from a trusted third party verifies ownership of the software. Certificates using the X509 standard (derived from the X500 directory specification) can be accepted universally. Certifi-

Digital certificates can authenticate the origin of software or the identity of individuals

cates come in four classes, or levels of verification. Each level requires more detailed background information in order to verify identity.

A trusted certificate authority issues certificates

Certificates are issued by a Certificate Authority (CA), which can be a trusted external company (such as VeriSign), a government agency (such as the United States Postal Service), or a corporate CA through their own Certificate Server (such as the Microsoft Certificate Server). A CA has two main responsibilities: maintaining a Certificate Revocation List (of invalid certificates) and acting as a repository for valid digital certificates, along with proof of identity and a public key for each certificate holder.

Digital certificates bind the identity of an individual, or data,[11] to a pair of electronic keys that can be used to encode or *sign* digital information. The use of digital certificates to verify key ownership thwarts people in their attempts to use phony keys or impersonate another. (Note that the key must be encrypted to protect confidentiality.)

Protecting Data with Encryption

Traditional methods of affixing a seal or signing documents to identify the source, authenticate the contents, and assure confidentiality are useless in electronic communications. Instead, a mark must be encoded in the data itself. Data encryption is the real life version of the secret decoder ring that spiked sales of cereal boxes in the 1950's. Today, instead of simple character substitution (A=Z, B=Y, C=X, and so on), complex algorithms use statistical and mathematical analysis to encode a message more securely.

At its most basic, encryption is systematically rearranging elements in a message to obscure the content to anyone but the intended recipient of the information. There are numer-

---

11. Technically, the identity is bound to the client or server, rather than a human.

ous encryption methods and products that are specific to applications, such as e-mail or credit card transactions.

Crypt

Based on a software implementation of the World War II German Enigma machine, crypt is a basic encryption utility for UNIX systems. Although not considered robust enough today to prevent an attack, it remains useful because of one of its features—it draws an excessive amount of CPU time during decryption, thus drawing attention to an attempt to decode a message. System administrators who watch for heavy use will spot this early warning.

DES (Data Encryption Standard)

DES is a UNIX encryption utility developed by IBM that relies on an alphanumeric string as a single key to both encrypt and decrypt a message. It was developed in 1977 and certified then as a U.S. government standard.[12] With a

Encryption and Governments

In France, Iraq, Iran, and some other countries, non-governmental encryption is illegal. In Russia, non-governmental-*approved* encryption is illegal. In the United States, certain encryption hardware and software comes under control of the Arms Export Control Act, as *munitions-related*. Export licensing requires a review by the National Security Agency, a review so lengthy that it has often exceeded the useful life of the software. Because encryption technology is often built into software, computer companies are lobbying to ease encryption export restrictions that are hampering commerce. Richard White, a civil libertarian incensed about the restrictions, had the RSA encryption algorithm tattooed on his arm, classifying his arm as a weapon that he may not bring into Canada or several other countries.

---

12. Although DES has been re-certified by the U.S. government many times, after the current certification period expires in 1998, it is doubtful that for government purposes, the system will be re-certified.

single key or symmetric system, both the user and the sender use the same key for coding or decoding. One drawback of the secret key system lies in getting the key into the hands of the person who legitimately should unlock the message (or file). During transport, the key could fall into the wrong hands. If you change the key, you have the same delivery problem all over again. In addition, the single key system does not address authentication or non-repudiation. With single-key encryption, there is no way of knowing which person used the key (since it's the same) to alter a message. Therefore, neither party can repudiate what the other may have done.

RSA and Public/Private Key Encryption

RSA encryption requires two matched keys, a public key and a private key

Drs. Ron Rivest, Adi Shamir, and Len Adleman created a simple cipher to name their dual key (asymmetric) system: they used the first letter of each of their last names. Rather than relying on a single key to code and decode messages, their system uses a private key (which the owner keeps secret) and a corresponding public key. What one key does, the other can undo. Either key of the pair can be used to decode or code a message (see Figure 4-4). So if you use your private key to code a message, others can use your public key (available on a key server or sent with the document) to unlock the message that comes from you. Conversely, others can use your public key to send you a message that only you can read. You can use your *set* of keys to secure a message to anyone, and you don't have the problem of sending (securely) a key each time you wish to communicate confidentially.

Use a Certificate Authority to validate the identity of the key owner

This takes care of securing the data, but still does not authenticate your identity. To ensure correct delivery of a public key, use a Certificate Authority. After you prove your identity to the CA, the CA will certify your identity to others who request verification.

Pretty Good Privacy (PGP)

Phil Zimmerman created this simple, but very strong, tool for encrypting e-mail through public key encryption. It is very tamper resistant. PGP is a blend of RSA and IDEA (International Data Encryption Algorithm).[13] PGP can also be used to create a digital signature through the encryption of characters that have been added at the end of the document. This allows you to verify that the digital signature and the document match. Attempts to verify the signature will fail if even one character of the document has been altered.

PGP has a colorful history as freeware encryption, and commercial versions are now available

Public/private key encryption.

Figure 4-4

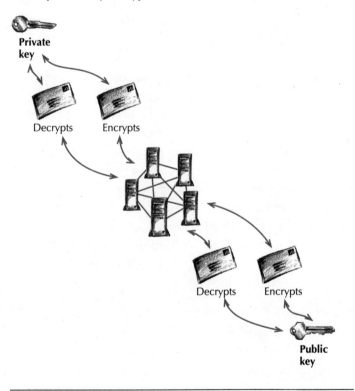

Private key

Decrypts   Encrypts

Decrypts   Encrypts

Public key

---

13. IDEA was developed in Zurich, Switzerland, by Xeujia Lai and James Massey.

Designing a Strategy

Comprehensive
security means
deterrence,
protection,
detection,
and response

A comprehensive security plan should include mechanisms for deterring invasions and wrong-doers, protecting data according to its value, detecting attacks and tampered-with data, and responding to threats with improved measures and retribution. Deterrence, protection, detection, and response—leave out any one of these four elements and, although you may be double-locking the doors, you'll be leaving a window wide open.

Set up deterrents

The first thing neighborhood watch groups hear from the advising police officer is: make your property unappealing to burglars. Deter them from trying to gain entry in the first place. To deter intruders from accessing your intranet, you could put out a sacrificial lamb or camouflage internal host IP addresses. The FBI's National Computer Crimes Squad recommends setting up a *no trespassing* warning (see "Official Assistance," page 126). But Kirby Leeper, Chief Technology Officer for Teleres Corp., averred emphatically by e-mail that it's important to stop them before they ever see a warning sign. Leeper relies on a gauntlet of firewalls, routers, and filters. "If they can get to a 'posted' sign that means they are talking to my computer already! If they can get there they can possibly figure something out. We stop their TCP/IP packets from even getting to our computers. They see nothing, nada, zip from us. We are not there. They must have tried the wrong address."

Protection includes
authentication and
encryption

Protect your data resources by securing them against unauthorized access and alteration. Use certification programs to certify the true identity of users and the source of incoming data. Use encryption programs to maintain confidentiality. Enforce security procedures as if the life of your business depends upon it. Protect the network administrator's information just as rigorously as financial data. To an intruder, getting hold of the keys to the building is a bigger score than just getting into one locked room.

CryptoAPI

Microsoft CryptoAPI is an application programming interface (API) that developers can use to build cryptographic functionality into applications without having to write their own algorithms. Cryptographic algorithms are not only difficult to write, but take special expertise. The CryptoAPI also contains certificate-based functionality that enables developers to sign a document, attach their certificate to it, and encrypt and send it to someone else. The recipient would use CryptoAPI's signature verification algorithm to decrypt it and verify the source.

In addition, because the CryptoAPI contains a service provider model that allows a developer to use a Cryptographic Service Provider (CSP) to supply the actual cryptography, it is easier for a developer to create an application that can meet different requirements for domestic- and export-strength encryption. A CSP can plug encryption of different strengths and types into the application, without changing the code.

Set up monitoring systems to detect attack patterns as well as the presence of intruders. Make sure intruders trigger first-alert alarms in your system. Software products available today (such as WatchGuard's Security Management System and AltaVista Firewall) can act as motion detectors and warn you of suspicious activity on your network. Regard these alerts as a gift; they will show you where you may be vulnerable.

Monitor intranet activity to detect unwelcome activity

Respond strongly both to invasions and to lapses of security. Make use of monitoring data to understand the type and location of vulnerabilities. It's hard to tell whether snooping is just idle curiosity or a scouting mission in preparation for an attack. Inform employees of computer security risks and tell them what they can do to prevent them. Implement procedures for continuous improvement of your efforts to deter, protect, detect, and respond to security threats.

Respond quickly and educate others

Custom design
security for each area
of your intranet

An intranet security system needs to be custom tailored to the value (lost productivity, lost opportunity) that would be associated with loss, leakage, or damage. Different areas on

---

Checklist for Designing Comprehensive Coverage for an Intranet

1. Decide who will design the system. Are your IT professionals proficient at designing, implementing, and managing new security technologies? Not sure? You might want to hire a consultant to work with an internal security team composed of representatives from IT and trusted users.

2. Identify what needs to be protected and why. Inventory all the supplies, hardware, software, documentation, and data associated with the computer system. Every version of keyboard, server, tape backup, modem, operating system, source code, and application has unique vulnerabilities. One little, inexpensive item found on every supply shelf that has probably wreaked millions of dollars of havoc is the floppy disk.

3. Determine who represents greatest risk and address how to handle each type of potential threat from internal, trusted external, and external intruders.

4. Secure all documentation. Where is network documentation maintained, and who has access to it? Product documentation for hardware and software describe security procedures for specific versions. Guard procedures for bypassing the administrator's password.

5. Evaluate the available options, costs, and technologies. Does the cost of defense square with the value of the resource? Do you know if you are guarding against data destruction or against losing control of information?

6. Define the process for developing, publishing, and enforcing security procedures. Procedures (including procedures for handling exceptions) are needed for network administration as well as users. Users will need awareness and skills training.

7. Build in the means (and monies) for monitoring. Review the time and location of intrusions so as to discern patterns and vulnerabilities. Plan system reviews on a fixed time schedule. Evaluate the relevance of old risks; determine new exposures.

---

your intranet will require different levels of security. Your network administrator's password files will need a Kevlar jacket, but the marketing department's stores of press releases can do fine with a lighter layer of security.

Setting Policies and Procedures for Users

For continuous protection, it is essential to set policies and procedures for handling data and managing users. Procedures must be rigorously maintained, preferably without the creation of a boot camp environment. Usually security is breached not because the lock broke, but because someone forgot to lock the door. It is generally easier to control the hardware and software factors than the human factors. Also, the human ones are usually more expensive to maintain.

Network administrative procedures need to grow in response to new learning about potential vulnerabilities. For example, if a review of logs showed an unusual amount of login attempts to the human resources servers between midnight and 4 a.m., then a change might be in order that would effectively block all access to those files, except for access by key managers.

Personnel controls are the restrictions and permissions assigned to individuals within the organization. Individuals are granted access to and prohibitions from certain information. A procedure for managing user profiles might specify a time period to update users' profiles after they have been reassigned. As an individual moves up through an organization, a higher level of scrutiny should precede the granting of a higher level of security access. In some situations even background checks and polygraphs might not be unreasonable.

The network cannot be designed solely around the need for protection; it must also be designed to serve the users. However, the best protection policies are those that are transparent to the user. Intranet users should not be aware of the fences—if they are, they'll be tempted to open the gates.

> Network administrators also need to live by procedures

> Security should be flexible and responsive

> Personnel controls should be regularly updated

> The best protection measures are invisible to the users

One of the most obvious security risks is the *Remember my password* checkbox. Many users check this box to save the time it takes to enter a password each time they log on. But, by doing so, they make it easy for anyone who sits at their workstation to impersonate them online. There is a simple solution—an administrator can use poledit to disallow saving the user authentication on a computer.

Setting Download and Upload Policies

Create a sandbox for downloaded files

Every organization needs to set policies governing the downloading of applications or files from the Internet. You could require that all software be downloaded into a sandbox environment, that is, a constrained run-time environment where the software cannot damage network resources.

Restrict downloads to files with digital signatures

Another security option is to allow the download of only digitally signed applets, ActiveX controls, or any type of file so that the origins of the code can be authenticated. Microsoft Authenticode has an accountability mechanism built into Internet Explorer versions 3.0 and 4.0;[14] Authenticode certificates identify the software publisher—the company accountable for producing it. Digital signage shows the origin, but not whether it is flawed. You can also insist that your developers have their code *signed* before they launch it on your intranet.

Floppy disks represent a risk

Some organizations have forbidden the introduction of *any* floppy disks brought from home into the network until network administrators clear them as virus-free. This can be a cumbersome process, but it is secure. Other organizations forbid the downloading of *any* software from the Internet. Still other organizations rely on the security notifications in browsers and instruct employees to set security levels to high.

---

14. With Internet Explorer 4.0, IT administrators can preinstall certificates and free users from having to stop and make a decision about software that has been already approved.

Evaluating the Costs and Risks

To get a picture of the cost of reducing risk in your organization, create a matrix to display the relative exposures, the cost of loss, and cost of mitigation. List, and then prioritize all vulnerabilities. As shown in Figure 4-5, the risk that someone will break into the operations lab and physically remove a backup tape may be low (B), but the risk that someone will gain access to an unattended online computer may be high (A). Then assign a cost for each loss of security and the cost of a corrective or preventative measure for each.

Draw a matrix of costs and exposure

Relationship between the cost of the loss of security and the cost of mitigating measures.

Figure 4-5

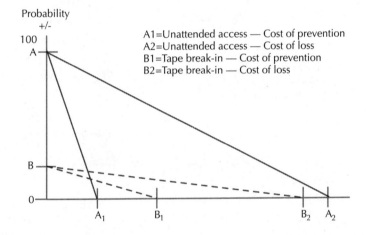

Probability
+/-

A1=Unattended access — Cost of prevention
A2=Unattended access — Cost of loss
B1=Tape break-in — Cost of prevention
B2=Tape break-in — Cost of loss

Be prepared to pay for security. This includes allocating funds and time for your IT personnel to keep up–to-date with other security professionals on the continuing flow of new viruses, new products, and new types of threats to information security. The National Computer Security Association (NCSA) is a trade association with a membership roster of more than 30,000. Their services include firewall testing, training, underground reconnaissance,[15] and security system

Fund security efforts adequately

---

15. NCSA's IS/Recon (InfoSecurity Reconaissance) provides information about security alerts and hacker/cracker/phreak research.

Microsoft Internet Explorer 4.0 Security Zones

Internet Explorer 4.0 includes a provision for network administrators to set up Security Zones on their intranets. Administrators can use the four predefined zones (Intranet, Trusted Extranet, General Internet and Untrusted) or they can customize the number and definitions of the zones. Each zone can have separate security settings specific to the source, protocol, domain name or directory of the Web site. As part of the Security Zones model, administrators can decide which third-party controls or other signed code to allow on their intranets. The Security Zones provision will make it easier for administrators to control network access and to reduce the *noise* of authentication notices by predetermining trusted sites that a user could access without interruption.

certification. The NCSA Web Site certification provides assurance that the organization's Web site meets minimum standards for logical and physical security. This validation could be important both to management and to extranet partners. To pass certification, your security system will undergo rigorous attacks from inside and outside your network. NCSA will send copies of their test criteria on request.

Hack your own system

Test your system, or better yet, bring in a *tiger team*[16] to try to break into it. Be sure to include a social engineering test. For example, let them walk in your front door, using the cover of being a temporary employee, and see how long it takes them to walk out with your strategy for handling a lawsuit or the most sensitive project files on your network. In the debriefing session they can tell you how they found the holes and how to plug them.

Official Assistance

The FBI and the Department of Defense are very concerned about the safety of organizational computing, both in

---

16. A tiger team is a group hired by an organization to test its security system.

National Computer Crimes Squad Recommendations

The FBI's National Computer Crimes Squad (NCCS) makes it their business to track computer crimes, and they recommend a complex mix of strategies that include:

- A login banner to serve as a *No Trespassing* sign and warn against unauthorized access (a very mild deterrent)
- Keystroke monitoring to alert you to unusual patterns, such as repeated login attempts, which may mean your system is under attack
- Telephone line strategies:

  Trap and trace—the phone company can trap and trace incoming calls from suspected intruders

  Caller ID—use it to identify remote login attempts

  Call Blocker—use it in conjunction with Caller ID to block calls from certain numbers at certain locations, such as university dorms, which probably have no earthly reason to dial into your organization
- Data encryption to scramble outgoing messages
- Firewalls acting as an access control system between trusted and untrusted networks

government and in business. After all, their concern for computing security is what spurred the evolution of the Internet in the first place. The Department of Defense has published their levels of security in *Trusted Computer Standards Evaluation Criteria*, also known as the *Orange Book*. The lowest level is D1 (a completely untrusted system), then C1, C2, B1, B2, B3, and finally Level A, which brings the security system itself under scrutiny. Unfortunately, security software packages on the market do not correlate to the DOD levels. If they did adhere to these standards, then it would be easier to define the level of protection different areas of your intranet require and to compare different vendors' offerings.

It's difficult to compare security software packages

Looking Ahead

Before there were computer networks, confidential information was locked away in file cabinets and on secured floors. But people still got in and the information got out. Security and surveillance techniques have matured, as have the ingenuity (and meanness) of the intrusions. In Japan, they have a saying, *business is war*. No doubt both your building security and your network security professionals would agree.

An army of security professionals and government agencies is making it its business to thwart the rising tide of risk. Events such as the National Information Systems Security Conference provide an opportunity for sharing research about attack trends, intrusion detection, and solutions. At the October 1996 conference held in Baltimore, Maryland, Steve Bellovin of AT&T Bell Laboratories identified as new trends password sniffing, sequence number guessing, connection hijacking, denial of service attacks, and exploitation of Web script helper application vulnerabilities. He is looking forward to IP layer (packet-level) encryption and even an *Internet Flight Recorder* that would record the last 30 minutes of network traffic so it could be analyzed when a problem strikes. But then hackers have conferences, too.[17]

The future, besides bringing new products to shore up defenses, will also bring new conceptual models of security. Many people have concerns that the present methods of access control are inadequate for distributed applications and groups. What is needed is a more responsive system with differing levels of trust and, more importantly, a *context* for the trust. Existing database systems have administrative controls for queries, but in complex group situations,

---

17. DefCon is an annual hacker convention, where hackers discuss their business within full view of the attending government agents.

the controls are often inadequate because queries are unable to specify a data object with precision.

One solution might be *task-based authorization* which could provide a better approach to access control than the current subject-object paradigm. While the subject-object paradigm focuses on the *how* of security, a task-based authorization system is a policy-oriented approach that focuses on *what* needs to be done. It could get administrators closer to granting just-in-time access, instead of static permissions.

Task-based authorization focuses on protection tasks

If you haven't been thoroughly put off building an intranet (or ever using any network again), the next four chapters describe how you can use an intranet for quick publishing, information management, knowledge-working, and distance learning. With an awareness of network security, you may be more alert to opportunities for rendering each of these intranet activity areas more secure.

Chapter Five

Using an Intranet for Quick Publishing

At a meeting at the Hitachi Corporation in Silicon Valley, the new CEO was addressing the troops in preparation for a final push to roll out a new product. He put up a slide that read *Speed is God.* He added with import, "And time is the Devil."

Many of the early-adopter organizations began their intranets with quick publishing. They looked at lengthy lead times for putting things in print and reckoned that by publishing quickly on an intranet, they could make use of time as a strategic element. Once they got their feet wet, they evolved towards more extensive business-critical functions.

While there is definitely an overlap between quick publishing and information management, this chapter focuses on basic publishing issues, tools, and opportunities geared toward *getting the word out*. Chapter 6, "Using an Intranet for Information Management," delves into acquiring, organizing, and distributing an organization's information base.

A sense of urgency is pervasive in business today

Quick publishing is typically an organization's first intranet activity

Quick Publishing Defined

Quick publishing is posting information on an intranet

Quick publishing is the posting of information on an intranet Web site—the *convenience store* of text, documents, audio and visual media. An intranet can be an agile tool for communicating news and information. With simple Web-based tools, it's quick to publish and quick for users of the intranet to get the information they need, when they need it, wherever they happen to be.

Brochure-ware and Bulletin Boards

Information is available for viewing, downloading, and printing

In the very simplest form, an intranet can offer *electronic brochure-ware*—perhaps an unflattering term, but an apt description of a useful electronic bulletin board of materials the organization already has in print. The information may include company policies, site and employee directories, company news, product or service announcements, and press releases (see "What Goes Online?" page 141). At the organization's internal Web site, the information is available on Web pages for viewing, downloading, and printing. As the use of the intranet matures, the bulletin board can grow to be a virtual meeting place for exchanging ideas and working together as well. But most intranets start out as an electronic bulletin board or *information parts store*.

The intranet becomes the information parts store

Traditionally, the term information store has referred to some sort of physical medium for storing information, like a disk drive, database, flat file, or Excel spreadsheet. But with the information parts store, an intranet is more than dead storage; it encompasses a way of handling living information, information that needs to be kept fresh and up to date.

Many documents may already have an identifying number

Most organizations already assign printed material an identifying part number so that it can be reordered easily, just like the parts in the maintenance department or in a catalog. So, whether it's a white paper on a resource management issue, an emergency procedures manual, an anti-virus software program, a PowerPoint presentation, or a corporate graphics package, the item belongs in the company's information parts store, that is, on the intranet (see Figure 5-1). Any item that helps employees do business belongs on the intranet.

Shopping in the information parts store.

Figure 5-1

This parts store is open twenty-four hours a day, seven days a week. And it's not disrupted by weather, limited by geography, or restricted by time zones. An intranet is everywhere you are.

An intranet is always open for business

As an organization's intranet grows, divisions and departments put up home pages and publish their own information. For example, the maintenance department might post Hazardous Materials Data Sheets, while the environmental department might publish the Spill Prevention Program and the Environmental Incident Emergency Response Plan (see Figure 5-2 on the next page).

Departments or divisions may publish their own Web sites

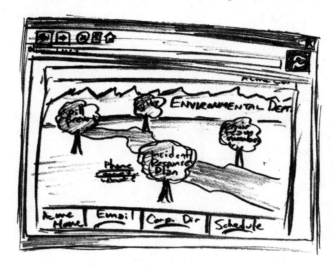

Bypass the print
shop and mailroom

With the addition of a little interactivity, users can read, browse, navigate their way around, follow links, and send messages responding to or requesting information. Unlike a paper brochure, of course, the information on the intranet can be updated and republished very quickly, without ever going through the print shop or the mailroom.

Advantages

Intranets reduce
time- wasting
activities

What is the one commodity you cannot buy, borrow, or make? Time. Development cycles are shrinking, customer patience wanes quickly—the *just in time* mantra really means *sooner than you previously thought possible.* For every advantage that quick publishing has over conventional print publishing, the bottom line is: it saves time over and over again. The table on page 136 illustrates intranet advantages.

Saving time
increases
productivity

Departments that publish and update manuals, catalogs, or directories will find their tasks easier if they publish the material on line. An intranet can simplify the process of keeping

What's the Problem with Print?

There's nothing wrong with print if you don't mind waiting to get your hands on a copy and then, once you get it, if you're not dismayed to find the information is out of date. It's a wonder there's a tree left standing, according to paper consumption figures quoted by John Warnock, CEO of Adobe Systems, at the 1996 CyberCommerce Conference. According to Warnock, the United States alone has a print habit of three billion pages per day and a catalog consumption of eighteen billion catalogs per year. While the purpose of producing this mountain of print is to provide information, the very nature of the printing business involves lengthy lead and distribution times. To be useful, information needs to be fresh. Stale produce and information belong in the trash (which is the destination each day of most of those three billion pages.) The 10th or the 10,000th person to visit a Web site will never complain about a lack of copies—Web pages are a renewable resource.

company documents up-to-date. By quick-publishing business-critical information on an intranet, an organization can greatly improve internal communications, save actual dollars, and save more of that nonrenewable asset—time.

"Sure, it will save me time," said Earnest Phillips, Communications Specialist for Weyerhaeuser, the largest forest products company in the world, of using an intranet to publish information. "What it can do, is let me do *more* in about the same amount of time it takes me to publish *one* communication in print. I can do several *types* of [targeted] publications—I can have one for salary workers, one for timberlands, and one for wood products. When I do an online version, as soon as the text is approved, then—'uh-oh a mistake,' fix it, save it, and—it's posted."

Some organizations like Georgia-Pacific West, Inc.—a wholly owned subsidiary of Georgia-Pacific that manufactures pulp, paper, and chemical products in Bellingham, Washington—are even aiming for *single document, single*

Intranets can be the sole source of some information

The Primary Advantages of Publishing On Line, Compared to Print Publishing

Feature	Advantage
process time savings	The process of online publishing takes less time than paper publishing.
real-time information	Because it's easy to keep online content current, a change in the Emergency Response phone number or the price of a product can get distributed immediately.
one source	One source of company-wide information reduces confusing misinformation and conveys a unified message.
materials and handling savings	Less paper to buy. There are fewer steps to publishing.

location. This means that some information will be available *only* on their intranet. That way, there is one source for the information. This approach saves time for those who are responsible for maintaining the information and for those who depend on it.

Before Intranets

Printing a publication requires many decisions

Every print publication that ends up in an employee's (or partner's) hands has to be designed, printed, bound, shipped, received, and perhaps updated. Each step may involve different suppliers. There are myriad decisions that must be made before the material gets into print and out to the people who need it. For some of those decisions, an intranet is not the issue.

Some materials, such as a policy manual, are relatively static; people get used to having a version that is not completely up-to-date. Other information, like a customer contact list, needs to be updated much more frequently if it is to be an asset, rather than a liability. In the past, if your organization could not furnish you with current information, you had to take the time to develop your own way to keep up to date or suffer the consequences. Using an out-of-date catalog to sell to a customer could end up costing your organization and hurting your credibility. Updating print publications could take a lot of time for the publishers, as well as for the people who received and filed the new material.

People were used to operating with out-of-date materials, but that could hurt business

Before organizations had the convenience of publishing and updating materials on line, they usually had to coordinate and manage a wider array of internal and external suppliers in order to handle publication and distribution of company materials. Organizations often outsourced large publications, such as an employee manual, so they could focus their attention on their core business. Then, if the material needed to be updated, the same large cast of characters would have to be reassembled to go through many of the same steps again. Now, in contrast, intranet publishing is more streamlined and involves fewer suppliers, as you will see in the "The Process of Quick Publishing" section (see page 148).

Many professionals become involved in print publication and distribution

Whether an organization published and distributed a document in-house or contracted with a supplier to do part or all of the job, it would take time during the design process to evaluate the economics of publishing options. Was it a large enough print run for offset printing? Small enough to make photocopies and let the mail room distribute them? What type of binding would be appropriate? If it needed to be updated very frequently, should the material go into a notebook binder. Or would it be more cost effective just to publish a new edition? Which was more expensive, a spiral binder or a notebook? Would the material fit in a two-inch

Print publications require many time-consuming decisions

notebook, or two and a half inches? A four-inch binder? Or two of the two-inch binders? Each of those decisions— distribution quantity, printing quality, packaging options— took time to analyze and then time to decide whether the effort should be handled internally, or whether time needed to be scheduled to go through a bid process.

On an intranet, there is no cost for additional copies

With an intranet, it doesn't matter how many copies you need, and quality issues translate to the look and speed of the site, rather than materials expenditures tied to each instance of publishing.

Is an Intranet the Key to a Paperless Organization?

An intranet can reduce some paper use, but not immediately

When you turn the switch and light up the intranet, don't burn your bridge to your paper suppliers. You will probably save paper in the long run, but it may not happen overnight.

Some organizations have measurable paper savings

Many organizations are counting up paper savings of seventy, eighty and ninety percent. The IRS reports that every time they sent out wage and tax information to a taxpayer on paper, it costs the department more than $5.00, but putting it online only costs them about $0.01. Whether or not you are able to add up significant savings of materials depends mainly on how you are using paper now and the spread of the intranet throughout your organization.

Although copying costs may increase, overall paper use will decrease

With more reliance on electronic communications, there is an accompanying increase in people's tendency to hit the Print button on the browser. So there is some shift in the *use* of paper, and who's doing the printing. But, this *print on demand* quantity is low compared to *distribute to everyone you can.*

Making the shift from paper to on line "If you have 3000 people getting a newsletter printed on paper, and 3000 people getting it on the [internal] web, you're still dealing with paper," said Earnest Phillips, Communication Specialist, Weyerhaeuser Company.

Saving Paper? Is That the Reason To Jump To an Intranet?

"That's the wrong approach," said Earnest Phillips, Weyerhaeuser Company. "If you say, 'It'll save paper,' you don't understand the medium. The purpose is not to eliminate [paper], it's to make information more accessible…You're not dealing with *as much* paper," said Phillips, "but it's really a question of access. When everyone has access, then you can think about eliminating the paper." When asked how many desktops will be linked, Phillips responds, "Ah, I didn't say we'd have a *computer* for every individual. Kiosks! Kiosks in the lunchroom—in places where people can get *access* to them."

Being *halfway there* to an intranet can add expense temporarily, because the organization is maintaining two communication systems, paper and electronic, for the same purpose. For this reason, many organizations choose to put on line first the documents that:

Put employee directories and safety manuals on line first

- Inhibit the flow of business when they are outdated
- Become outdated very quickly, such as employee directories
- Are costly to produce or update

Who's on First?

Which groups are the first to go on line? Those with a minimum level of technophobia and a willingness to break a little new ground. Usually, it's a group that can see the technology as a tool for solving a communication problem and improving a process.

The first groups on line are those who view technology as a tool

In many organizations, the communications and human resources departments are first to buy the advantages of an intranet and publish their information on line. Both these departments bear the heavy burden of issuing timely information. In addition, they usually see the opportunity not only to improve communications, but also to automate and improve their business processes. (And of course, the United Way chairman can hardly wait to reach out on line!)

Communications and HR departments often go first

In April of 1996, some departments in Weyerhaeuser, with a boost from the Information Technology department, jumped on line. Corporate Communications put up a *News and Info* site on the new intranet. But they purposely did *not* label it *Corporate Communications*. "People could care less who did it," Phillips said, "Our site is based on *news* and *information*, so that's what we called it."

Allow employees to use the intranet for routine information

Two sides of the HR coin Besides easing the formidable expense of publishing and distributing paper documents, a human resource department in particular can operate more efficiently by freeing its staff from answering commonly asked questions about benefits and compensation. Instead, employees can find this information for themselves on the human resource intranet site. Some human resource departments are also shifting the burden of performing some routine processing tasks, such as updating job change records, to the employee whose job has changed. After all, these employees are the ones who *own* that data.

Concerns about confidentiality and distribution deter some human resource departments

On the other hand, some HR departments approach an intranet with caution for two reasons. First, their databases contain very confidential information, and they have to be assured that the data will be completely protected and not fall into the wrong hands (see Chapter 4, "Risk and Mitigation Strategies"). Second, to comply with fairness regulations, they must have a high level of confidence in their mechanisms for distributing job postings. So they are often heavily invested in maintaining and updating numerous formats—job or information hot lines, *fax-back* systems, newsletters, special event flyers, and printed job posting announcements. For this reason, they may not welcome an additional format at first.

Nevertheless, an intranet can be an effective compliance vehicle. Once an organization is *wired*, timely distribution is easier and quicker, and it can be more robust.

Northrop Grumman

After the Northrop Company merged with Grumman in 1994, and then a year later added Westinghouse Electronics, the company grew from an aerospace company located in California to a nation-wide aerospace and electronics firm with 45,000 people in five operating divisions spread over 100 locations and joint venture partners worldwide. Publishing their job announcement newspaper, *Horizons*, was getting to be a larger and larger operation.

Looking ahead to an eight-fold increase in publication costs in two years, the company put together a Web version of *Horizons* for their intranet. They also replicated it outside their firewall on their WWW site. Twice a month, they post all job openings to both locations. Because not every individual in the company has a computer, computers have been placed in building lobbies and other places where the *Horizons* paper copies used to be distributed.

Northrop Grumman's online *Horizons* is more than just a list of jobs. Because the site has a link back to the employment database, job seekers can search and cut the data in several ways. They can search by payroll grade or skills. They can also submit a resume and an application on line, and it will be routed electronically to the appropriate employment office within the company.

What Goes On Line?

An intranet provides an expedient way to leverage the content that an organization already owns. Sometimes people are surprised: "Wow! Look at all this stuff." Frequently, within a large organization, information is available that others could use if they knew it existed. After the intranet is up and running for a while, usage patterns reveal a lot about what employees want and need.

Publishing information online often makes it more visible

Every organization will have different criteria for what gets published on line. Some will keep tight reins, allowing only *business-critical* information. And others will grow into a business/community environment. For quick publishing, the focus is getting what you need and getting on with your work.

Each organization has its own criteria for posting content online

Many departments
have materials that
they can publish
online

Below is a list of several types of information that lend themselves to quick publishing on an intranet. This list, arranged by departments within a generic organization, represents one way to spin a Web, but there are many other workable structures. It depends on which department or division in an organization owns what information.

A List of Intranet Quick Publishing Contents

Administration

- facility locators (with downloadable maps)
- technical library resources
- safety data (bulletins, manuals, and achievements)
- how-to information for getting business cards, ordering safety equipment, placing purchase orders, scheduling meeting rooms, reserving a company vehicle, making travel arrangements, and so forth.

Corporate Info and News

- corporate policies and procedures
- annual reports
- company missions and goals
- press releases
- industry-related news clippings
- issues and position documents
- product announcements
- legislative and regulatory updates
- company announcements
- holiday schedules
- special events (blood drives and company picnics)

Departmental and Team Home Pages

- product news
- manuals
- project status
- new projects
- R&D
- benchmark information
- laboratory results
- research seminar news and summaries
- training opportunities
- team job postings

HR Info

- searchable employee phone directories
- skills and expert directories
- benefits information and enrollment opportunities (health plans, compensation, vacation balances, 401K programs)
- employee surveys (and results)
- special recognition
- job postings
- employee status changes
- employee manuals
- child care programs
- commuting options
- classified bulletin boards (items for sale, housing, events)

Imagine the changes that would flow from having all this information up to date and only a few mouse clicks away. Imagine how that would change the employees' productivity, and their relationship to their work as well.

Following are snapshots of different organizations listed under content type on their intranet:

News: BG&E News has always been a popular attraction on *Route 96*, the Baltimore Gas & Electric intranet named after a main highway in Maryland. After the announcement of a proposed merger with Potomac Electric, Route 96 became a source of information for employees about the merger. That site had quick links to mission, vision, and value statements. The day before a vote to accept or reject the IBEW union, the Information Systems department sent out an e-mail message that they would publish the results on line. "As results were tallied, they were pushed to desktops on a marquee at the top of the Route 96 home page," said Kim Ethridge, V.I.P magazine editor, Corporate Communications Dept., "Information Systems just sat there and watched the counters."

Employee directories: HarperCollins When HarperCollins used to publish their employee directory on paper, it was a major undertaking. They published ten different versions twice a year. Now that the information is on line, employees can find their colleagues no matter where they are, and the information is always current. The HarperCollins intranet, developed in late 1995 and deployed at the end of 1996, also helps to cut software distribution costs and to stream-line activities in employee communications, training, sales, marketing, and executive management.

Employee directories: Warner Brothers Features Animation The most frequently used feature of the Warner Brothers Feature Animation's fledgling intranet is the phone directory. It's not just a listing of names and locations, though. It contains photos of individuals and more details, if the em-ployees have completed a questionnaire. It also has maps to show where an individual works.

Document distribution: Harris Electronic Systems Company Harris Electronic Systems Company, a $3.6 billion global operation that ranks #400 on the Fortune 500, started its intranet in 1994. To reduce printing and shipping costs, the company initiated Electronic Document Distribution. Staffers are converting paper documents to electronic documents (stored in the PDF[1] format), creating and posting a hyperlinked table of contents, and employing Adobe Acrobat for transferring the PDF documents. On average, according to the logs, the Harris site for publications is accessed about 17,000 times a month.

Scanning documents can add more information to theintranet

Manuals and compliance: BC Hydro Canada's third largest utility launched its intranet as an experiment in 1995. By 1999, the company's internal Web is destined to be "the only way to publish," said Bill Fernihough, Engineering Supervisor in the BC Hydro Apparatus Projects Department and intranet activist. By law, facilities that use chemical products are required to have Material Safety Data Sheets (MSDS) readily available. With five mouse clicks and a couple of keystrokes on the intranet, employees in BC Hydro can use the MSDS Search function and get to those documents. MSDS is only one of the manuals on line. BC Hydro has published the equivalent of 7800 documents on their intranet and has eliminated the need to update individual copies of numerous manuals.

BC Hydro has simplified distribution of vital safety documents

To distribute maintenance procedures the old way, recounts Fernihough, "It was print, make labels, print envelopes, mail, open the envelopes, update binders. Then send mail advising of the update. We'd send them to 170 people, although only 30 needed them, because it's easier [sending 170] than keeping track of who needs to see it, or taking the risk that someone who does, doesn't have access."

Manuals and compliance: London Underground The thirteen volumes of the London Underground Railway Safety Case manual must, by law, be maintained by each of the

---

1.   PDF (Portable Document File) is the format created by Adobe Acrobat.

General Managers on this extensive subway network. To comply, they updated thirteen 4-inch binders each month. "Most of time the Safety Case is meant to guide you to other manuals and other information [such as the Working Reference Manual]," said Alec Bruty, consultant for the London Underground. "The Safety Case is the rule book you have to comply with, and the Working [Reference] Manual tells you how to comply with it—[for instance] how to turn off traction current to make the site safe." The manuals cover every aspect of safe operations, including safety policies and risk assessment—risk to customers, work force risk, contractor risk and hazards, and psychological stress. Fortunately, the prodigious manual was already in an electronic form for printing. Lotus Notes was considered but rejected because of its high cost (£2 million). An intranet solution, with the NT operating system and Microsoft Internet Information Server, dropped printing costs by £80,000 to a cost of £50,000 for a trial by 250 users. The online safety manual is a living document—a source of easily accessible, up-to-date information.

Volumes of rules are quickly accessible on the London Underground intranet

Manuals and compliance: Bemis Company Bemis Company Inc., a $1.5 billion manufacturer of flexible packaging and specialty-coated graphics products, put their manufacturing system's troubleshooting and disaster recovery manual on line. The information had been printed and distributed to all their facilities across the country, but it was difficult to keep up-to-date and slow to distribute. Using Microsoft Access, SQL Server, IIS, Windows NT, Internet Explorer 3.0 and FrontPage, they were able to update it centrally. No more worries about the right people having the right version of the printed manual: everyone has access to real time information.

A troubleshooting and disaster recovery manual is on line and accessible

Support services: Coors On the CyBEERweb, the Coors Brewing Company intranet, the Guidebook is the place for computer support services. It's the one place employees visit to change their password, find out more about Internet access, or to connect with the Help desk for specific problems.

Computer support has a Web site on the Coors intranet

Product Information: Bank of Hawaii At the Bank of Hawaii, customer service representatives can show prospective bank clients a description of all the available bank products and services right on the intranet. The information is always current; out-of-date brochures are a thing of the past. And because the keyboard is on the service representative's side of the desk, there is no real risk that customers could drive through the bank's intranet on their own.

Product information is kept up-to-date on an intranet

Just-in-Time Information

In a race between finding information on a printed page somewhere and looking it up electronically, the bytes will win every time. A major financial services group put up a Top Five Issues area on their intranet. As illustrated in Figure 5-3, each issue gets a brief synopsis. Some staff members routinely check the area, just to keep up to date. But for the telephone service providers, the area is a fast way to get to an answer to a question that a customer may raise. Often before the customer has fully articulated the question, the phone representative has jumped to the Top Five Issues Web page and has linked down to the #3 issue. From that screen, they can provide, with no delay, a cogent response that delivers the company's point of view.

Intranets can make it quicker to answer customers' questions

Top Five Issues—just-in-time information.

Figure 5-3

The impetus for the city of Vancouver to build an intranet came from the outside, in a manner of speaking. The city has had a site on the World Wide Web since 1994. Some city employees found it was quicker to use their browser to log on to the Internet and go to the City of Vancouver Web site to find information they needed, instead of opening one of the proprietary applications to search one of the city's various internal databases. It was only a matter of time before the information available on the outside was brought inside, to an easy-to-use intranet.

"It has definitely changed our culture," said Scott Macrae, Communications Manager for the city of Vancouver, of the impact their new intranet has had. "People were saying, 'How could we serve customers differently?' And they were asking, 'Why do we have to keep repeating this [information] and printing it? Why can't we have one good copy, that we have confidence is the right one?'"

The bylaws of the city of Vancouver? The city's law department began to see the intranet as a solution to the problem of republishing the city bylaws. "They're the guardians of all bylaws, so they get to thinking, 'Instead of every time a bylaw is amended, reconsolidating [the bylaws], sending it out as an amendment, and putting it in the right binder. It would be better to have *one* document.' The staff needs this as much as the public."

The Process of Quick Publishing

The first few steps of quick publishing mirror the process of producing paper documents or a videotape. Whatever the medium, you still need to define the scope of the project and the customer's expectations, and then organize the content. What is different is the ease with which you can test and change the display or the content. Linear communication processes, such as video or print, are difficult and expensive to test in a prototype stage and to change once they're in their final form. The following section highlights the main steps in the process of building a Web site on an intranet. The steps are illustrated in Figure 5-4.

The process of quick publishing.   **Figure 5-4**

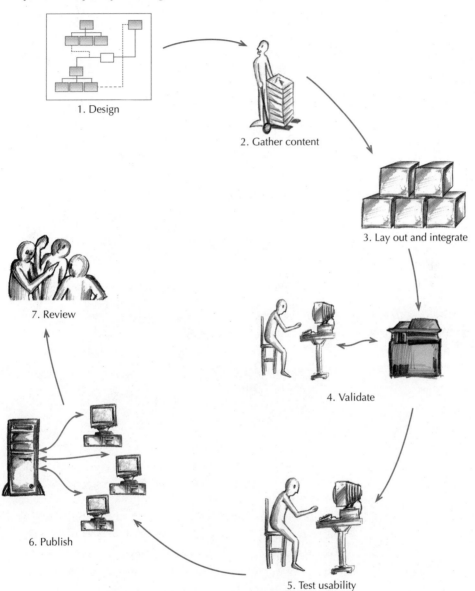

1. Design

2. Gather content

3. Lay out and integrate

7. Review

4. Validate

6. Publish

5. Test usability

1. Design it. The design phase includes defining the purpose of the communication, analyzing the audience (or your customers), and planning the product. In the case of a Web site or home page, this means also designing the site map, the navigation flow and functionality, as well as the *look and feel* of the site. It also includes building a prototype to test design and functionality.

2. Develop and gather the content. This may include converting existing documents (such as a word processing document), selecting graphics, text, audio and video segments, and creating new elements.

3. Lay out and integrate the elements that will function on the site. (Where *are* those graphics?)

4. Review, validate, and publish in a staging area. (This is the dress rehearsal site.)

5. Test the site for functionality and user acceptance. (In this phase, people outside the development group are usually invited to *bang on it* to see if they can *break it.*)

6. Publish on a designated server. (This is *show time.*)

7. Get feedback, reevaluate the design (Step #1) and audience assumptions. Revise content or design as necessary to meet communication objectives.

This process is basically the same whether the site is a home page for a project team—with hyperlinks to team members' pages and status reports—or the library resources site for an entire organization. The Web pages could be created by an experienced, professional Web design consulting firm or by one of the team members.

Comparing Paper and Intranet Publishing

Compare publishing on paper vs. publishing on the intranet: not only are there fewer steps to quick publishing, but also many of the steps can be accomplished more quickly. The table below doesn't include all the steps for offset printing, but hits the highlights.

While the table shows the difference in the number of steps, it does not reflect the more subtle opportunities for saving time by publishing and distributing materials on an intranet, instead of in print.

Publishing on Paper	Intranet Publishing
1. Plan and design	1. Plan and design
2. Develop content	2. Develop content
3. Create layout	3. Create layout and integrate
4. Create negative and plates	4. Review and tweak in staging area
5. Check sample press run	5. Test functionality and links
6. Send to printing	6. Move content to online site
7. Review press run	
8. Send to folding, binding or packaging, if required	
9. Ship (mailroom, post office or carrier)	
10. Receive and distribute (mailroom)	
11. Make changes or updates	7. Make changes or updates
12. Repeat steps 2, 3, 4, 5, 6, 7, 8, 9, 10	8. Repeat Steps 2, 3, 4, 5, 6

HTML Authoring Made Easy

The basic framework for Web pages is HTML (HyperText Markup Language). A browser interprets HTML codes and displays the information. Web pages can also use ActiveX controls and Java scripting to add functionality, such as electronic forms and other special services. But a page begins with HTML coding.

Pages authored in HTML can be very simple or can contain small applications

| The purpose of HTML coding has evolved from very functional to highly interactive | Originally, the purpose of HTML coding was page structure, *not* page layout. However, as Web authors enjoyed using the layout features, browser makers began to stray from the standards sanctioned by the World Wide Web Consortium (see "Open Systems and Standards," page 63), the de jure standards-setting body. The market drove the creation of newer (and competing) versions of browsers with their own (nonstandard) enhancements, which could only be seen with their browser software. With an intranet, you can legislate the use of a particular browser and eliminate the problem of incompatibility before it arises. |

| HTML tags specify, then browsers interpret, how information is to be displayed on the page | Basically, HTML language has a very simple construction. It consists of a series of tags that govern both the organization and the layout of a page, and was originally designed to display text only. Generally, tags come in pairs; tags bracket the information that is affected by the tag. The tags used in HTML have the same basic function as tags hidden in word processing programs, that is, the structure of the display with headings and other page elements. (Word processing programs send these instructions to a printer.) But the two differ in that it's the browser that interprets the HTML code. So an *H1 (heading)* in one browser may be 24 point Garabaldi, flush left; but another browser may display *H1* headings in 18 point Arial. |

| HTML has been stretched into a design tool | Each new version of a browser has offered new ways to display and manipulate data that will appear in the browser. Pages can now contain small programs, such as Java scripts or ActiveX controls, that perform specific actions (see "Automating Data Updates," page 180). But basic HTML authoring—producing a simple Web site with hyperlinks, without the animated flourishes or sophisticated data-retrieving functions—is easy to do. |

HTML Code

Following is a simplified example of HTML code. There are two main sections: the head section and the body section. The title and metadata[2] appear in the head section. The body contains the content. The entire document begins with <HTML> and ends with </HTML>.

```
<HTML> <HEAD> <META HTTP-EQUIV="Content-Type" content="text/html; charset=
iso-8859-1" >
<meta name="GENERATOR" CONTENT="Microsoft FrontPage 2.0">
<TITLE>Publications Team Report  October 1997 </TITLE>
<BODY background="images/backgrnd.jpg" bgcolor=#FFFFFF">
<H1 align="center".>Project Status</H1>
<P>The Publications Team has the following active projects:
<table border="1" cellpadding="3" bordercolor="#000000">
    <tr>
        <td><strong>Project</strong></td>
        <td><strong>Leader</strong></td>
        <td><strong>Completion status</strong></td>
    </tr>
    <tr>
        <td width="100%">Create new Web design for  WWW site</td>
        <td width="100%"><a href="mailto:BradH"> BradH </A></td>
        <td width="100%">75%</td>
    </tr>
    <tr>
        <td width="100%">Evaluate feedback mechanisms</td>
        <td width="100%"><A HREF="mailto:DevH"> DevH </A </td>
        <td width="100%">90%</td>
    </tr>
    <tr>
        <td width="100%">Analyze series potential </td>
        <td width="100%"><A HREF="mailto:StuS"> SteveS </A> </td>
        <td width="100%">85%</td>
    </tr>
    <tr>
        <td width="100%">Recommend new titles </td>
        <td width="100%"><A HREF="mailto:TyG"> TyG </A></td>
        <td width="100%">60%</td>
    </tr>

</BODY>
</HTML>
```

---

2. Metadata is data about data.

Microsoft Internet Explorer interprets this code, and produces the following display.

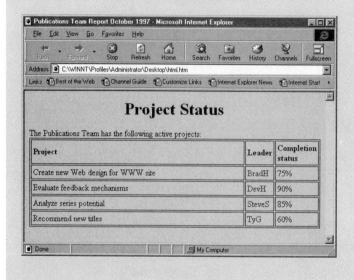

Web pages can display multimedia and documents in other formats

Web pages include text and media files. You can create links to almost any file format—a graphic, video, animation, sound file, or Microsoft Office file. For example, when you click a link to a Microsoft Word document (in other words a link to a .doc file), the browser loads the portion of the Word application needed to display the document.[3]

Scripts my be incorporated to add sophisticated features

Web authoring can be simple or very complex, depending on the goals for the site. If there is a lot of embedded functionality to support transactions, such as manipulating or retrieving data, the HTML coding may include Visual Basic or Perl and look more like sophisticated computer programming. However, if the information and the presentation style are fairly straightforward, the HTML coding will be simple.

---

3. Whether Word takes over the browser and displays the document within the browser window or displays the document within its own window depends on the implementation.

Basic HTML is easy to learn Because everything in an HTML document is written as text (with tags), you can use a simple text editor such as Notepad or WordPad to create HTML from scratch. (Some refer to this as the *brute force* method.) However, because HTML tags must be precisely correct (if you open a tag, you must close it), most Web authors prefer either to use an HTML authoring program or to create a document in an application they're familiar with, and then convert it to HTML format. For instance, Microsoft Word 97 and other software applications offer the option to save a document as an HTML file. IE 4.0 can also be used as an authoring tool. With IE 4.0, it is as easy to change a page as it is to change a word processing document. Granted, Web-masters and developers can create many special features for Web pages but anyone can publish a simple Web page for an intranet to get the information on line. This enabling, *anyone can* aspect of intranets delivers the power to everyone.

You can also use conversion programs or Web authoring tools to create a Web page

When choosing software for developing Web pages, insist on development tools that have open standards. Beware of proprietary tools that *must* be used to revise the site, or in the future, you will be locked into using those tools and unable to take advantage of other innovations that those tools do not support.

Opt for Web authoring tools that adhere to open standards

You can also use the *View Source* command on a browser to see a text file of the HTML coding that underlies any Web page, on the Internet or an intranet. Many people have gotten their start authoring Web pages by copying a text file from a page that they liked and inserting their own content between the tags. It's probably a sign of the maturity of the Web design industry that some text files now contain copyrights, which make it illegal to copy the work of the person who designed that page or to use it without permission.

To see the HTML code for a Web page, use the View Source command on your browser

Because the rudiments of HTML are easy to teach and easy to learn, almost anyone with some computer experience can

Basic HTML authoring may become a routine business skill

learn how to author or update a simple Web page. Today we take it for granted that anyone in business has the basic skills to use a computer. Perhaps the day is not too far off when we will also assume that anyone in business knows the basics of updating a Web page.

Scott Macrae, Communications Manager for the city of Vancouver, has been a leader in getting an online presence for the city of Vancouver. However, by his own admission, he's not a programmer. "The IS [Information Systems] people don't have that geewhiz factor about intranets. To them, I guess it's just another network. Whereas for non-geeks like me, it's, 'Holy Moses, I don't know anything about computers, but I can put up a Web site!'."

Standards and Trends

Create simple, effective Web pages

The recent trend on the Internet is for simplified sites. People fighting information overload are asking for less doodads and more real content. The message is cut to the chase. In addition, the small screens of the new hand-held computers cannot display extensive graphics.

Pages can proliferate very rapidly on an intranet

When intranets get large, really large, the traditional structure of numerous small HTML files can become extremely cumbersome. The number of pages on an organization's Web site can grow to unbelievable proportions. Ilene Lang, CEO of AltaVista OnSite computing, said that they had sent forth a Webcrawler (an automated intelligent agent) to find out how many pages their intranet site contained. After an hour and a million pages, they turned the crawler off. The sizes of intranets vary as much as a return on investment. If an intranet grows organically, as they usually do, it's not uncommon not to have a page count.

If a Web site is very large, it can be very time-consuming to make fundamental changes to all the pages on a site. The title portion at the top of each file on a Web site begins with nearly identical coding to define the look and attributes of the pages on that site. If you want to change an attribute, such as the font style or the color of a banner to reflect a new corporate color logo, every single page on the site has to be modified. You can use a text editor to change all the files in a group. However, instead of creating numerous small HTML files in the first place, the trend is to create one long file with internal links pointing to locations within that file. This structure serves the contiguous nature of Web design and eases the repetitive task of updating numerous HTML files. With the single file design, only one page is downloaded, so that helps to increase the response time when a user goes from internal link to internal link. However, if that one HTML file includes references to several ancillary files (such as GIF files for graphics), repeated trips to the server to download each file are still required. IE 4.0 has built-in features that accelerate the process of loading pages into a browser, such as allowing developers options for allocating bandwidth consumption.

Create fewer files by making them longer files with internal hyperlinks

We've grown accustomed to the term *Web page*, a presentation of specific information in a Web browser. Actually, while the page metaphor still works for describing sites on an intranet or the Internet, the concept of physical pages (with links to other pages) is in transition. As you'll see in the next section, dynamically generated pages are easy to update.

Create page shells to hold real-time data

Static and Dynamic Pages

In the beginning of HTML programming, all Web pages were static. A static page is created in advance. When you type a URL (Uniform Resource Locator) address or click a link (which points to a URL), the browser sends the request (through the motherboard, the netcard, and the modem) to the server, which then *serves* the page back to the browser on your computer.

Static pages are frozen dinners, dynamic pages are short order cooks

Pre-specified content is data that is *hard-coded*, that is, the information is written in the text file. When the information becomes out of date, static Web pages have to be updated by hand. Static pages may be appropriate for information that does not change frequently, such as an organization's mission statement. However, worming your way around coding tags to make changes can be tedious.

Dynamic pages are generated *on the fly*, drawing information from a database, embedded logic, or other data store

Dynamic pages maintain the structure of the information on the page, but the actual data is held in a database or another file, which is more convenient to update than an HTML page. Forms can be created with CGI (common gateway interface), Java scripts, Active Server Pages (ASP), or ActiveX controls. In other words, the page acts as a shell for content.

Generating pages dynamically does not guarantee the data has been updated recently

It's important to recognize that being able to draw data dynamically doesn't guarantee that the data (in the data store) is up to date. Unless there is a process and a means for getting updates into the data store, a page may generate out-of-date data. One of the attractive features of an intranet is the capability for multiple users to update data dynamically, as well as view dynamically generated pages.

You can use Web forms to retrieve data into a dynamic Web page

When a Web page offers a form[4] that you can use to make a specific request, or provides you with separate links for specialized data (for example, a choice of foreign languages or a hyperlink to another document), special instructions are encoded in the request sent to the server. The server interprets the special instructions and processes the request, usually with the help of a scripted routine that accesses the data and selects data that matches the specific instructions. The server ultimately returns the custom-tailored data to your browser.

Rob Bilson, Senior Webmaster for Amkor Electronics Inc., a global leader in semiconductor IC packaging, assembly and

---

4. A "form" on an intranet does not need to look like a job application. A form is an input device that offers text fields and other controls.

testing, uses dynamic pages to create his *What's New* page on AANet, the Amkor intranet. "It doesn't physically exist. All the information comes from databases." Bilson uses the same tool to update, add, or delete items from the database that feeds the *What's New* page (see Figure 5-5).

Amkor's What's New page is dynamically generated

The "What's New Administration" tool in the Amkor Tool Box.

Figure 5-5

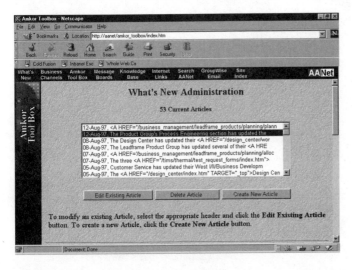

To publish information on the *What's New* page, Bilson uses a form, as shown in Figure 5-6, on the next page. "When I create an entry in the 'What's New' database, I have a [electronic] form I fill out. I submit the form and it goes into the database. When someone clicks on 'What's New,' they get an HTML table [Figure 5-7, on the next page]. The date is on the left, and on the right is a blurb about what's been changed, and links to that information."

In addition to custom-built publishing tools, there are a growing number of tools available from vendors that enhance displays of data on a Web page. Some of these tools, like Chart FX control from Software FX, can generate a chart display of statistical data (see Figure 5-8, on page 161). The chart control is embedded in the Web page. When an interactive form is filled out to specify parameters, a multi-

Sophisticated data displays are supported by custom-built tools

Figure 5-6   *The Amkor Tool Box offers a form for the "What's New" page.*

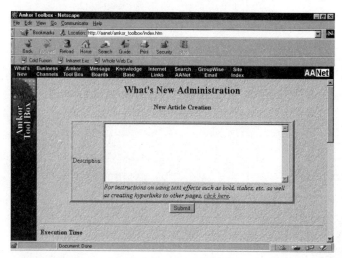

Figure 5-7   *The "What's New" page is generated dynamically.*

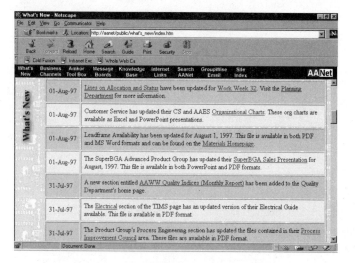

colored chart is generated on the fly. The viewer can change
the type of chart (such as a bar chart, pie chart, or scatter
chart) and even explore *what if* scenarios, perhaps to see
what factors would need to change for sales to be boosted
by a certain percentage.

The Chart FX Design Time Control (as shown here with Microsoft Visual InterDev) automatically generates the code (text-based scripting) to integrate a chart in a Web page.

Figure 5-8

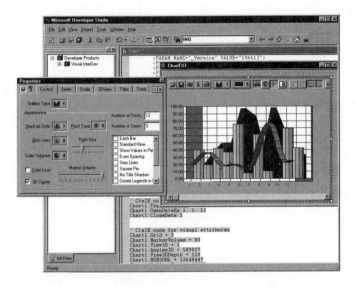

Dynamic HTML (DHTML) is an object-based model of HTML. Both Microsoft and Netscape have proposed to W3C slightly different standards for HTML, and have incorporated these approaches into the 4.0 versions of their browsers. DHTML gives authors the ability to update dynamically the contents, style, and structure of Web-based content. HTML originated as a standard for text and cannot accommodate today's demands for interactivity, multimedia content, and the accompanying need for bandwidth conservation. The Document Object Model Working Group is an industry consortium working to define a neutral standard for DHTML.

DHTML is a proposed standard for providing better interactivity than HTML

Looking Ahead

The definitive characteristic of an intranet, which makes it different from all other information technology solutions in the past, is that anyone can publish. You don't have to master complicated publishing tools. You don't have to have

It's easy to publish and distribute information on an intranet

prior programming experience. Anyone can do it. Sure, you can embroider your site with blinking, flashing, flipping, popping, scrolling knick-knacks, but that's adding glitz, not value.

Intranets give us more time by reducing the amount of time we spend that adds no value

As employees save time by having quicker access to the information they need to do their jobs, their company will save money. How much? Do the math for your organization. What if an intranet could save each employee a total of thirty minutes a day?

230 (work days a year) x 30 minutes/day = 165 hours/ year

N (number of employees) x 165 hours = ___hours/ year savings

What would your company do with the extra time? What projects would get to market quicker? What services could you improve?

Give empowerment more than lip service

Until an organization allows and encourages divisions, departments, and teams to publish (to put up their own Web pages), the organization remains entrenched in the command and control way of thinking. You may have given lip service to *empowerment,* but it's an empty promise.

While it's easy to appreciate the benefits that could accrue from being able to publish information quickly, that's not always enough to cause an organization to *stop the presses* and begin to build that intranet. An intranet can also offer the means for multiple users to update information *dynamically* using forms (built by Webmasters or software developers) right on an intranet Web page. This is a way to acquire up-to-date content. And operating with current data leads to better productivity. In the next chapter, we'll examine using an intranet to manage information: to acquire it, to organize it, and to distribute it.

Chapter Six

Using an Intranet for Information Management

From the point of view of information technology managers, information needs to be acquired, organized, and distributed. From the point of view of IT's information customers, the main issue is *access*—getting the right information, right when they need it, wherever it resides. Distributing and accessing data are two sides of the same coin. When an organization *webifies* its data, information can be delivered and accessed faster and more efficiently. (The word *webify* may not be in Websters' dictionary yet; it's just one more of those newly minted, avant-garde words to express retrofitting your information resources with Internet-based technology.)

The goal of information management is to reduce cycle time

As Charles Wang has pointed out, to be able to provide just-in-time information you have to set up the same structure that allows just-in-time materials delivery to work.[1] For an intranet, this means you need structured systems for capturing

Structure information for just-in-time retrieval

---

1.   Charles Wang, *Techno Vision*, page 140.

and integrating all types of information, and this includes ideas—ideas that could lead to improvements in products and services. An intranet can store this kind of intelligence.

Anyone with a browser and permission can take part in information management on an intranet

No doubt you already have a network that has some or many of the functions an intranet can provide—ways to organize and share database information and to exchange e-mail and participate in discussion forums. But on an intranet, with its native interactivity and connectivity advantages, you will enable anyone in your organization to update and access information if they are within reach of a computer with Internet-based protocols and permission. For information to be used as a strategic asset, structured and unstructured data must be brought under an organizing principle of some kind.

Information management is a means for acquiring, integrating, and distributing information

This chapter looks at how the intranet advantages of interactivity and connectivity can contribute to building an asset—an information base that runs across your organization. The "Acquiring Types of Data" section (see page 169) looks at data as a resource, what data is, and different ways to build that resource, such as linking to other information resources and updating data dynamically. The next section, "Organizing and Integrating the Data," (see page 182) focuses on ways to integrate legacy[2] database applications and to apply Web advantages to creating Web applications. The last section, "Easy Access to Information" (see page 194), covers seeking and sending information, and remote access.

Who Needs What Information?

There are three types of information customers in organizations today: task workers, information providers, and knowledge workers. Each group uses data in a different way.

---

2. Legacy systems represent the stored knowledge of the past, information that must be maintained and accessible.

Task workers need information to carry out a specific task, like placing a phone call or entering an order. Typically, they need *just-in-time* information. They may need to find a variety of data, such as customer names, shipping preferences, product information and availability, and electronic order forms (e-forms). But, when they're talking on the phone to update a customer's profile information, they don't have time to open different database programs to access repositories of different types of information.

Task workers update or verify data

Information providers are people such as customer representatives or help desk support personnel. They need access to a wide range of data to do their jobs, and they need it on demand. Their success depends on getting their hands on just the right information to solve a problem or win a customer. Their needs for data vary, but frequently they need to drill down quickly to find the right detail.

An information provider's role is to supply data

Knowledge workers use information either to collaborate or to coordinate large-scale activities. Their information needs range from being able to communicate one-to-one or one-to-many to using data for decision-making. Knowledge workers frequently require more bandwidth (to handle multimedia) than do information providers or task workers. (See Chapter 7, "Knowledge-Working".)

Knowledge workers use data for decision-making

Task workers, information providers, and knowledge workers all want the same thing: they want to shift to *access-based computing*, and away from *data processing*. They want the software and the hardware to get out of their way and let them get at their information. They want a front end that's a portal, not a barrier.

Employees want barrier-free access to information.

What managers want is to reduce time delays, errors, and labor costs by empowering employees to wait on themselves in a self-service information environment. They want *one-touch* information handling, which means they want to reduce the number of people who touch data by having the

Managers can increase productivity by improving information handling

same employee who creates a *transaction*[3] enter the data directly into the database. They, too, want to eliminate information middlemen as much as possible. Managers also want employees to be able to find the resources they need quickly, without waiting for someone else. Reducing dependencies saves time.

The problem is that it's easier to build the house of your dreams from the ground up than to remodel the house in

---

Dixons Mastercare Speeds Service via Their Intranet

Dixons Mastercare is the largest electrical retailer in the United Kingdom, with 800 stores selling a wide variety of brand goods, household appliances, business products, personal computers, and software. Their scope of technical support is one of the most extensive in Europe. The retailer uses its intranet to deliver more responsive service to its *information providers,* who in turn provide technical support for Dixons customers.

Dixons' *Quality, Service, Promise* project has encouraged customers to call in for help. Dixons' PC Service supports all their business products, including 38 brands of desktop PCs, laptops, fax machines, more than 1000 peripherals sold by PC World, and software products. At the Nottingham Call Centre, 235 customer-facing support staff field about 2700 calls a day.

Dixons has moved its service arrangements from an Access database to real time in SQL, and in doing so, has eliminated a huge manual file. So when a call comes in, technicians are ready with an online procedural database that has all the service arrangements, all the promises, and all the vendors' changes. For instance, Compaq went from a one-year, to a three-year, and back to a one-year service agreement. By checking the purchase date, the technician knows immediately if the customer has to pay or if the goods are still under the original warranty, and if the customer bought an extended warranty. Technicians can instantly check if a vendor has made upgrades available and can make those available to the customer. A change made at headquarters in Hammel Hampstead is available in the Nottingham Call Center in a few minutes.

---

3. In this context, a transaction is any effort to alter or manipulate data.

which you're living. Any information architect will say the same. The problem facing information technology managers is a complex and inefficient LAN or WAN network: too many isolated sources of information and too many copies of the same information in different locations on their networks. Well, you hope it's the same information.

Existing data management systems are complex and inefficient

Divisions and departments within an organization frequently maintain duplicate sets of information. Employee lists may exist in several databases, for instance, one in payroll and one for security clearances. There may be several separate lists of customers, one maintained by marketing, one by sales, one for invoicing, one for shipping, and one for service and support. Duplicate records consume twice as much time to create, manage, and maintain; they also increase the opportunities for errors. If a customer's name is entered in a *customer order* database, but spelled differently in the *work order* database, that customer may fall through the cracks.

Databases containing duplicate information lead to problems

Without the unifying influence of an intranet, an organization's information assets may reside locked in numerous databases, in file cabinets, in folders in someone's desk, or in piles on top of a desk. Getting access to information from disparate data sources may require employees to negotiate a different operating system or launch a different software program, and proceed through a sometimes counter-intuitive hierarchy of folders and subfolders. These are tasks that take time to learn and time to perform. Learning new software is not a trivial endeavor. And someone has to do the training—and the retraining. The intranet solution is to consolidate and publish as much information as you can.

Without integrated databases, you can't be sure where to look

IT challenges Administrators who are converting their networks to intranets face three specific challenges (or you can call them opportunities) concerning data resources:

- Managing legacy systems and integrating them with newer dynamic databases.

- Corralling unstructured information, such as e-mail or graphics, into a common information system.
- Making the flow of information quick and easy for their customers.

There are other fundamental issues to be resolved about blending the attributes of client/server networks with Web-

The High Cost of Document Management

One solution for bringing legacy data stored in older hardware and software systems into an intranet is to convert it to run on a new system. Any way you cut it, data conversion is expensive.

American National Standards has defined the lifetime estimates and optimal storage conditions for paper and microfilm, but these characteristics have not yet been defined for computer media by either national or international standards organizations. A report on document life cycle management[4] issued by the Association for Information and Image Management International (AIIM)[5] estimates that an electronic document storage and retrieval system installed *today* is likely to be replaced or significantly upgraded within five to six years. Recopying documents is an expensive undertaking, if you consider the cost of the replacement media, computer time, and operator time.

For example, with an average data transfer rate of 700 kilobytes per second, a collection of 30 gigabytes of optical disk storage (one million electronic document images) would take twelve hours to recopy. The report also estimates that at five to ten cents a page (typical service bureau rate), converting a collection of one million documents to a different format can cost $50,000 to $100,000. But if information is not converted, eventually the length of time it takes to access information will erode productivity.

---

4. Document life cycle management is the process by which businesses and government agencies maintain electronic documents relative to legal and fiscal requirements for retention periods.

5. AIIM International is the leading global association bringing together information management professionals and providers of digital document technologies.

based technologies, such as maintaining transaction-processing support in the stateless environment, (see "The Problem of Statelessness," page 187). IT staffers have decisions to make about choosing platforms, families of server products, scripting languages, and which Web applications to build and which to buy.

Managers and communicators have to decide *how to decide* what type of content belongs on the intranet and who can and shall publish. They will want to examine when information should just be rendered accessible, and when it needs to be *pushed* (see "Webcasting—Push Technology", page 201). On the other hand, they also have to keep alert to balancing the growth of the intranet with the capacity to manage and maintain it.

Acquiring Types of Data

Data isn't what it used to be. It used to be just rows and columns—numbers and lists. It used to fit tidily in tables, charts, and databases. Not anymore. Data includes photos, maps, audio, video, word processing documents, whiteboard drawings, animations, presentation slides, as well as text and numbers. Those types that are not already in digital format can be converted, and any information that can be stored digitally can be made available through a Web browser.

Data can be created and stored in many different formats

Structured information, like left-brain thinking, has defined pathways and logic; unstructured information is more like right-brained activities, more communication-oriented. Both are valuable aspects of an organization's intelligence assets. Both belong parked on an intranet.

Structured and Unstructured Data

Databases contain structured information. But there's a wealth of valuable information floating about that is not inside an existing database and not already organized or contained within easily accessible structures.

Data is either structured or unstructured

Generally, unstructured information comes from communication—some way to express a point or concept (see Figure 6-1). Unstructured information springs from messages, anecdotes, documents, brainstorming sessions, *what if* scenarios, back-of-the-envelope ideas, drawings on a whiteboard, graphics, sketches, spreadsheets, field intelligence, e-mail, and online forms. Unstructured communication is more informal. (In dress code terms, more *casual Friday* rather than *meet the customer* clothes.) But the seeds of the next success in your organization may lie within one of these data forms. Most of the information your organization owns is in the form of unstructured data.

Figure 6-1   *Unstructured information is people-oriented information.*

Inventory your
information
resources

If you want to *fill the shelves* of your intranet quickly with rich data, look at how information is gathered (or not gathered) in your organization today. Then look at the other information that is not easily accessible. Look for both structured and unstructured data. There is probably a great potential for corralling the paper, databases, sounds and pictures, as well as free-form information, into a browser-accessible format on your intranet. You can also harvest research data, seminars, briefings, and product announcements from your partners' Web pages or extranets. (Your competitors' Web pages may have information of value to you, too). What opportunities are you now missing? What could you do with a wider information base?

Cull all sources for accurate, up-to-date, relevant data. The goal of data acquisition is to have efficient, reliable processes for gathering accurate, up-to-date, relevant data in any format from any source. As you will see throughout this chapter, there are numerous sources of data, both on line and in isolated databases, and there are many different ways to acquire relevant content for your intranet.

Find what's most relevant and up-to-date

Harnessing Unstructured Communication

If you are able to capture unstructured communication without killing it, you will bring home a bounty to your organization. That's because intranets are built on standard Web protocols, a commonality that makes it easier to capture and access different types of unstructured data.

Many brilliant ideas go to waste if there isn't a way to capture them

E-mail Because e-mail is such a swift way to dash off a note, it's sometimes easy to forget that an e-mail message is a business communication. Bill Fernihough, Senior Professional Engineer, Technical Support, Apparatus Department, BC Hydro, remembers when the word-processing department handled all the correspondence for the utility. Records of all correspondence were meticulously maintained. "No one dashed off a note to a supplier," said Fernihough. " If there was a problem with a piece of equipment, the engineer and the vendor would commit to paper the evolution of the resolution to the problem....Nowadays, you may work out a problem together by 'discussing it' through e-mail."

Information messaging is unstructured data

Usually, last week or last month's e-mail blurs into history. Fernihough added, "Actually, in the old days, when you took over a job, the first thing you did was sit down and review the files. It could take several days! Nowadays, the history of a problem and its solution may be in my head, wherever I go, but it's not necessarily recorded where someone else can find it."

Too often, vital information resides in someone's head

Newsgroups and forum folders can be used to organize and save information

This information in someone's head could represent an asset loss for the organization. E-mail can be stored in folders, and conversation threads can be stored in discussion forums, such as the Public Folders in Microsoft Exchange. Fernihough suggested another solution for capturing e-mail, using newsgroup technology. If newsgroups were named "…with file numbers, we could copy every e-mail note to the 'newsgroup filing system.'… Anyone could just log on to a 'file' using a newsgroup reader."

Use e-mail with Internet-based standards to reduce barriers

Many IT departments want to standardize e-mail across their WANs and LANs. Due to mergers, acquisitions, or independent-minded departments, they are saddled with a boatload of different e-mail applications they have to maintain, and a move to make changes can swamp that boatload with internal politics. (Some people get very, very attached to the features of the e-mail system they have learned to use.) So the IT staff struggles with either maintaining separate e-mail

How Private is E-mail?

It's not as private as a letter. Neither individuals or organizations may shield e-mail as private information. Once e-mail is composed, it's stored on a mail server. Hitting the *send* icon doesn't move the mail, it triggers a *you have mail* message on the recipient's computer. Then the recipient reads the master version on the server, where it resides until the nightly backup procedure stores it (usually off-site) safely on magnetic tape on another computer. E-mail is long-lived. Then there is the *copy* icon. Who knows where your mail will go?

A 1996 United States federal court ruled, in Smythe v. The Pillsbury Company, that e-mail messages sent by an employee cannot be considered confidential. Michael Smyth was fired after his e-mail, critical of Pillsbury, was read by management. He sued, claiming his rights of privacy had been violated. The moral of this story is that any e-mail message should be treated as if it's written on company letterhead.

systems or using gateways (either from a third party vendor or through features built into the e-mail applications) to *make* them connect. An intranet can reduce the technical (but not the political) problem, because e-mail that uses Internet-based protocols can operate across different platforms.[6]

Discussion forums Beyond sending multiple copies of an e-mail message or subscribing to a listserv,[7] there are other ways a team or interest group can share (and preserve) concerns and solutions. They can use discussion forums or online chat areas.

Use a discussion forum to pass on a solution or raise a question

While you may already be using discussion forums on your network, using a forum on an intranet is easier. For example, you can use the browser controls to bookmark a forum for easy access and use the browser's Back button to view a previous message. Participants can fill in an e-form to initiate or contribute to a topic. As illustrated in Figure 6-2 on the next page, a form could have a drop-down list box of

Use of intranet browsers, bookmarks, and forms provide added benefits

Will E-mail Change How People Communicate?

With an intranet, more people in your organization will be using e-mail instead of making a quick phone call, and they could start seeing a change, not necessarily for the better. Just as the telephone changed the *look and feel* of communication, so has e-mail. Some experts say the stylistic brevity of e-mail contributes to the tendency toward short attention spans. You get used to the quickness. Type a quick query. Dash off a response in a flash. It takes longer to place a call, exchange a few pleasantries, and then get to the point. Just like using a TV remote to flash through channels, you get used to nailing the *scroll bar* to zip through a message.

---

6. The primary Internet mail protocols are SMTP, IMAP, POP, and POP3.

7. LISTSERV is the name of a popular mailing list program. Majordomo and LISTPROC are two others.

subtopic areas and a text area for entering comments. The purpose of adding structure is to enable anyone with access to the forum to sort and retrieve ideas.

Figure 6-2   ***Form for participating in a discussion forum.***

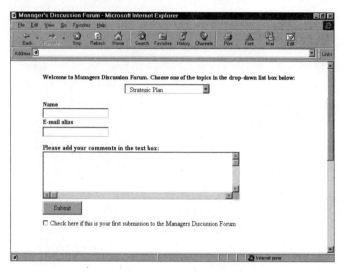

Use a business discussion forum to focus on a topic

Forums can be on *community interest* topics, such as child care or water sports, or on critical business subjects, such as:

- Benchmarking
- Market strategies
- Best practices
- Losses or threats
- Competitive information
- Emerging issues

The ARAMARK MIS Council posted meeting notes, then added comments

Membership is sometimes restricted to a particular group within the organization. For example, the MIS (Management of Information Services) group of the ARAMARK Corporation comprises the heads of eighteen different business units. On the ARMARK intranet, StarNet, they post information, such as contracts and solutions, to share among themselves.

Within the full MIS group, the MIS Council, made up of vice presidents, created their own forum to post proceedings from their meetings. This forum grew organically as Council members added comments and information. The Council also issues assignments to MIS work groups, who use the intranet to work collaboratively (see Chapter 7, "Knowledge-Working").

Inter Relay Chat (IRC) Another Internet protocol useful for intranets is Inter Relay Chat (IRC). Unlike e-mail and discussion forums, which are *time-delayed*, IRC supports real-time text-based electronic *discussions* between two or more participants. (It's a good option for people who think with their fingers.) The chat text captures a written record of ideas.

IRC is an Internet protocol for multi-user, text-based communication

Building an Information Base

You can acquire unstructured types of information by linking other data formats to a Web page and by selectively connecting to sources on the Internet. What existing information can you harvest for your intranet? What connections do you already have?

You already know that, besides creating Web pages or converting existing documents to HTML, you can create a hyperlink on a Web page to connect information that is not in HTML format, such as a Word or a Portable Document Format (PDF) file.[8] BC Hydro and many other large companies rely on PDF as a quick and painless way to acquire a large volume of information for their intranet. Some organizations have undertaken large scanning projects to bring information into their intranet. The Adobe Capture plug-in, which is part of Adobe Acrobat software, uses character, font, and page recognition (supporting multiple languages)

Include internal information in your intranet by linking and scanning

---

8. With Adobe Acrobat software, anyone—an engineer, an artist, or an author—can create work in any application, then convert it to a PDF file.

to create searchable, Web-ready files. Fujitsu bundles Adobe Acrobat software with the Fujitsu ScanPartner 600c, a high-resolution desktop scanner that automatically converts the scanned material to Adobe PDF files.

Link to content-specific Internet Web sites

Selective links from intranet Web sites to Internet news media, information providers, trade journals, industry organizations, and partner Web sites or their extranets can expand your information resources. For instance, links to up-to-date weather information on the World Wide Web may benefit insurance and transportation interests.

Link to trade publications on the World Wide Web

The Coors Brewing Company's intranet, *CyBEERweb,* has an extensive online collection of articles and magazines available on their library Web site. They also have links to trade publications available on the Internet, such as *The Canadian Journal of Plant Science* and *Cereal Chemistry.*

Connect to information providers

Material from online providers, such as Dow Jones (News/Retrieval), Lexis-Nexis, and Knight-Ridder (Dialog), is easily imported to an intranet, as HTML, PDF, or Microsoft Word files. On your intranet you can set access restrictions to comply with agreements made with external information providers.

Competition Between Online Archives is Driving Down the Cost of Information

Traditional business databases such as Dow Jones (News/Retrieval), Lexis-Nexis, and Knight-Ridder (Dialog) have gone on line. Some of these big online database information companies saw their sales drop when a plethora of newspaper and magazine Web sites began giving away (or selling for a very small fee) articles for which the large service providers used to charge $20 or more. They have come back with improved services and better search capabilities. For business customers, this means more information is available in a digital format.

Another way to expand your information resources is to link to partners' Web sites or to sites of industry groups. Air Products and Chemicals, Inc., operates the Chemical Information Data Exchange (CIDX) Web site, as shown in Figure 6-3. CIDX is education-oriented and promotes the use of technology within the chemical industry. Their first focus was EDI. As Figure 6-4 on the next page illustrates, the *Products and Services* Web page contains a link to the EDI Implementation Guidelines developed by CIDX members. Only the listserv discussions are restricted to CIDX members.

Harvest information from partners' extranets or industry groups' Web sites

The Chemical Information Data Exchange (CIDX) Web site is an informational site for the chemical industry about using technology.

Figure 6-3

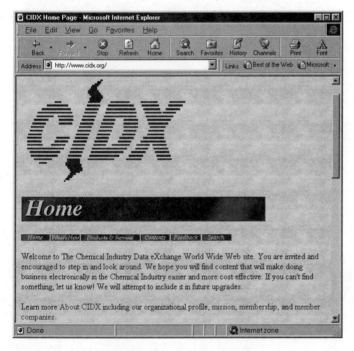

Dynamically Updating Data

In Chapter 5 ("Static and Dynamic Pages," page 155) you saw how dynamic Web pages could return data on the fly. This section focuses on updating or adding data dynamically in an intranet environment—one more way to acquire information resources for your intranet. (In this context, *dynamically* means *in real time* as opposed to updates that are processed in batches.)

Figure 6-4

The CIDX Products and Services Web page includes hyperlinks to the EDI Implementation Guide and other chemical industry information.

Online survey forms can update databases dynamically

Mary-Ellen Fremuth, Webmaster for the Lexis-Nexis intranet, reported in the Reader's Web section of the online Intranet Design Magazine that, after Microsoft Exchange was rolled out to the entire company, an online form sent results to a Microsoft Access database. This is *one-touch* data—the survey recipients input their own data, which could be used to create several different reports.

What type of data would you like to see that is fresh daily? If you were running a product promotion, would you like to see sales figures daily, or bimonthly?

Mainframes store data in indexed text files or relational databases. Consider, for example, the gathering of customer profile data, including their preferred method of shipping and the name of the purchasing contact. The old way of building data stores (see Figure 6-5) was to employ someone to gather the data by phone interview or to fill in a form, and that person would hand off the data to data-entry clerks, who would enter the customer profile changes in the org- anization's database. The interval between updates was measured in weeks, rather than minutes. Any day during those weeks, a truck could be hitting the highway towards an out-of-date address.

Data entry was a labor-intensive effort

The process of building data stores took a lot of people and a lot of time.

Figure 6-5

Customer list database

Shipping database

Client/server computing pioneered dynamic updating. The processing power on the client machine enabled several update activities, such as returning totals, data validation, and checking against rules. This shortened the interval between updates. Putting a *Web front end* on a database increases productivity even more for the following reasons:

- If an organization has a heterogeneous mix of UNIX, Macintosh, and IBM-compatible personal computers, there's no problem—one Web-based application fits all. Anyone across the organization with intranet access can contribute.
- Building one common interface takes less time for developers than creating interfaces for each type of computing environment.
- Web application pages are stored on the server until they are requested by the client, so the IT staff doesn't have to worry about distributing or installing applications or supporting users who do.

Automating data updates Developers have several ways to automate the process of updating data. Common Gateway Interface (CGI) scripts, Internet Server Application Programming Interface (ISAPI), and Active Data Objects (ADO) run on a server, while Java applets, ActiveX controls, VB scripts, and Java scripts execute on the client side. These solutions can be used solo or in combination.

Probably the most common solution has been to write a CGI script that runs on the server. (You may have noticed the CGI designation as part of a URL.) When the user enters the data in a form on the Web page, the CGI script sends a command to the server to handle the update. In a validation process, the server checks the new data and either updates the database or returns a message. The downside of CGI

Developers Can Create Interactive Forms Using

- Scripting languages (Java scripts or VB scripts)
- ActiveX controls
- Java applets
- Common Gateway Interface (CGI)
- Internet Server Application Programming Interface (ISAPI)
- Active Data Objects (ADO), on Active Server Pages (ASP)
- Microsoft Internet Explorer 4.0 (using data binding)

scripts is that they tend to create a bottleneck: because they are not compiled,[9] CGI scripts take longer to run. In addition, for every user who performs that operation, a separate script (and separate process) is started, further slowing performance. An Internet Server Application Programming Interface (ISAPI) filter, which runs on Microsoft products, and NSAPI, for Netscape products, functions in the same way as a CGI script.

A quicker server-side solution for developers working on an Active Platform is provided by ActiveX Data Objects (ADO), which run on a server in Active Server Pages (ASP), to access and manipulate data in a database server. The ADO returns a standard HTML stream to the browser and populates fields of a record set. In "Managing Data Objects," page 185, you will see how objects can be managed across a distributed intranet environment.

Microsoft's Active Platform technology is another server solution

With ADO and data binding, as you'll see below, Web pages can be intelligent enough to connect to a data store, retrieve the data, display it, and (depending on the design) allow users to add, delete, or update the data.

---

9. When an uncompiled script is run, each line of code must first be verified and translated into object language before the machine can execute it.

Data binding is an open standard technology included in Internet Explorer 4.0 to speed delivery of information from a data store to a Web page. It promises a more efficient use of network resources than traditional server-side Web page presentation and data retrieval. With data binding, the HTML page is treated like a template;[10] and Data Source Objects (DSO) act as object brokers to supply data to that page. After downloading a record set, DSOs can sort, filter, and update data on the client, without another call to the server. DSOs reduce server load by not repeatedly accessing data; they generate their own HTML and eliminate the need to maintain user state (see "The Problem of Statelessness," page 187). Data Source Objects instruct the server to deliver a flat file asynchronously, in a way that is similar to the way GIFs are delivered incrementally. So a page is rendered more quickly than when a page is prepared on the server and transmitted in its entirety to the client.

Organizing and Integrating the Data

Information that is
accessible is a
strategic asset

Think about data or information as a *raw material.* Harvesting reliable, accurate, and timely information will build your organization's *intelligence,* which in turn will be used to manufacture decisions. To get the most out of your intranet, whether you are planning to serve one division or to implement an enterprise-wide intranet and extranet, it's crucial to have strategies and tools for organizing the content you wish to make available. Continuing under the broad topic of information management, this section explores ways to organize and integrate the data.

Before you embark on a full scale intranet, it's a good idea to assess the status of the structured information in your organization. Data can be identified by location (desktop or

---

10. The template is defined by HTML extensions, proposed to the World Wide Web Consortium (W3C).

server) or by the database structure (relational or object-oriented). Databases can reside on mainframes, servers, and desktops. Data may exist in a Microsoft Access database, a Microsoft FoxPro, an Oracle, or a SQL database. Tabulate where your data resides and the formats in which it exists. Review the software products that work with these formats. How easy to use are they? How effective are they?

Analyze the data strategic asset sources of your organization

Just as organizations have been able to speed up their processes by flattening the steep slopes of their management hierarchies, information architects may wish to do the same flattening, and for the same reason. Instead of maintaining isolated data islands, you can structure an efficient, lively repository of up-to-date data from legacy systems and new *web-lications* (another term not yet in Webster's, no pun intended) using Web-based technologies. One strategy is to integrate as much data as possible and keep the network up and functioning smoothly.

Aim to create an integrated, up-to-date information resource

Viewing Information

In the beginning of this chapter, you saw that task workers, information providers, and knowledge workers used data in different ways. However, their needs often overlap and they need to see different aspects of the same data stores.

Proprietary databases organized data in containers

Information stored in proprietary databases affords only a single view, the view for which the product is intended. As shown in Figure 6-6, on the next page, the containers isolate groups of items.

With an intranet, information can be organized to support multiple views into the data. As Figure 6-7 on the next page illustrates, many departments or individuals can use the same core information, but each may *view* a different slice of it. Integrating data in a common Web and allowing multiple views into it increases efficiency.

Figure 6-6   *Information locked in proprietary databases.*

Customer list
database

Shipping
database

Figure 6-7   *Multiple views into a customer database.*

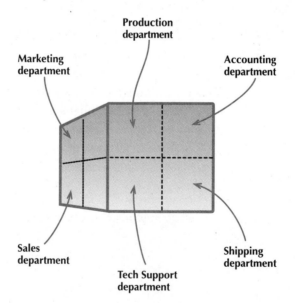

Production
department

Marketing
department

Accounting
department

Sales
department

Shipping
department

Tech Support
department

Intranets support
multiple views into
information

The John Deere Waterloo Works Division is implementing a
visual front end to a dynamic parts database, and has extended the usefulness of the information to several different
departments. On the intranet, employees can see a picture
of the part and read a detailed description. They can find

the size of the part, the bill of materials, and a list of operations that workers used to put the part together. Different people in the organization will use the database in different ways.

Engineers will be able to develop bills of materials automatically for their designs. Purchasing departments will be able to send out a picture of a part to vendors for quotes. Shop workers will be able to review how a part is put together. Each employee will draw a different view of the information. Having it available quickly and easily in a browser will increase the productivity of each group.

Managing Data Objects

When information management technology moved from batch online transactions to dynamic transactions, the shape of information structures changed. Instead of information being perceived as records that *belonged* to a department or a division, such as customer records, billing records, or shipping records, an item of information could be regarded as an *object*. For instance, a *customer object* has specific attributes like a name, a delivery address, a billing address, a district, an identifying number, a shipping preference, an account manager, and so on. Different departments or divisions may *view* different attributes of the object, or see it from a different angle, so to speak.

Different departments need to view different attributes of a data object

Creating and using objects in the distributed environment of an intranet (or the Internet) is more complex than in a traditional client/server environment.[11] There are protocols for managing objects, but the inherent stateless nature of HTTP had to be overcome to accomplish distributed computing.

Handling objects in a Web-based environment is more difficult than on a traditional network

---

11. Instantiation raises questions in a intranet or Internet environment, such as whether the object was created on the client machine or the remote server.

CORBA, DCOM,
and RMI are
competing standards
for managing objects
in a distributed
environment

CORBA, DCOM, RMI Standards There are three competing standards for managing objects in a distributed environment (intranet or Internet): Common Object Request Broker Architecture (CORBA) and Microsoft's Distributed Component Object Model (DCOM), and Remote Method Invocation (RMI) with Java. These standards are for managing object-to-object communication over a TCP/IP network.[12]

CORBA uses object
request brokers
(ORB)

CORBA is a standard proposed by the Object Management Group (OMG), a vendor alliance that first introduced CORBA 1.1 in 1991, well before the Internet and TCP/IP networks took center stage. CORBA 2.0 was released in 1994. CORBA is classical object-oriented programming and has gained wide platform support. CORBA defined the Interface Definition Language (IDL) and the Application Programming Interfaces (API) that enable client/server object interaction within a specific implementation of an Object Request Broker (ORB).

An ORB is middleware, such as Tuxedo by BEA Systems, that keeps track of the location and capabilities of objects. To ensure interoperability, ORBs use Internet InterORB Protocol (IIOP), an implementation of the General InterORB Protocol (GIOP), on top of TCP/IP. The usefulness of IIOP may transcend CORBA; any architecture that implements IIOP can communicate with any other IIOP-compliant architecture.

DCOM uses services
to facilitate object
communication

DCOM enables software components to communicate over a cross-platform network by using the services available on each platform to implement the necessary activities, such as concurrency, multi-threading, and security. The transport and security mechanisms are based on the already-familiar Distributed Computing Environment (DCE) standards.

---

12.   There is also a Java solution for managing objects over an intranet or the Interenet called Remote Method Invocation (RMI). Java 1.1 allows object serialization and database access. JavaSoft has a component model called JavaBeans; however, the JavaBean Enterprise architecture is still under development.

Microsoft developed DCOM based on the Open Software Foundation's DCE-RPC specification. DCOM will work with both Java applets and Microsoft ActiveX components, and it is supported by a growing number of vendors. Microsoft has submitted its object technology (COM, DCOM, and ActiveX) to The Open Group (parent company of a number of standards organizations, including the Open Software Foundation), so that it can become an industry-wide standard. Platform support for DCOM is more limited than that for CORBA, but it is growing as the base of NT servers and Win32 developers grows.

The DCOM and the CORBA roads may eventually come together, or not. In the meantime, the solution will be CORBA to COM bridges, from vendors such as Iona Technologies.

RMI is Sun Microsystems' implementation of the distributed object architecture, much like Microsoft's DCOM or OMG's CORBA. A Java applet or application inherits the RMI classes built into Java.

The problem of statelessness In a traditional client/server environment, when a client makes a request of a server, the two establish a connection that they maintain during a session.[13] Once the session is opened, the two can do business back and forth—exchanging data—until one closes the session.

> A client and server maintain a connection while they exchange data

One of the biggest limitations of the HTTP protocol is the absence of *active sessions.* Clients and servers on the Internet or an intranet send messages using HTTP, which is a stateless protocol. On the Internet or an intranet, when a server responds to a client request, the connection is opened and then closed immediately. Out of sight, out of mind. The server does not stay connected (or maintain that state)

> Internet connections are not persistent

---

13. A session is the time interval during which the client and server are interacting.

waiting for a reply or further information from the client. In fact, a Web server cannot detect whether information the client sends back as a response actually came from your computer or someone else's.

DHTML can get around the problem

There are solutions to overcome statelessness, which otherwise would be an impediment to updating data. Dynamic HTML (DHTML) is employed in Internet Explorer 4.0 as a solution to manage communication and data retrieval. But the first solution came from Netscape.

Cookies get around the problem of statelessness

Netscape originated the *cookie* as a workaround to the problem of statelessness A cookie acts as a session identifier. The often-maligned cookie is a small file sent by the server during the first connection. The browser caches the cookie on the client machine for the use of the server that furnished it. With each connection thereafter, the browser returns a copy of the cookie to that server, as a token of recognition. On the back end, the server uses the cookie to identify the client each time. Some people see cookies as a security risk, because they have the ability to store information on your hard drive.

Cookies identify the client machine

The client machine collects the cookies. The problem is, the cookie identifies the individual user, but is stored on the client machine that originated the transaction. So you may have cookies stored on your laptop computer that are not on your desktop computer, and vice versa. You may have many, many cookies taking up your cache on your machines.

Without an expiration date, cookies stay stashed on the client machine

The Microsoft Web server solution for the problem also involves sending a cookie, but a session object in an Active Server Pages (ASP) script manages the cookie The developer writing the ASP script specifies the length of time for the session to remain open by setting the session object's time-out property. The session object can also delete cookies that do not have an expiration date when the browser is closed.

The London Underground

The London Underground uses Active Server Pages (ASP) e-forms to maintain their Incident Notification Process, which is part of their safety record. When an incident occurs, employees fill in an e-form that immediately adds the item to the database. Over the course of dealing with that incident, they may come back to the database several times and add more information as it becomes available. Through the Microsoft Index Server with the Web browser, the incidents in the database can be searched and sorted.

Document management compatibility standards Managing different types of applications in a multi-vendor environment has always been a challenging endeavor. The need for standards will continue to escalate, if we are to keep pace with intranet technologies.

Standards continue to evolve

Working with the major document management vendors, a task force of the Association for Information and Image Management International (AIIM) developed Open Document Management API (ODMA) standards for intranet extensions. The technical specifications provide a framework for linking ODMA-compliant document management systems to intranets, so that system administrators can provide transparent, security-controlled access with a browser from any client (including personal computers, network computers, and WebTVs). This is another case where, as innovative technology evolves, the effort to standardize it moves hand in glove. Vendors and their customers need standards to avoid the technological isolation that plagued the mainframe era.

ODMA standards are technical specifications for document management

Integrating Data

The purpose of integrating databases is to handle in more productive ways the information that resides in your organization. In the past, when you wanted to get information out of a legacy database, you harnessed your team of software

Integrating databases used to require extensive programming

developers and they wrote hundreds and hundreds of lines of code to do it. Using an intranet opens up additional options. Database vendors are working to incorporate Web-based enhancements in their products (so their customers won't defect to other products and database solutions). Meanwhile, software developers are designing Web front ends to databases and other data stores so their customers can interact with the data through their browsers.

If a database is ODBC (Open Database Connectivity) compliant (and most are today), then there is already a common ground to build communications links between databases across multiple platforms and different product families.

Mainframe vendor solutions Mainframe vendors are responding to their customers' attraction to intranets and are providing middleware to improve interoperability between disparate computing systems and to present database information to a browser. With this middleware, IT staff can organize data sources across the intranet. It is like building sky-bridges between the buildings that house various sources of information.

IBM developed the Component Broker (CB) Connector (formerly code-named Business Object Server), which can encapsulate information and transactions from almost any computer and convert them to self-contained objects. CB Connector is compatible with Common Object Request Broker Architecture (CORBA) as well as with Java and ActiveX clients. Brokering the components of computing (objects) can bridge the gap between mainframes on the back end and the desktop at the front.

Oracle has developed a middleware software product, the WebConnect Pro module from OpenConnect Systems, that enables their database servers to connect legacy applications to Web servers. In this middle ground, data coming from the server is packaged in an HTML Web page before

Middleware helps bridge the gap between a client computer and multiple databases

IBM's Component Broker (CB) Connector converts encapsulated information to data objects

Oracle's middleware solution connects legacy applications to Web servers

being passed to the browser. With another tool, Open Vista, users can reformat the look of the material or combine multiple COBOL green screens in the original application into one screen on the browser. Oracle's Network Computer (NC) will also use the technology. It will provide the NCs with terminal emulation capabilities, allowing them to tap directly into legacy applications.

Intranet database Web applications Vendors are building browser-based, relational database products. One such product is Netiva, a server and developing tools package that builds Web application databases for Java-enabled browsers. Netiva Software developed DataPage technology (patent-pending), which allows users to create multi-user intranet relational databases and enables them to import data from desktop databases, such as Microsoft Access.

New software products build multi-user relational databases for a Web environment

Databases built with Netiva (by *users*, not programmers) run in a browser, but perform more like an application written with Microsoft Access or PowerBuilder than an HTML application, chiefly because Netiva allows dynamic validation.[14] This product was not built for high-density, enterprise transactions, but scaled for fast data sharing between workgroups or departments. Plans are to add ODBC connectivity and SQL drivers for connecting the Netiva Server to back-end databases.

Building Customized Web Front Ends

To give their data customers unified access to multiple sources of information, software developers build customized Web front-end intranet applications. Whether they need to link legacy databases or connect several sources of data, by building an intranet application they can eliminate barriers between the data and those who need it.

Unified front ends eliminate barriers

---

14. Dynamic validation is the real-time, on-the-spot interactive process of validating information. For instance, you can dynamically check whether a part is in stock, before finalizing a purchase order.

Beth Israel and Deaconess Hospital merged When Boston's Beth Israel and Deaconess Hospitals merged in 1996, and patients were encouraged to visit either hospital, they expected that their records would be accessible from either one. But the fact that the hospitals merged didn't mean the databases automatically would.

Each hospital had
its own legacy
database system

In fact, Beth Israel's records were ensconced in data structures of a 1960s program language unique to the health care industry, with an even more esoteric data manipulation language known as MUMPS (Massachusetts General Hospital Utility Multi-Programming System). On the other hand, Deaconess records were in a Sybase relational database that used SQL. Because the two database structures had so little in common, they had no way of talking to each other.

Developers joined
the two systems
together with a
common interface

The customized solution, now at the prototype stage, came from a Windows-based visual development tool called Visual M, from InterSystems, which could help build a common interface. The system uses ActiveX components to query the MUMPS database and a mix of InterSystems technology, other third-party components, and Visual Basic to query the Deaconess database. Application servers at each hospital can pull and translate data into a uniform format that a consolidating server (working in concert with Microsoft Internet Information Server) can deliver to a Web page. The system relies on Microsoft encryption technology to secure transmission between the application servers, and on Secure Sockets Layer (SSL) between the servers and browsers. And all the patients will know is that, wherever they go, their records will be there.

A Web front end
provides a unified
interface to
numerous data
sources

Seattle Times connects newsroom research resources
When the newsroom needs facts, speed and accuracy count. The 290 people in the newsroom at the Seattle Times newspaper rely on research databases and directories. Before their shift to an NT platform with IBM-compatible or

Macintosh computers, the newsroom (like most newspapers in the country) had a mainframe-based ATEX system with terminals. Tom Boyer, Database Editor for the Seattle Times newsroom, built a Web front end for ATEX, so reporters can pull data from it into *Café*, their new newsroom intranet. Now, through one interface—their browser—they have access to multiple sources of data. They can access PhoneDisc (a nationwide phone directory), a *virtual Rolodex* contact management application, and a portion (so far) of their own text-searchable story archives. It's far easier for them to use the browser interface than to learn to use (and relearn) the other computer and paper archives.

For instance, when news comes in of a fire in a warehouse, it's easier to use Tom Boyer's *intranet appliance* to find out who owns the building at 1178 East Side Street than to use a paper version of a reverse phone directory. That's especially so if the reporter is not in the newsroom, where the directory is. It's a lot quicker to use remote access, and the time saved can make the difference in making a deadline.

Remote access keeps the office resources available to reporters in the field

Besides this newspaper's application of new technology, their deployment of a database expert–an IT person—*right in the newsroom* is worthy of note. Boyer is an employee of the newsroom, not a member of the IT staff. Many large organizations have begun to attach technical specialists, such as communicators and information technologists, right to the department or division. In this position, they *know* the business they are supporting.

An IT person on the newsroom staff is news

Dixons Mastercare adds multimedia to the information base Dixons Mastercare PC Services has taken advantage of the interactive capabilities of Web pages to create a multimedia reference guide for product support. PC Services is building its intranet information base by adding product write-ups, video clips, and stills of hardware and software they support.

Add video and stills to create a Web-based multimedia reference guide

Visuals make it
easier to identify a
"thingie"

With a video or still camera, staffers take pictures of the connections in the back of hardware. Then, as support technicians talk to customers, they can access that page on their intranet and see what the customer is seeing; the problem with that *thingie* is easier to solve. They also build sequences of software screens to mimic applications, so they can instruct a customer as to what button to press next. "We use FrontPage to create the pages…. We capture screen shots and add hot spots to act as buttons," said Keith Martin-Smith, Director of Dixons PC Services. "The one thing we can't emulate is, 'I've got this error message!'"

When an enterprise's intelligence is organized and integrated in a data-rich, multi-user, interactive Web environment, the opportunities to compress time and improve processes really expand. When access to information is flattened, it flows faster. The next section explores how IT can assure easy access to information on your intranet.

Easy Access to Information

Too little structure—
or too much—makes
it hard to find
needed information

Unfortunately, as the Internet has expanded, the concept of *access to information on the Internet* has become an oxymoron. Anarchy is a frustrating organizing principle. In a traditional client/server environment, there is plenty of structure, with multiple servers and server directories and folders and subfolders, but the inherent problem with nested, hierarchical information is lack of visibility. You have to learn and *remember* where information is located. For someone who has just joined a project, and doesn't know the lay of the land, this is a barrier to getting information.

Safeco uses an
intranet to organize
data enterprise-wide

SAFECO Insurance Corporation's Senior Business Systems Analyst, Ken Fenwick, touts the intranet as a means for removing barriers and thereby saving time. "What it [the SAFECO intranet] has allowed us to do—we realize that knowledge is an asset—is to disseminate knowledge across the organization very quickly, very effectively and to remove the barriers to finding information…. An intranet can catalog, provide directories, and search engines for a full text search. It allows you to share across the *whole* enterprise, and solve the issue associated with knowledge chaos."

"Let's say instead of storing that information on a Web server in HTML format, with a search engine and indexes in place that makes navigation to knowledge very easy, we took that same piece of information and stuck it in a directory on a file server, and you have to find where the file server is, where the directory is, and what do they call the document? It's looking for a needle in a haystack."

Indexing to Facilitate Access

One of the basic tools that help prepare information for retrieval is indexing software. Intranet indexing tools come in all sizes. For an NT platform, the Microsoft Index Server is a free, downloadable component of Windows NT Server 4.0.[15] The Adobe Catalog software only indexes PDF files. One advantage that Adobe currently has over its nearest competitor, Tumbleweed Software Corporation's *Envoy*, is the automated scheduling feature, which is especially useful for sites with large volumes of PDF files.

Indexing software sets up information for retrieval

For personal computers, AltaVista's Personal Extensions, a handy index and search browser-based product, searches across 200 file formats on your desktop—word processing documents, PowerPoint files, desktop databases, e-mail, and even e-mail attachments—and can extend a search to Usenet and the Internet, too. As shown in Figure 6-8, on the next page, an ideal search routine should be able to target any and all of your information resources.

Index and search programs are also available for personal computers

---

15. Microsoft Index Server works in conjunction with Windows NT Server 4.0 and Internet Information Server 2.0, and creates an index in seven languages.

Figure 6-8   *Sending Rover to search all information domains.*

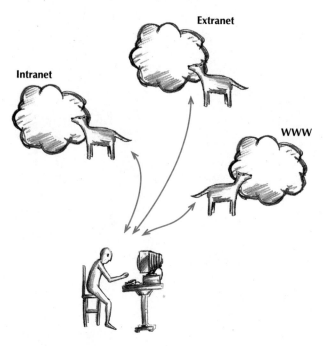

Searching for Data

There are four primary ways to organize a search: keyword search, smart search, hierarchical category search, and parametric search.

- Keyword searches work well with relational databases. However, keyword searches give no feedback about why a query failed to return results or returned too many to be useful. It's a guessing game to see which filters will return the result you want.
- Using smart searching you can create filters with two or more search criteria to filter. Boolean searches are smart searches. Searching on a text string, such as a phrase that appears in a document, is another type of smart search. Using *AND* or *NEAR* can give association, but not context.

- Hierarchical category searches start within a context. For example, if you are searching for a certain electric motor in a product catalog, you might look under Equipment, then Motors, then Electric. The more intuitive the categories (to the user, not the search designer), the easier the search.
- Parametric searches allow you to search by specific parameters that define the object, for example, style, part number, location, or size. If you know the part number or speed of the electric motor, you can find it more quickly.

How can you speed up the search process? Combining a parametric search with a hierarchical category search is one way. Many search engines offer keyword searches within a category.

Neither humans nor computers are perfect search engines. As it is, *human engines* lack speed, but make up for it with *intentional* processing—understanding context and the intent behind a search.

The perfect search engine would be a librarian-computer combination

Electronic engines have the computational speed, but lack discernment. They can recognize only text and static Web pages. Search engines cannot access databases; they are confounded by dynamic data. They step right over multimedia information; they can index a text caption for an image, but cannot see the difference between a 1000-ft. view of the Juneau ice fields and a rumpled white linen napkin on a tabletop. (See Chapter 14, "Looking Further Ahead"). The next section describes new product features that can increase productivity by making it easier and quicker to filter search results on your intranet.

Features to look for in search software The most exciting new direction in commercial smart search products is toward visual displays of search results that show relationships of information, instead of just returning the long, long lists of

New search products focus on contextual information and visual displays

results. SemioMap, Excite, and AltaVista's Live Topics are all taking this approach in different ways.

- SemioMap, developed in Java, has advanced indexing and summarization features. It thoroughly indexes data, identifies repeated concepts, and displays the results in a graphical user interface.

- Excite has a uniquely visual display. It has a scatter/gather interface; the search clusters the results according to conceptual connections, and you can scatter/gather those results into subcategories. A unique feature is the display on the left-hand portion of the screen that indicates the relative length of each document. The number of dark spots indicate the prevalence of the keywords.

- LiveTopics, a new component of the Private Extensions products by AltaVista Internet Software, dynamically generates a suggested best-guess group of topics to use in further refining your query. For instance, if you searched on the word *filter*, the results could return 232,400 entries. But LiveTopics might group the results under signal, packet, camera, air filtration, and so on. Using the visual interface, as displayed in Figure 6-9, you can exclude categories that don't interest you and focus on the topic area that you meant in the first place.

Spiders and agents
locate data

Spiders—benefits and blockades Spiders are software programs that search Web pages for index information. They don't crawl anywhere; they are server-side programs that automatically download and examine Web pages (including the metadata tags[16] in HTML files) for keywords and phrases. (Spiders, like intranets, are misnamed; they should have been called English Pointers or Golden Retrievers.)

---

16. A metadata tag is an HTML tag that contains information about the data on that page.

LiveTopics groups search results under logical categories, which you can include or exclude in a more refined search.

Figure 6-9

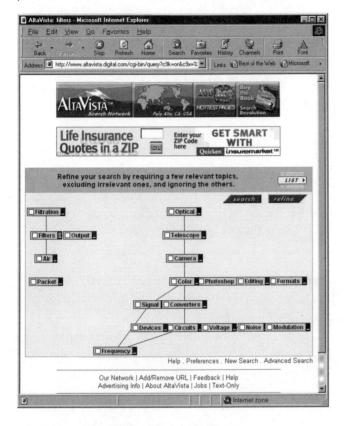

They retrieve indexing data with their respective URLs and store them in the search engine's database.[17]

Spiders can cause a drain on network resources by their relentless indexing activities. Also, you may not wish to have a spider index certain secure sites on your intranet or extranet. The Standard for Robot Exclusion specifies a way to block spiders from accessing a Web site (see *To Block Spider Access to a Site,* on the next page).

Block spider indexing with the Standard for Robot Exclusion

---

17. To many, the term search engine refers to a Web site (such as Yahoo and Excite) that provides Web search capabilities. Actually, what each one provides is a program that accesses their database of keywords, titles, and URLs of Web sites that they have indexed.

To Block Spider Access to a Site

The Web Robots FAQ on the Webcrawler.com WWW site describes how to block spiders. The simplest way to block spiders is to write a structured text file to inform spiders that all or portions of your server are off limits. Add these two lines to the /robots.txt file on the root level of your server:

User-agent: * (name of a spider)

Disallow: , / (specifies path that is disallowed; if no path is listed, then the spider named has full access).

Repeat these two lines for each spider. As long as the spider program recognizes the Standard for Robot Exclusion (and you should not install a spider on your intranet that doesn't), this code will keep spiders away.

Intelligent Agents—the next step to productivity Agents can be client- or server-based programs. They operate more independently than indexing robots or spiders. Personal agents can be directed by a user to pull information or perform helpful tasks. For instance, they can monitor Web pages and inform the user when updates occur.

Agents take advantage of the linking and associative features of the Web environment to find information. Developers of search technology are attempting to infuse more intelligence into their search activities—fuzzy logic, concept mapping, or relevance ranking—to match the evaluative processes of humans (see Chapter 14, "Looking Further Ahead").

The interface to a Web application is an access point

Developing customized search interfaces for intranets Powerful search engines cannot solve all issues of access. The interface of an application is a point of access. And, to the user, if it's not intuitive, efficient, and congruent with the flow of work, it won't work well.

Traditionally, business software has been built from the rules up. That is, the developer starts with the logic process and builds a structure that will *contain* the information. While developers strive to *organize* data, users just want to *interact with data.* Their view of information is a series of relationships. Because of their immersion in their content, they see logical groupings that a developer unfamiliar with their work environment might not see at first. (Well, users fail to appreciate elegant code, too.) An awkward interface, although visually beautiful, can slow productivity, while a well-ordered one that leads a user through the application environment can speed tasks.

Users see the contextual relationships in the data

"The great thing about using a Web, is that you can conceivably build as many interfaces as you need," said Tom Boyer, Database Editor for the Seattle Times newsroom. "Sometimes it takes less time to build a special interface (for accessing Web-based information) than it would take to train people to use an interface they're not comfortable with…. For example for PhoneDisc, the telephone directory, we have four different interfaces: an easy interface for quick look-ups, an address-searching interface for reverse address look-ups, a power interface with all the fields, and a special interface for looking-up by the phone number. We can build as many as you want… If someone can't learn to use an interface, instead of training and retraining, build them an interface that they *can* use. We can build a new one in a half an hour."

You can create multiple interfaces or access points

Webcasting—Push Technology

As noted in the beginning of this chapter, the flip side of access is the distribution of information. Push technology, or Webcasting, is a valuable tool for managers, especially in these days when the mass of available information can turn into a blur. Managers can focus an individual's attention on *must see* information.

Push technology is a tool for managers

Before push technology, most corporations had only one vehicle to get the *same* message to all employees at the

Deliver a single
message to everyone
at the same time

same time—they tucked a message inside the pay envelope.
But that doesn't work well for publishing time-critical information. Webcasting has matured to the point that managers
wishing to send information directly to a group of employees, or all employees, find it to be a better alternative.

PointCast pushes push technology PointCast led the way in
push technology on the Internet. Users with Internet access
could specify their news areas of interest (such as technology news, headlines, individual stock prices, and sports) and
as information became available, PointCast would offer to
download items from its news channel resources relative to
that list.

PointCast was a lively screensaver. When a user's screen
was idle, news bulletins (and ads) would appear. Many
information technologists credit PointCast with introducing
managers to an information-rich Web environment. However, there were two problems.

First, early versions of the program garnered far too much
bandwidth at the expense of network resources. Early push
technology was, in truth, an elaborate pull system. The
service actually sent a notice to each subscriber that some
news or information that matched the pre-selected criteria
was available, and the user clicked to retrieve (pull) that
information. You and many others might have been retrieving the information from the server at the same time, hence
the problem with bandwidth and load management.

The second problem was the distraction factor. Having your
workday disrupted (brightened would be the word employees used) raised the question: Was this service business
critical? Actually, no. Few employees needed the glamorous
interruptions.

Frustrated with diminished network performance and concerned about employee performance, many organizations

Managing Load – a Historical Perspective

The problem of managing load is one the utility industry knows well. Back in the *oil panic* winter of 1973–74, the television stations in Britain sought to do their part in reducing the use of electricity. So they agreed to cease broadcasting after the evening news at 10:00 p.m. Unfortunately, in nearly every household in the land, after they turned off the *telly* at 10:00, at 10:01 p.m. they turned on their electric teakettles. To modify the load curve, the television stations staggered their sign-offs at 10-minute intervals. Load management is a serious concern for information technology managers.

either restricted the program or banned it from desktops. Since then, PointCast and other follow-on programs have slimmed down the technology to deal with the problem of overburdening the business network.

Intranet product developers (and managers) digested the PointCast experience as a *lesson learned.* For an intranet to be useful, it can't *bury* its users or their network. Unchanneled, any deluge of information is liable to drain, instead of gain, productivity; if you're too busy just keeping up, you can't move forward.

Unicasting and Multicasting Unicasting technology, which sends a single data channel (or message) to each user (see Figure 6-10, on the next page), was the source of the problem of overloaded bandwidths. Thousands of individual messages prompted thousands of individual actions at virtually the same time.

The solution is multicasting, an Internet protocol that can feed a *single* data stream to *multiple* users (see Figure 6-11 on the next page). Multicast technology has real business value as a messaging device. It can be programmed to run in the background unobserved. The technology can work in two ways: an organization can send an alert notification

Newer technology solves bandwidth problem

Unicasting sends one message to each subscriber

Multicasting sends the same news to everyone at the same time

Figure 6-10   *Unicasting sends a single signal to each recipient.*

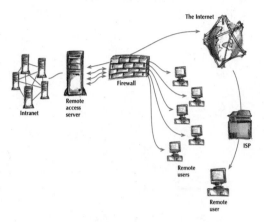

straight to the desktop[18] or an employee can subscribe to receive certain information updates when new data becomes available.

Figure 6-11   *Multicasting feeds a single data stream to multiple users.*

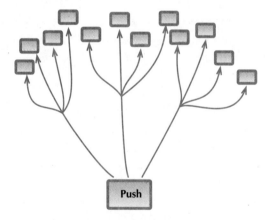

For managers, push technology is a means for distributing *must see* information on a timely basis. Users can receive the data without any action on their part. Notifications sent via e-mail can go unnoticed in the daily avalanche of e-

18. As an alternative to posting a notice on the lunchroom wall or mass-mailing an e-mail message.

mail. Push technology gives managers a tool for sending general announcements and specific data right to the desktop.

When the Corporate Communications department for the Coors Brewing Company switched to using push technology, they were able to discontinue sending a twice-weekly fax package of news clippings. With the old system, the information was always at least a day old by the time it was packaged, faxed, and delivered to the individuals in the company who could use the information. Now, every Wednesday and Friday they *push* the clippings over the Coors intranet, *CyBEERweb*, and on to the desktops of those who need them. The information is fresher and the process is easier.

Quick publishing can replace fax packages of news clippings

When Air Products and Chemicals, Inc., a worldwide supplier of industrial gases and chemicals, installed Microsoft's Internet Explorer on 1000 desktops, they set it up so that when employees boot their computers each day they open to *Air Products Online* in the browser. That raises the question, said Steve Cameron, Manager of Communication Programs, "Do you put the corporate news as part of the boot? Or do we ask, 'Do you want to open your CorpNews now?' You have to consider how invasive you want to be."

Overused, push technology may numb employees to important communiqués

The use of push technology needs to be tempered. If you begin shouting at employees from their desktops, they may tune out that channel also.

Use push technology sparingly

Requesting Information

Employees can sign up to be notified of certain events or information as it becomes available. For example, a claims adjuster for an insurance company can request to be notified whenever there is a change in company policy about handling catastrophe claims or when extreme weather is expected in a specific geographic region. A dispatcher with

Subscribe to sites or channels that alert you to timely information you can use

Internet access might subscribe to traffic or weather alerts in a specific geographic area.

Channel technology can push updates and internal news

An internal news channel can keep employees informed of competitive information—information they can use. Not only can a manager push messages or news to a group, but IT administrators can also push software updates through a channel. Web pages can also be updated through channel technology.

An interview study of 150 information systems managers conducted by the IP Multicast Initiative (IPMI),[19] a multi-vendor forum, found that the main interests for corporate uses of multicasting are audio and video streaming, push applications, electronic software distribution, multi-point conferencing, and Web-site replication.

Reaching—Remote Access and Productivity

Today's flexible work schedules and extended workdays are increasing the demand for remote access. Employees in the field and telecommuters at home—more and more employees—are *rasing* into the corporate intranet or extranet. (To *ras* is not to joke, it is to connect to the Remote Access Server). Remote access technology has been available on traditional LANs and WANS, but the benefits of speedy access to information, coupled with the ease of collaboration, make it especially attractive on an intranet.

Support people and network staff will need additional training

While telecommuters who use an intranet may have fewer support needs, because of the ease of the browser interface, they may need increased technical support while they are mastering remote access. Increased remote access means additional training for the support staff, too. Help desk people need to know how to troubleshoot modem problems, and network staff may need to know more about large

---

19. IP Multicasting Initiative is a vendor group pushing business applications of multicast technologies.

modem pools and remote access servers. Maintaining logs of user problems can reveal common problems and solutions. These solutions can also be posted on a Web site, which will encourage remote users to help themselves.

As part of evaluating the design of an intranet, consider the network load from remote access connections. How many people will be granted remote access? Will they be coming in on 28.8 Kbps or ISDN and T-1 lines? How frequently are telecommuters likely to access the network, and for how long during each session? What types of resources—conferencing, messaging, data access—will they be needing?

Telecommuting will affect network load

It's hard to measure the productivity gains from telecommuting, but it's generally agreed that it often boosts employees' morale to be more in control of their time; they tend to be happier, and that leads to their being more productive. Dial-up access keeps them connected to files on shared network directories and e-mail. With intranet collaboration products, they can engage in virtual meetings and work productively with others in their organization (see Chapter 7, "Knowledge-Working"). From a customer's office, they can have access to Web sites—containing their organization's catalogs, presentations, price lists, production schedules, and shipping status—through a single Web-based interface, the browser.

Location-free access works to improve morale and productivity

There are several ways to set up intranet access and security for remote users. As shown in Figure 6-12, on the next page, a user could come in through a simple dial-up access line to a remote access server, or over a Virtual Private Network. A new VPN server product by Aventail Corporation can connect both telecommuters and extranet users. The server runs Socks version 5, the IETF (Internet Engineering Task Force) standard for distributed network security, on top of the Microsoft Winsock API layer. Because it has authentication and encryption at the session layer, it lets authorized users send and receive data across the firewall securely.

Socks v.5 is a standard for distributed network security

Figure 6-12   *Remote access with a dial-up connection.*

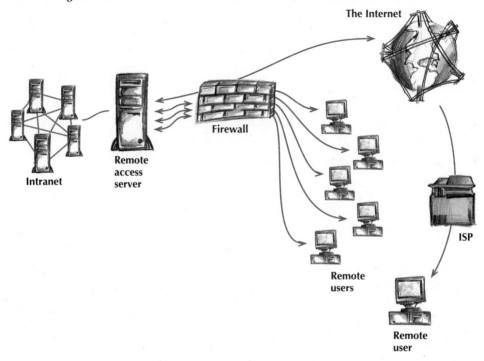

The Internet

Firewall

Intranet

Remote
access
server

Remote
users

ISP

Remote
user

Teleres example of secure remote access Working for the Teleres Corporation in Dayton, Ohio, meant that Phil Jennings was often on the road. And the road could lead to Bellevue, Washington, or it could lead to Tokyo, Japan. With an able IT staff behind him, Jennings could be assured of seamless access to his files over the Teleres intranet, wherever he was.

Remote access can retrieve files that a phone call can't

From a phone connection in Tokyo, Jennings can use remote access to check a contract (in a Word document format) on the file system in Dayton. This is something that he can't call in and ask a secretary to look up, because the secretary won't have access to certain confidential files and therefore can't retrieve them. Behind the scenes, the Microsoft Index Server, which automatically builds search indexes from a file server, can search anything that is produced in the Microsoft family of products.

For security, the contract document has embedded meta-data codes that specify who has permission to see the file. Jennings' name appears in the metadata. The secretary's doesn't. A search can be initiated for the contract document, but the Web server will not display the file unless the seeker is authenticated as Jennings.

Metadata codes in the contract restrict access to named individuals

Looking Ahead

This chapter covered a lot of ground—exploring the types of data and the ways to acquire it for an intranet, organizing legacy and dynamic data, creating custom Web applications, and ways to access and distribute information. This is the groundwork—building the information base that is rich and accessible.

The next chapter explores how an intranet can provide the means for using these intelligence assets to fuel teams' efforts to produce better products and services. You'll see how teams have used new intranet products and technologies to increase their productivity.

Chapter Seven

Knowledge-Working

Francis Bacon (1561-1626) said it first, "Nam et ipsa scientia potestas est." Or, if your Latin is rusty, "Knowledge itself is power." It's still true.

Today, the knowledge of the group gives power to an organization, but only if the group is highly focused and can work unimpeded by technical or geographic barriers. Over an intranet, the goal for knowledge workers is to leverage the information assets of their organization and turn them into profit-generating products and services. In other words, knowledge for knowledge's sake isn't important; the knowledge must lead to action. And quickly.

Intellectual capital must be focused and accessible to be effective

The core business questions need responses. How are finances doing? How are projects doing? What are the scheduling, or manufacturing issues? Are we in compliance? Why not? The answers reside in a database somewhere, waiting to travel up the chain of command. With the Web activity afforded by an intranet, you can get the big picture with a browser—some say it's the first tool that is executive-proof.

Focus on core business questions and answers

This chapter focuses on improving the productivity of knowledge workers through conferencing and decision-support tools on an intranet.

In the 1980s, students invented their solution to information overload: study groups or *knowledge networks*. Students pooled their knowledge and studied together. (And maybe that's why they had time to devote hours to surfing the Internet and meeting people around the planet for virtual conversations and gaming.) Industry, now made up of many of those graduates, is comfortable with work group collaboration as a route to more than a passing grade.

Definition

Business gurus have come up with various terms to describe an organization that has reinvented itself to succeed in the digital economy, terms such as *learning organization, virtual corporation, networked organization, cluster organization, relational organization, crazy organization,* and *intelligent enterprise* (see *The Digital Economy* sidebar). Generally speaking, the terms all define organizations that re-orchestrate their business processes around streamlined collaborations.

The term "knowledge-working" describes using up-to-date data to make decisions

While there is nothing wrong with the word *collaboration*, the term *knowledge-working* is more inclusive. First, it focuses on knowledge workers, who use information either to collaborate or to coordinate large-scale activities. The term also implies using the organization's knowledge resources (ideas, people, and materials) efficiently to make decisions and build products or services. (To review the difference between task workers, information providers, and knowledge workers, see "Who Needs What Information," page 165.) In some cases knowledge workers collaborate in project development. Whether it is an engineering design for an airplane or a virtual reality theme park attraction, an intranet can provide data and video conferencing for virtual team meetings. Intranet decision-support tools can also give managers the knowledge they need to coordinate large scale activities.

Global IT expert Don Tapscott followed his popular book *Paradigm Shift* with *Digital Economy, Promise and Peril in the Age of Networked Intelligence*. In this book he explores how organizations that harness the speed of information can transform their organizations and invent new ways of doing business to succeed in this new "knowledge economy." Early in his book (p. 12), he recites the litany of authors' new names for a reinvented company. The full list (authors and names) includes Peter Senge, "learning organization"; Davidow and Malone, "virtual corporation"; Peter Keen, "relational organization"; Tom Peters, "crazy organization"; D. Quinn Mills, "cluster organization"; Charles Savage, "human networking"; Russell Ackoff, "democratic corporation"; James Brian Quinn, "intelligent enterprise"; Michael Hammer and James Champy, "reengineered corporation."

Working in a Virtual Space

Much of the knowledge-working on an intranet takes place in a virtual environment. As overused (and often misused) as the term *virtual* has become, it is a valid word to describe that *out of place* location where business goes on between two or more people who are all somewhere else. The best minds for the job can meet together in a networked virtual environment, regardless of where they are sitting. Intranets can give you location-free, hands-on meetings that are quick and responsive, moving with the agility of a cutting horse, rather than that of an oil tanker.

"Virtual environment" means a shared space

Before Intranets

The father of all groupware[1] products is Lotus Notes. Notes made Lotus the *come-back kid* when their Lotus 1-2-3 spreadsheet program began to lose its luster. The attractiveness of Notes made Lotus attractive to IBM, which acquired it.

Lotus Notes was the first groupware product

---

1. For more information about groupware, see *Understanding Groupware in the Enterprise*, by Joanne Woodcock, another title in the Microsoft Press Strategic Technology Series.

Other proprietary products followed suit. Microsoft Exchange became one of the leading collaborative computing products. Now, in this intranet era, Microsoft and Netscape have created platforms for intranet development and activities, and Lotus has transformed Notes into Domino for developing and running groupware applications across intranets. (Chapter 12, "Implementing Your Intranet," covers intranet platform issues.)

Traditional groupware products that enabled collaboration across LANs and WANs were often difficult to learn and did not scale well. The following table compares features of traditional and intranet groupware.

Comparing Traditional Groupware to Intranet Collaboration

Features	Groupware	Intranets
platform choice	platform-specific	publish across wide variety of platforms
package or build-to-suit	complete package	administrators can mix and match components
price to purchase	expensive	cheap
scalability	difficult to scale	very scalable
interface	sophisticated, unique for each product	simpler, universal to all intranet applications
Protocols	TCP/IP and other protocols	TCP/IP and other protocols

Intranet Opportunities for Knowledge-Working

Two conditions have to be in place before an organization can benefit from knowledge-working tools.

- An organization must attain (or at least be striving for) a degree of cultural readiness.

- The suppliers of conferencing equipment (hardware and software) must offer standards-based products that are interoperable, so users won't be frustrated when *my conferencing software won't talk to your conferencing software.*

The standards-based products are here, and more will follow. The cultural readiness is up to individual organizations. In 1994 when ARAMARK, a national food service provider, began an ambitious five-year mission to grow 10 percent per year, they knew they couldn't get there with business as usual.

Open standards and cultural readiness are a must

The ARAMARK culture was very decentralized; there were eighteen divisions, but there were Culinary Managers and General Managers in each. One of the strategies to achieve their five-year goal was to improve communication among the divisions, and the intranet became one of the means. The first focus was to publish newsworthy events and information. The next objectives were to improve horizontal communication across the company, and then provide a forum for collaboration. Teams that cross division lines, and state lines, are now beginning to work together with the intranet technology. The ARAMARK PC Help desk team is responsible for identifying best practices. The team uses a discussion forum on *Starnet* to share ideas and stay on track with their objectives. "We've got to demonstrate we can use this technology effectively," said John Kallelis, Vice President of Information Technology, ARAMARK. "But the biggest issue is cultural. We have to change. People are not used to working this way."

Team workers need to get used to collaborating with technology

Although ARAMARK personnel were used to working in a team environment, they had not been used to using technology to enable collaboration. But the speed and reach of intranet communications was immediately attractive and generated enthusiasm for the intranet. The IT department took the *it has to be easy* approach and made sure technol-

The intranet enables speed and a wider reach

ogy got out of the way of the business at hand. "They [users] have to get to the services [on the intranet] easily, without a lot of log on and sign off... Information is a couple of mouse clicks away." Also, as you will see in Chapter 10, ("Choosing the Project and Developing a Marketing Plan," page 275), they made careful choices as to which groups to include in the initial pilot projects. Word gets around. Other pilot projects are in the works, and one division is exploring building an extranet.

Knowledge-working needs a team environment to thrive

The prerequisite for using an intranet for knowledge-working is that the organization must have a team-oriented culture. Ask not only *does it have work groups?* but *does the culture support the concept of sharing information*? It may sound like a trivial distinction, but without a team-oriented work ethic, the incentive to become comfortable with virtual meetings may not be there (see "What are the Challenges," page 230).

Conferencing

Depicting information can make it easier to grasp

Communicating with pictures increases understanding, so it can save time, which will save dollars. Visual aids can give a quick overview of a situation and make it easier to get to the details that need attention. Each type of conferencing—data, voice, or video—can make a unique contribution to knowledge-working, and as you'll see in Chapter 8, to distance learning. Adding conferencing across an intranet requires evaluating network configuration, client processing power, audio and video hardware, and conferencing software.

Data conferencing costs the least bandwidth

Being able to put the same information in front of you and your team members—on a shared whiteboard or by sharing a document—means you can see, compare, and interpret the data before you (see Figure 7-1). The data could be a spreadsheet, a word processing document, a PowerPoint presentation, a chart, a graphic, engineering designs, or a video. You can confer with each other immediately in order to take action.

The T.120 protocol is used for the transport-independent multipoint data conferencing needed for whiteboards, application-sharing and viewing. Many products, such as NetMeeting, include data conferencing as part of their videoconferencing package.

The T.120 protocol is used for multi-point conferencing

Sharing a document on a whiteboard.

Figure 7-1

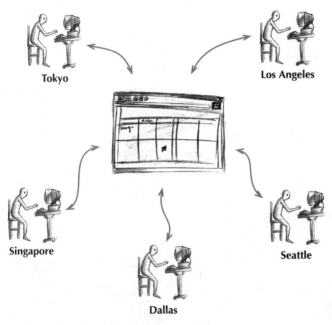

Tokyo

Los Angeles

Singapore

Seattle

Dallas

Streaming media technology, pioneered by RealAudio, opened the door to delivering data, audio, or video files in real time or on demand. It was a breakthrough in overcoming technical limitations that had thwarted use of video for collaboration. Long download times and small video windows hampered effective communication.

Streaming technology has enabled delivery of higher quality video

Unlike database files, which are small repeating structures (records), stream-oriented files (text, audio, video) contain streams (or flows) of characters. Streaming requires the client and server to work together to create an uninterrupted flow. Rather than waiting for an entire audio or video file to

The display begins before all the data has arrived

download from the server as illustrated in Figure 7-2, the client buffers a few seconds of it, then starts displaying it as shown in Figure 7-3. Microsoft Internet Explorer 4.0 uses streaming technology to speed downloads of data.

Figure 7-2   *Downloading an entire audio source file.*

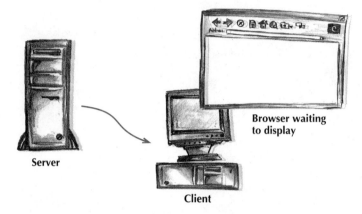

Server

Browser waiting
to display

Client

Figure 7-3   *Data streaming—client buffers a few seconds of audio data, then begins to display it.*

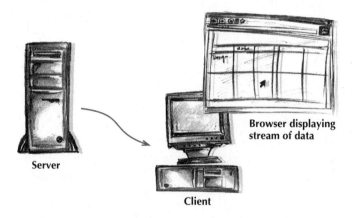

Server

Browser displaying
stream of data

Client

Conferencing Equipment Standards

There are a number of international standards for conferencing equipment that have gained broad industry support.[2] *Industry* in this case includes not only software and hardware vendors, but also the telecommunications industry. More proposals for standards are coming. The table below describes the relevant protocols for different types of conf-erencing, and whether the standard was approved by the International Telecommunications Union (ITU) or the International Engineering Task Force (IETF). Even though these are not Internet protocols, they are important on intranets, enabling users to take advantage of the conferencing capabilities of collaboration products.

Market leaders are assuring their products are interoperable

Conferencing Protocols

Protocol	Standards group	Function
T.120	ITU	set of protocols for transport-independent, multipoint data conferencing
RTP (and RTCP)	IETF	Real-time Protocol (and Real-time Control Protocol)
H323	ITU	set of protocols for audio, video, and data conferencing over TCP/IP networks
H324	ITU	(as above) for analog phone lines (POTS)
H320	ITU	(as above) for ISDN lines

Although these conferencing protocols are now in place, there has not yet been enough time for significant formal cross-testing of equipment and software from the various vendors to assure that they actually do work seamlessly together as they should. Because some of the protocols leave some areas open to interpretation, complete inter-operability is not absolutely assured at this point. By checking with specific vendors to see if their products have been tested together, you can proceed with assurance.

Thorough cross-testing has not yet occurred

---

2. At the "Hacking in Progress (HIP) '97" open air conference held in Amsterdam, August, 1997, the importance of using products that adhere to protocols became very apparent. A videoconference link to the New York hackers conference, "Beyond Hope," was spoiled by a bad connection. The videoconferencing product, PictureTel, was a proprietary, not a standards-based conferencing system. (PictureTel's newest product, LiveManager 3.0, is compliant with H323.)

Off-the-Shelf Products

While the last chapter showed that many organizations are relying primarily on custom-built applications for use on their intranets, there are a number of off-the-shelf intranet-ready groupware products on the market today, including a host of new products that support conferencing.[3]

Some of these products are not browser-based, nor do they require that you run them on an intranet. Any two or more persons can collaborate over phone lines using Microsoft NetMeeting, for example. However, it's both easy and beneficial to integrate those products into an intranet. For instance, an engineering team home page, besides including team information and project reports, could contain a link for NetMeeting, making it convenient for team members to access the collaboration tool. It would be like putting conferencing equipment right into a meeting room.

Figure 7-4   *Microsoft NetMeeting.*

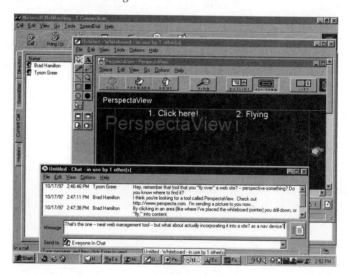

---

3. For video conferencing, an organization also needs server software, client software, and video hardware.

NetMeeting and MeetingPoint

Microsoft NetMeeting is client software that supports data, voice, and video-conferencing (see Figure 7-4). With it, people can extend a phone call to include image and document sharing with others. They can communicate by writing messages back and forth in the chat text area, or by voice-conferencing. Two or more people using the voice conferencing feature can also take turns marking up documents or images for data conferencing. With the addition of a video-capture card and camera, you can also have a face-to-face meeting from computer to computer. The Microsoft Internet Locator Server (ILS) provides the means to connect users' names with their IP addresses on the intranet. This makes it easy for users to find each other. ILS Directory services get around the problem of dynamic addressing and provide up-to-date connection information so that users can contact each other.

Because it has been built on an open standards-based platform, the software can *collaborate* with products from other hardware and software vendors. Microsoft NetMeeting was the first real-time Internet phone voice communications client that supports international conferencing standards. For instance, the T.120 protocols from the International Telecommunications Union (ITU) is also supported by telephone companies, bridge manufacturers, videoconferencing vendors, and service providers.

White Pine Software Inc. produces a server software product, MeetingPoint, which works with a variety of clients, including Microsoft's NetMeeting, Netscape's Communicator, Intel Corp's VideoPhone, and their own CUseeMe software for videoconferencing. MeetingPoint runs on both NT and UNIX servers. It uses the H.323 protocol for audio, video, and data conferencing over TCP/IP networks.

A key question for network administrators is: How does the software affect network load? (And how much additional load will videoconferencing put on the network staffers who have to manage it?) MeetingPoint optimizes bandwidth use during videoconferencing in two ways. Using multicast technology, MeetingPoint distributes different streams of traffic according to the types

The impact of conferencing on network demand must be addressed

Video Bandwidth

As defined by the *Computer Desktop Encyclopedia*, video bandwidth is the maximum computer screen display resolution, expressed in megahertz. To calculate bandwidth, multiply the horizontal resolution by the vertical resolution and then by the number of refreshes per second. For example, an 800 x 600 x 60 refreshes computer display absorbs a whopping 28.8 MHz of bandwidth. By comparison, the limit in television broadcasting is 3.58 MHz.

of connections that participants have, and administrators may set bandwidth limits for network segments. But what if video shares a data channel with critical data traffic (as MeetingPoint does)? Will the data stream slow? That depends—which is the standard response about any change to any network. Granted, intranets can support higher bandwidth demands than the Internet, but long before a group within an organization embarks on widespread videoconferencing, the network administrator needs to be involved. Network administrators may choose to run a separate pipe to support videoconferencing.

Virtual Meetings

Video conferencing used to be a formal information exchange.

Before intranets, many organizations were already using videoconferencing as a vehicle to deliver presentations and to conduct meetings. Some organizations dedicated rooms as videoconference centers, with hard-wired connections, multiple monitors and cameras built into cabinets, copy stand camera, fax and phone support, and row-like seating arrangements. Generally, these rooms were located near the executive offices, and not near the engineering offices or the shop floor. Even if the equipment was housed in a mobile cabinet, the cart would reside in the conference room on the executive floor, not on the shop floor, or not even in the engineering department. Originally, videoconferencing was meant for reporting or formal discussions, and not often used to *do core business.*

Northrop Grumman—Cameras on the Shop Floor

Northrop Grumman fully supports the teaming concept. They built Team Communication Centers (TCC), next generation videoconference rooms that can handle fifteen to eighteen members of a team with full video, voice, and data-collaboration capabilities. Team members can either dial in remotely or from their desktops and share in the voice and data elements of a meeting. "From video-conference rooms and defined sessions, we have moved to teams that are far more flexible and agile, and may involve team members in Team Communication Centers, at their desktops, or in a hotel room," said Richard Atkinson, Chief Communications Technologist, Northrop Grumman Corp. "It's how we wish to do business." At Northrop Grumman they have taken the camera out of the videoconferencing *box*, and can use it on the factory floor to send video images to a meeting in progress.

In one instance, the factory was an aircraft manufacturing retrofit facility in Melbourne, Florida, and the engineering team was in Bethpage, New York (see Figure 7-5 on the next page). Video images along with data elements (CAD/CAM work procedures, parts lists) were fed over the Northrop Grumman Corp. intranet to show the engineering team what it looked like when the work crew in Florida opened up a twenty-year-old airplane. Before, without the blending of intranet technology with video delivery, the team had to fly from New York to Florida to see it first-hand, incurring expenses and losing productivity while traveling. "Now through video," Atkinson describes, "They can see it *semi-first-hand*. They [the team] can make an immediate decision. And they can use the video and photos, and at the same time, jointly work on CAD/CAM and schematics. This enables the teams to deal with a problem from their remote

Now video conferencing takes place on a desktop, in a meeting room, or in a hotel room

Remote cameras can provide information to improve a process

site, and keep moving on." The ease of accessing these diverse formats of information through one interface—the browser—keeps the technology from getting in the way of the collaboration. The Web-based technologies accelerate the speed and depth of collaboration.

Figure 7-5   *A team in New York and another in Florida shared video images, drawings, and parts lists over the intranet.*

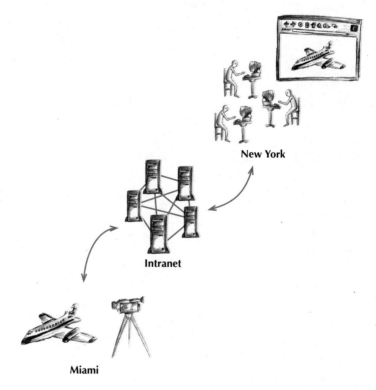

On the Northrop Grumman intranet, they also use Net-Meeting on personal computers and equivalent products, such as Hewlett Packard's SharedX, on their UNIX equipment. They continue to adjust and grow network segments to support intranet services, such as videoconferencing, as the needs of teams evolve.

Workflow

Groupware is information-centric. As illustrated in Figure 7-6, the focus is on the data that is developed, distributed, or discussed. Workflow is process-centric (see Figure 7-7 on the next page), addressing issues such as: How does the process work? What is the sequence and timing for the pieces to fit together? Workflow products include message routing and document sharing. Structured workflow applications can automate critical business functions—such as shipping and billing statements or purchase authorizations—according to business rules.

Groupware is information-centric; workflow is process-centric

Groupware focuses on the data.

Figure 7-6

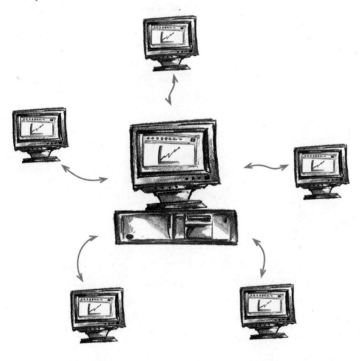

Figure 7-7   *Workflow focuses on the process.*

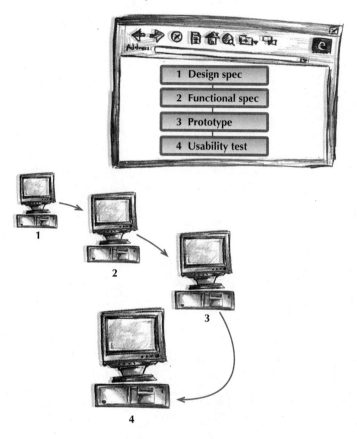

Workflow software
automates and
manages processes

Workflow software automates tasks performed by individuals or by the group, such as generating periodic status reports that can be shared (electronically) with team members,
key managers, and other departments. For instance, an
engineering report may be automatically shared with the
design and production departments. Sometimes the fewer
the people who *touch* workflow, the more streamlined the
process becomes. Alert mechanisms that flag an incomplete
action step are blame-free, and can focus the group on
creating solutions. Workflow applications can be used
behind the scenes to manage a development process or can
be used to manage the flow of business, as you will see in
the next section.

Emery WorldWide's Intranet Inventory Management System

In 1996, Emery WorldWide won a contract with the United States Postal Service for the delivery of USPS second-day airmail. As part of the requirements for this project, the USPS requested that Emery provide an inventory management system that tracked the pickup, delivery and on-hand inventory of second-day priority mail containers. The project involved about twenty geographically dispersed Emery sites around the United States.

Emery's solution was to build a workflow application to run on their corporate intranet, using remote object technology to track the mail containers. They built the inventory management application using Java 1.1 as the development language, and used Remote Method Invocation (RMI) for managing objects on a distributed network.[4] RMI is Sun's implementation of DCOM or an Object Request Broker (ORB), as discussed in "Managing Data Objects," page 185.

The inventory system used local static data[5] encapsulated in RMI objects, and saved transaction time by transferring only dynamic data (data that has changed) back to the corporate data servers. In addition, since the data was encapsulated in the remote object on the local hard drive, it was available without a call across the network to the server each time a user needed to use the inventory-management application. The production servers at corporate headquarters downloaded data to a data warehouse, which created daily reports and data transfers to the USPS and Emery personnel. The design increased application performance by 700 percent compared to a design without remote objects.

Emery WorldWide won a contract that required an inventory management system.

Emery's solution was an intranet workflow application using remote objects

Using remote objects increased application performance by 700 percent

---

4. Remote Method Invocation is the Java method for distributing remote objects over an intranet or the Internet. Using an RMI call, a Java applet running on a client can control a Java server applet.

5. Local static data is usually code tables or reference data, and can be on the client machine. It can be significant in size and volume.

An important cost-saving feature of the project was the way in which data was transmitted from the remote container-handling sites. Each workstation ran NT 4.0 and was connected through an RF (radio frequency) card to network hubs, then to T1 lines across the Emery corporate WAN to a server in Portland, Oregon. Using RF transmission saved having to install, synchronize, and manage additional servers for each remote location.

Using RF transmission saved the cost and installation of servers at the remote sites

Without an intranet, the traditional way to implement an inventory tracking system would be to install servers running applications at each of the distributed sites. Each client machine would have to implement a message queuing process (instead of RMI) to coordinate with the corporate server receiving the updates from the distributed sites. Message queuing systems are notoriously difficult to implement. Due to lower hardware and software requirements, the intranet solution cost half as much as a traditional client/server solution, and was much more efficient, too.

A traditional client/server network solution would have required elaborate message queuing

For Managers—Program Management and Decision Support

Fulfilling the responsibilities of project management means managing an increasing load of information in a shorter and shorter period of time. In the last chapter, you saw that integrating legacy databases and building with dynamic databases could create a just-in-time knowledge base accessible from a single user interface, a browser. This section addresses how that information, available on an intranet, can be used for decision support.

Intranets tools can be used for decision support

Executives have to rely on others to contribute information that they need to make decisions. In many cases, what the information providers are doing is *filtering* data, so invariably the messages (that come up through channels) carry some distortion. The result is that executives are handed information that they cannot always trust. And this often

When status information passes up the chain of command, it is often diluted

leaves managers in the dark; you can't fix a problem unless you know it exists.

"With thousands of people working on something, how do you know, day to day, if they're going in the right direction?" Richard Atkinson asked rhetorically. Northrop Grumman Corp. uses a Web-based program management matrix to assure that executives have up-to-date information that they can trust. One matrix program covers five areas: customer satisfaction, schedule, subcontractor data, performance data, and project health indicators. The color-coded health indicators—red, yellow, or green lights—are generated automatically by the system, according to thresholds that are fed by other data systems.

Color-coded indicators are generated automatically

On a Web-based program management matrix, executives use a browser to drill down in a color area to a chart. From there, they can get descriptions and photos that describe the situation. Atkinson explained how the system can speed resolution of an issue. "If I were an executive, and saw *red*, I'd go to the person who owns the *statusing*, then to the person who owns the process. You can trust the system. If it's reporting wrong, we can change the thresholds."

A red color area signals a problem

The common way to use health indicators in an automated computerized system is to allow problems to *drive* the color. It's like an automatic red-green railroad signal that the train engineers see as they're rolling down a track. If it shows green, the track isn't *sort of* clear; it *is* clear. So, if you've got green in all areas of a category but one, that category's status will show red to indicate there is a problem that has not been cleared. "Human nature is just the opposite," said Atkinson. "If 90 percent of them are green, it's green forever! You don't see the red."

Systems (other than human systems) can deliver bad news effortlessly

The larger the project, the more opportunities there are for it to get off the track. A few years ago, during Northrop Grumman's work on the B2, teams worked to shorten the cycle time between being aware there was a problem and bringing it under control. The gap can be as much as three weeks. "What we wanted was not to spend two weeks under the assumption, 'We're ok,'" said Atkinson. The solution was a Web application, so executives could see at a glance how everyone was doing by scrolling down through the colors of fifty different programs that made up the B2 effort.

A matrix view can shorten the time frame for spotting problems

What Are the Challenges?

One of the main challenges of relying on any system for knowledge-working, is being able to count on the reliability of the information. This problem takes two forms. First: is the information on the intranet the latest version? In other words, has it been updated and are there controls in place to assure that the correct version of a document is on the intranet? And second, is the information accurate? How do you achieve a level of confidence that you are offering good information?

A knowledge base must contain accurate, reliable information

Currency and Version Control

On an intranet, there are several ways to attack the problem of ensuring the currency of your data. As you will see in Chapter 13 ("Updating Web Pages and Controlling Change," page 337), users must be made responsible for updating the content on their sites. In the previous chapter ("Dynamically Updating Data," page 177) you saw how easy it is on an intranet to use scripting or controls to update data dynamically. Another tactic is the use of hyper-links on the many relevant Web sites that can *point* to the latest version of a document; the department that *owns* the document maintains it on their Web site and takes charge of keeping it current. Setting up a channel is another way to ensure everyone in the information chain receives notification of the latest information. Having one accessible source of information simplifies the problem of out-of-date documents proliferating.

Use procedures to ensure document control and point to current data

It's easier and quicker to publish information on an intranet than to publish it in paper form, post it on a file server, or enter it into a traditional database. It's easy to publish, and easy to access. At Boeing, all the designs and changes stay electronic. On their intranet, which they've had since the days of DARPA, propagating changes to the end user is faster, and takes fewer steps than with paper or a traditional client/server network. When updating takes place automatically, you can be sure the software remembers to do the updates, even if people don't.

Software never forgets to execute automated updates

Accuracy of Knowledge Base

If you have many individuals contributing articles to a knowledge base, how do you offer users a level of confidence that the information is trustworthy? Ken Fenwick, Business Systems Analyst, SAFECO Insurance Corporation, surmised that airline passengers would hope that an engineer had read the latest copy of the document on the stress dynamics of wing design before sitting down to work, and not some version that was out of date.

Put in place a plan to verify the accuracy of content

Dixons Mastercare, the product support arm of the U.K. electric products retailer, encourages all technical support personnel to use e-forms to post solutions or *workarounds* on their intranet; this builds the knowledge base, and saves other technicians from reinventing the wheel. Unlike posting on a traditional client/server network, on an intranet it's easy to post discoveries—and quick to access them. (This builds enthusiasm for sharing information among peers, and they end up producing better results.) But to ensure that technicians can rely on information in the shared knowledge base, the senior consultants read through all the postings each day and, if necessary, edit them for accuracy.

To maintain accuracy, have experts monitor postings to knowledge repositories

Heather Campbell, Director, Project Management and Consulting Group for CIBC Architecture and Consulting Services in Toronto, Canada, has recommended a content-

Use a content-rating
system to label the
trustworthiness of
information

rating system that they employ at CIBC. A gold star signifies
information that is considered 100 percent accurate. A silver
star denotes information that is 100 percent accurate in the
context for which it was created. For example, if it was
created for the financial services field, but you were planning to use it for the health care field, you'd have to verify
its appropriateness. No rating indicates information that has
not been verified, and you would need to do that.

Solving the Downside of Collaborating

Most organizations spend time and money figuring out the
software, the hardware, and the cables and connections, but
precious little time imagining how employees are going to
take to doing business in full collaboration.

Ease the transition to
virtual meetings by
scheduling a face-to-
face meeting first

The digital age may be here, but most of us grew up in the
industrial one. We're used to face-to-face meetings. Getting
the most out of a virtual meeting may take some adjustment.
Generally, it helps if a geographically diverse team can meet
in person at least once, then when they meet over their
desktops for conferencing, there will already be a more
personal connection. Most teams agree that after meeting in
person, the desktop conferences cease to be a barrier to
good communication.

Users may or may not need training to become intranet
power users, but they will need conflict resolution training—the *soft* side of collaboration. Besides the acclimation
to a collaborative environment, arguing a point effectively in
virtual space is a necessary new communication skill. When
employees work through their disagreements, they can
strengthen products. Better to have employees arguing about
the demerits of an approach (instead of walking out of a
meeting) than to have customers set forth these arguments
and walk away from a product.

When Arno Penzias, Lucent Technologies' Chief Scientist, addressed students at the New School for Social Research, in New York City, he cautioned them about the downside of remote conf-erencing. "The first message is: I'm too important to come there," he said. "My first job as a speaker is to get you to like me." This begins the bond of trust, which underlies good communication. But it's difficult to do at a distance. Penzias pointed out that without engaging face to face (in real space), you have to overcome the lack of prox-imity, lack of eye contact, and inability to see body language very clearly. He explained how a good speaker watches an audience, and if their arms cross, if their heads are cupped in their hands, or worse, if they begin to nod off—the speaker knows it's necessary to change something to reconnect.

Changing meetings from in-person to virtual changes interpersonal dynamics

Looking Ahead

If an organization sells only *fill in the blank* opportunities as interactions, then the real message is: color *inside* the lines—no innovation welcomed here. Innovation, like finger painting, can be messy. Many organizations are learning new ways to get people together across time and distance. Learning, after all, is a search for a new structure. If we cling to the molds we've always known, how will we know or learn something new?

The next chapter, "Distance Learning Systems on an Intranet," explores how you can use an intranet to deliver training and education. While some of the conferencing technologies discussed in this chapter are applicable to distance learning, there are also new tools and issues to explore.

Chapter Eight

Distance Learning Systems on an Intranet

In the ancient Iñupiaq culture of the ice-bound North Slope of Alaska, resources were scarce. At the isolated whale camps and caribou hunts, each hand-made tool had to serve many purposes; the hunters had to extend every advantage. One tool, many purposes.

In the last three chapters you've seen how an intranet can be used for quick publishing, information management, and knowledge-working. It is also an efficient tool for creating, administering, and delivering training and education throughout an organization.

To be competitive, organizations must increase the speed and reach of learning. Corporate training budgets have been shrinking, but because technology and business practices are changing so rapidly, the need to update skills and information is growing. Faced with the need to do more with less, learning administrators are looking for ways to leverage both learning costs and their instructors' expertise. The goal is to deliver effective learning that is also cost-effective.

Learning systems must be both cost-effective and learning-effective

Certificate and
degree programs are
offered on line

Because intranets can offer access, with their easy-to-use interface, to a wide array of capabilities and updatable resources for administrators, instructors, and learners, an increasing number of corporations, academic institutions, and government entities are turning to Web technologies to implement location-free learning systems. Universities and commercial training providers are offering certificate courses and degree programs over the Internet, and corporations are using their intranets to deliver in-house training.

Intranet distance learning systems have the potential to achieve the rich interactivity and flexibility promised, but not delivered, by previous computer-mediated learning systems. As you will see in the "Foundations for Web-Based Distance Learning" section (see page 238), with the earlier efforts, lack of network connections left the student isolated. Absolute bandwidth limits of other training media soon curtailed choices in how content could be displayed.

This chapter reviews the prospects for developing, delivering, and managing learning via an intranet. After reading this chapter, you will be able to define intranet distance learning, and to weigh the pluses and minuses. You will be able to compare and contrast an intranet distance learning system with other training and instructional models, such as face-to-face instructor-led courses, computer-mediated learning, and traditional distance learning. Part of the course is understanding how instructional models differ, and how intranet distance learning uniquely serves today's team-based cultures. Finally, you will be able to discuss how the features of Web-based technology contribute to the creation, administration, and delivery of effective learning systems. There will not be a quiz.

There are several ways an organization can take advantage of Web-based training opportunities. You can build your own distance learning system, you can send your people to school at one of the online learning centers on the Internet, or you can subscribe to a learning service. For instance, Bell Canada sent its IT staff to school at Mentys,[1] an Internet-based training center. They studied TCP/IP and C++, and then came back and applied what they had learned to turn their old client/server network into an intranet—an intranet that now serves 40,000. Another outside training option is a commercial learning service that can build a learning structure and provide templates that your organization can use to personalize your own training program.

You can build your own training site or send students off to school on the Internet

What type of training needs are you currently filling (or not filling)? Do you need to deliver practical skills training, or to change how people approach their work? How convenient and cost-effective is your current training model? Are costs for travel or facilities a large part of the training budget? How is your current training most or least effective? Have you addressed team learning opportunities? How important is training to your employees?

Assess your current training system

Computer World Survey Shows Employees Value Opportunities for Training

A survey by *Computer World* magazine entitled *What makes a company a great place to work?* found that companies that routinely provided opportunities for training and development scored high as a measure of a *great place.* Of the 100 companies selected as the *best places to work,* 40 offered 7–10 days of formal training a year.

For individuals, life-long learning is essential in the effort to stay ahead of the job market (rather than get left behind). For companies, updating their employees' skills on a continuing basis is crucial to remaining competitive. In addition, as companies embrace the high performance work-team model, team learning has grown increasingly important. A team-based culture calls for new approaches to learning.

---

1. Mentys is an effort of the Global Knowledge Network and the Canadian Human Resource Council. It offers technical courses, networking, programming, JAVA, and client/server to TCP/IP over the Internet.

Definitions

A distance learning system is dynamic and interactive

Web-based distance learning is a multi-faceted, multimedia learning system that uses the interactive, dynamic, and collaborative capabilities of Web technologies for creating, delivering, and managing individual and team-based learning. It is the same as Web-based training (WBT) or Web-based instruction (WBI).

Web-based training and Web-based instruction are basically the same

The term Web-based training in the broadest sense includes not only improving skills in a work environment, but also changing attitudes or expanding knowledge. The term Web-based instruction is used in academia. This book settled on the term *Web-based distance learning*, to focus on results and intranets.

Web-based distance learning is a complete learning system

Distance learning began as a system for linking remote sites through one-way or two-way audio or video conferencing to deliver classroom instruction.[2] The sites were connected over a mix of cable, telephone lines, and satellites. Yesterday's distance learning was a *delivery* system, but with today's Web technologies, distance learning has the capacity to be a comprehensive *learning* system. The system can include administration, curriculum development, assessment, course and resource delivery, plus tutorials and collaboration.

Foundations for Web-based Distance Learning

Educational institutions and corporations realized the cost benefits in bringing quality instruction to isolated communities. Compressed video signals produced jerky images on a television monitor, a far cry from the television broadcasts it purported to be. Nevertheless, students in remote locations

---

2. The main purpose was to deliver classroom instruction, but US WEST and others used the technology to serve business conferencing and judicial arraignments.

could simultaneously share the same classroom discussions and instructor expertise.[3] Corporations could offer their employees continuing education classes and even the opportunity to join a college or university degree program in another location. For enterprises, distance learning was also an opportunity to leverage (or justify) an investment in teleconferencing equipment for presentations or group meetings.

Today's intranet distance learning evolved from a blend of computer-mediated instruction and distance learning

Computer-Mediated Learning

Computer-mediated learning encompasses any remote learning opportunity that is computer-enabled, including CD-ROM, interactive videodisk, and computer-based training (CBT) training.

- CD-ROMs disks are a highly portable delivery format that is appropriate for self-paced instruction, but provides no opportunity for interaction with peers or instructors. Without the capability to connect to a network, a student can use tests only for self-assessment.

- Interactive videodisks can store thirty minutes of full-motion video but are unable to support data processing or network capabilities unless used in conjunction with a computer.

- CBT emulates the classroom style, presenting content, exercises, summaries, and quizzes. If the computer is connected to a network, tests can be administered and scored, but there are no tools or means for collaboration. Many industries have used CBT as a vehicle for training and for competency exams, such as a real estate license.

---

3. In remote areas like the 88,000 square miles in the jurisdiction of the North Slope School District of Alaska, distance learning solved quality-of-instruction issues and stretched educational resources. In less isolated locales, urban schools could use distance learning to expand the variety of their offerings.

Computer-mediated products gave students the freedom of self-directed learning, but they lacked the network connections or communication tools that would have made it possible for a learner to receive feedback or to exchange ideas. In addition, inherent bandwidth limitations restrained the use of the learning elements to a continuing series of trade-offs.

> *Computer-mediated learning is self-directed, but lacks network connections*

Web-based distance learning is the next step in the evolution of computer-mediated training. Using Web-based technologies, you can create a structured, interactive learning environment in a virtual space. Web-based distance learning programs vary as to the level of collaborative learning, the quantity and types of learning resources, the nature of assessments (or testing), and the amount of interactivity. Learning applications vary as to the ratio of the amount of material to be downloaded to the student's computer to the amount available off line.

> *Create an interactive learning environment in a virtual space*

Learners visit a Web site on their intranet to find course materials, resources, multimedia presentations, schedules, and pre- and post-learning tests. On that site they can use messaging and collaborative tools to communicate with their instructor and fellow students. Because Web-based distance learning systems are built with Internet-based protocols, learners can access their online learning environment from an IBM-compatible personal computer, Macintosh, or UNIX machine. One course, many ways to reach it.

> *Distance learning takes place in virtual classrooms built with Web technologies*

Some Pluses and Minuses

Web-based distance learning utilizes the full range of intranet activities—quick publishing, information management, and knowledge-working. For example, instructors publish course materials on line, training administrators can update student records dynamically, and students can work collaboratively on class projects. The key advantages to

> *Supports collaboration and team-centered learning*

using an intranet for Web-based distance learning should resonate by now. They are its

- Flexibility (location and scheduling)
- Ease of maintaining and updating
- Potential for collaboration to enhance team learning

There is one more advantage that sets Web-based distance learning apart from other computer-mediated training. An intranet distance learning system can meet the criteria of a complete learning system, which integrates course and student administration, course content development (curriculum development and content authoring), delivery mechanism, tutorials and interaction, testing and feedback, plus auditing and reporting mechanisms.

Integrates content, collaboration, and administration

Web-based training offers a flexible approach to learning. As with other computer-mediated learning systems, learners may work at their own pace and on their own time schedule (assuming the curriculum design permits this), without traveling to a learning site. Because the classroom is an intranet Web site, it's always open—any hour of the day, any day of the week—and accessible from work, home, or a hotel room. (Instructors may appreciate this latitude as much as students.)

Available any time, from any location

On the minus side, desktop delivery can't ensure an appropriate learning environment. Although a worker's own environment is comfortable and familiar, it may be disrupted by distractions and interruptions from co-workers, customers, or managers, not to mention by the telephone.

Distractions may exist in the work environment

Depending on your network—actually on your segment of network—bandwidth can be a problem in delivering full motion video on demand. Bandwidth limitations can restrict instructional design or at least cause some tradeoffs between number and size of graphics or videos and speed.

Infrastructure can limit video delivery

And, training must be designed to the lowest common hardware denominator—a 386 will not run video. (But trainings can be on any platform.)

Distance learning is not for everyone

Web-based training is not for everyone. Technology can be distracting, especially when it doesn't work. Technical support must be built into the learning environment. Further, some learners need more face-to-face interaction and feel alienated when a computer replaces a human interface. Their outlook will affect their performance in a Web learning environment.

Furthermore, because of the inherent flexibility, individuals who do not have the discipline or the ability to structure and manage their time may have trouble completing their course work. For them, making time to complete assignments independently, beyond the glare of an instructor, can be overwhelming.

Web-based Distance Learning Environment

Students, instructors, and administrators access different interfaces

A distance learning application resides on a server and, like other Web applications, presents different views—interfaces—to the different types of users. Training administrators, instructors, and learners each take advantage of dynamic and interactive capabilities of the intranet environment.

Administration tasks can be automated; students can register on line

Training administrators can publish course descriptions and prerequisites, class schedules, instructor biographies, commonly asked questions, and registration information with applications on the distance learning Web site, as illustrated in Figure 8-1. Students who visit the site can register on line using interactive forms that dynamically update the class list database by adding their names and identification, and can assign a password and identifier to be used during the duration of the class. The password system serves both to close the doors to unauthorized students and to monitor student activity on the site. This feature would be especially important if the course led to certification and had special requirements.

Distance learning Web site contains course descriptions, schedules, instructor biographies, and registration information.

Figure 8-1

Instructors use Web authoring tools and convert documents from other formats to prepare course components in HTML and publish them on the distance learning site. Once an instructor designs, creates, (and tests!) a course, it can be instantly available to learners in any location around the globe who have access to the intranet. No waiting for the team to travel, adjust to a different learning environment and perhaps a different time zone. No worries if the room is too hot, too cold, or the instruction period is too long, or not long enough. Students control their environment and their pace.

Web-based distance learning is an efficient delivery mechanism

As illustrated in Figure 8-2, on the next page, a course site can include a resource area (for articles, lectures, media, and presentations), a communications area that links to threaded discussions and chat, collaboration tools, and messaging features for contacting the instructor. Updating

To students, the learning Web site is a classroom, library, and field trip

course materials on the intranet is easy and instantaneous, the same as updating any database or HTML static page on the intranet. Putting a hyperlink to new resources in a *What's New* area would continue to add interest to the site. Instructors can also use push technology to send special notices to students about upcoming events, changes, or reminders. For instance, an instructor could notify students about a NetShow presentation that they could see *live* on a certain date or download later (see *NetShow Streaming* sidebar).

Figure 8-2   *Resource site for a Web course.*

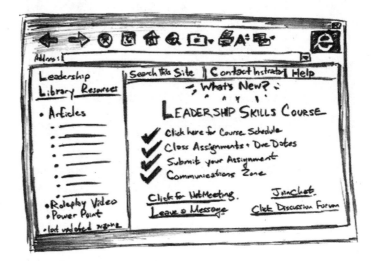

The distance learning Web site serves as library, media center, study carrel, classroom, drop-in center, break-out room, message center, appointment calendar, test room, and even book store. HTTP links can point to Internet sites (if Internet access is provided) or links to other resources. The idea is to create a warm, lively, self-service environment where students feel motivated to find the resources they need. One more thing that every site should include: a prominent Help button. While there are cost savings associated with getting out of the bricks and mortar and into the online world of learning (see "Cost Effectiveness—What

Help buttons and technical support are necessary

NetShow Streaming

NetShow is a presentation format that delivers audio and video content in a *Web* environment. The NetShow server stores and delivers media content, while the NetShow Player resides on the client machine. NetShow uses Microsoft Active Streaming Format (ASF) to prepare the media content for streaming to the client. Streaming allows the content to be played as it is fed to the client and to be discarded to make room for more. With this technology, video broadcasts can be downloaded without either the jerky results of compression or the interminable wait for a large file to download completely before playing. So video presentations—the president's speech or a fascinating subject presented by an expert—can be delivered live or downloaded later like any other file.

Can You Save?" page 249), one cost that will go up is the cost of computer support, especially in the first few weeks of a new class.

Instructors value the flexibility that Web-based distance learning offers, both for their own schedules and for what they may offer to their students. They may hold regularly scheduled chat sessions, but they are not tied to a classroom appearance or to a travel regime. In addition, because the course material is posted on a Web page, they are more able to react to students' needs and adjust course content or offer different learning resources than they are in either an in-structor-led or computer-mediated learning situation. It's very simple to add either a document (in any format) or a hyperlink to supply additional learning materials. In this way, instructors can serve more as guides or coaches to a learning experience.

The flexibility enables instructors to respond to students' needs

The students' view of the classroom is also a Web page. That's home base for finding a video presentation or a nar-rated Microsoft PowerPoint presentation, an article or test, or other students to commiserate with!

Motivated and self-directed students do well on line

Electronic Performance Support System (EPSS)

Electronic Performance Support System (or on line performance support) has been touted as the ideal just-in-time training aid. EPSS is support that is available electronically for a task that's facing you, without your having to ask someone else for help. A Web-based EPSS (WBEPSS) can include cue cards or wizards to walk you through a procedure, task-based templates of *best practices*, context-sensitive help, knowledge-base, agents, Web-based training modules, and virtual reality or augmented reality display. In a pilot project at Boeing, workers ready to work on the wiring harness for a 777 wing can view the wing through an augmented reality display. The display projects a virtual image of the wiring pattern on the wing and, as the technicians move their heads, the view of the wing and schematic changes, too. The schematic that they're seeing is the latest that the engineering department has put into the system. There are no delays, just up-to-date information, right *where* they need it.

Team members can work together, on their own schedules

The interactive capabilities of the intranet support collaborative learning. Class members can leave messages for each other on an electronic forum or listserv, and can use collaboration tools to work together on projects. Freed from the time constraints of classroom instruction, learners in different time zones can post messages or join discussions. Learners can use chat rooms for either scheduled or spontaneous discussions in *real time*. From a link in the learning environment, using products like NetMeeting, they can work together, wherever they are, on a document or plans for a project.

Integrated, dynamic databases ease burdens of administration

Administrators use the dynamic features of intranet environments to manage student records, including attendance, test results, and progress towards certification requirements. Student records can be forwarded automatically to external certification boards or institutions. In addition, administrators can monitor site activity and, by evaluating patterns of activity, determine which learning activities are most highly utilized and which should be revised.

Learning Models for Teams or Individuals

There are three learning models commonly used for delivering training or instruction. In each, the role of the instructor and the expectations of the students differ.

- Instructor-led training takes place in a classroom environment, with an instructor imparting ideas and knowledge by delivering lectures, administering labs or exercises, and leading discussions.
- Student-centered courses are particularly appropriate for skills training. The emphasis is more hands-on and practical. The instructor guides and demonstrates.
- Team-centered learning focuses on a transformation of the group, such as how to improve a process or to overcome traditional thinking to create a solution or design a product

Web-based distance learning can accommodate all three.

Matching Learning Objectives to Learning Models

Regardless of which type of technology you choose for developing, distributing, and managing courses, the learning objectives must always be aligned closely with the learning model. For instance, you wouldn't expect to rely on a lecture format to teach knee surgery. (You would hope surgeons have some hands-on, practical application of their training before practicing medicine on you.)

Objectives should match the model

Nor would you expect learners in a team-centered model, such as a group of researchers or a product development team, to reach a new understanding if the height of their *group experience* is sitting side by side to listen to a lecture together. For a team to achieve their particular learning objective (creating a new mental model of a problem to solve), they need to experience the give-and-take and breakthroughs that can only come from group interaction. But

Team interaction can take place in a shared virtual space

they don't have to meet face to face; they can achieve this on line in a shared, virtual space.

The table below summarizes the relationships between the three main types of learning delivery models and their respective learning objectives. Notice that different resources are appropriate for each type of instructional environment. And in each, the instructor plays a different role.

Comparing Features of Three Different Learning Delivery Models

Delivery Model	Learning Objective	Resources	Instructor role
instructor-centered	transfer information	lecture, video, audio with graphics	primary resource
student-centered	acquire skills	lecture, video, audio with graphics, task simulations, exercises	guide and support
team-centered	change mental model	group exercises, listservs, chat areas	facilitate group process

Web-based learning can accommodate multiple models and objectives

Many courses may contain more than one learning objective; each module may contain a different objective. For instance, the learning objective for an introduction to a safety course on Lockout Procedures could be *to transfer information*. If the training were given to a team, the learning objective for one module could be *to change model*, to build safety into the mindset of the team. The role of the instructor changes with each delivery model. An intranet can meet all three learning objectives.

Modular Courseware—
Learning Objects

One way the Web and new trends in learning are in alignment is the focus on component models. An efficient way to build and deliver training is by creating small components that can be configured into many different training purposes. Ken Fenwick, of SAFECO Insurance Companies, noted that they took their model from the textbook publishing business. Fenwick reports that textbook publishers will deliver a custom designed textbook—this chapter from here, that one from there—a book tailored to the specific needs of the customer. Training can be *published* in the same way.

Similar to textbook publishing and software development, creating small components is the key

The trend is toward *infonuggets*, the title of an article by Jack Gordon on the www.trainingsupersite. Rather than full-fledged courses, which copy the classroom model of the whole enchilada of training, small chunks fit well with just-in-time training and cause less disruption in the work place. The online library then becomes a storehouse of quick video refreshers and checklists, as well as structured tutorials with exercises or classes.

Small chunks suit just-in-time training needs

The modular approach appeals to managers—15- or 30-minute chunks devoted to leadership, team-training skills, and customer-focus skills can be digested in available time periods, without elaborate scheduling and coordinating. Again, the flexibility of the medium has moved far away from one-size-fits-all training.

Cost Effectiveness—
What Can You Save?

Because Web-based training brings the learning resources *to the students*, instead of bringing all the students *to the training*, there is the potential for significant savings in the cost of travel—airfare, hotels, per diem expenses—plus the time. There's a certain adjustment period necessary for

Online learning saves travel time and expenses for instructors or students

Benefits Summary for Learners, Teams, Instructors, and Administrators

Just like intranets as a whole, each population in a learning environment—learners, teams, instructors, and administrators—will have a different point of view on the benefits of online learning.

- Learners respond well to the flexibility and accessibility. Learning resources are a few keystrokes away—every day, all day.
- A team's use of collaboration and messaging tools will help craft an experience that can enhance team productivity. Exploring and discovering information builds self- and team-reliance.
- Instructors appreciate the ability to update course materials quickly.
- Administrators value the efficient delivery, ease of maintenance, potential for course evaluation, flexibility, and opportunities for cost savings. Traditional instructor-led courses have recurring infrastructure costs and travel expenses.

Although administrators, instructors, and learners will use different interfaces and may appreciate different aspects of Web-based distance learning, they all will have occasion to use many of the same types of Web-tools and features, such as interactive forms, messaging, and hyperlinks.

individuals to become comfortable (and therefore attentive learners) in an unfamiliar environment. But more importantly, you no longer have to bear the cost of the lost productivity incurred when a worker is taken out of the office.

Students can go directly to the information they need to learn

According to Bill Ryan, Director of Instructional Technology, Lakeland Community College, Ohio, who has researched learning effectiveness of different delivery systems, "Many organizations have found between 40 and 60 percent cost savings by the tighter instructional design (of Web-based training). The *Web*-based model allows students to by-pass information that's not needed, and to focus on what they do need."

No more classrooms to build, heat, and light; no more expenditures for building maintenance, security, or food service. No need to install computer hardware and software dedicated to training, nor overhead projectors, video playback and display equipment, computer projection or audio systems. Nor cables, microphones, desks, chairs…

Eliminate physical plant costs

There are also savings on printing, publishing, and distributing materials. A four-color brochure is much cheaper to produce on line than on paper. And it's cheaper to change if a name is misspelled or the schedule changes.

Save paper costs

Adapting to a Virtual Teaching Environment

The online world requires communication skills that differ from those that are standard issue for stand-up instructors in a classroom. It may be a new way of learning for the students, too—no eye contact, no hand gestures.

Instructors will do very little *presenting* in an interactive, more-coaching-less-teaching environment. Instructors need to become knowledgeable about building course content with Web-based media. Course materials that may be repurposed for a Web-based learning environment—the PowerPoint slides, video clips, audio materials—can all be posted on the Web site. However, the instructional design must change to use and support the interactivity afforded by the Web environment. For instance, an instructor may control the learning path by making certain material a prerequisite before a student gains access to other material.

Classroom instructors will need new computer and communication skills

Experienced classroom instructors need to make some adjustments in order to reach students in a virtual class. They will need to learn new ways to encourage and support learner participation. Studies show that most learners want this type of interaction, rather than pure self-study. Some classes require active participation in discussion forums, to prevent students from *hiding out in the back of the virtual room* and letting others do the *talking*.

The instructor must adjust to guiding participation, not controlling it

Instructors coach,
students construct
their own solutions

Intranet distance learning instructors are more like coaches, directing and giving structure to the learning experience. They play more of a *facilitating* role, leaving students room for discovery. This is particularly true in a team-based learning environment, where learners need to be handed the tools with which they can construct their own solutions. Most likely, a motivated team will even find new ways to use the tools the learning environment provides.

Looking Ahead

Now that you've read about the different activities that an intranet can support, and some of the technologies that make them possible, the next step is to explore an intranet life cycle. The next five chapters explore planning an intranet—defining the purpose and the audience before using the technology, building a pilot project, building a business case, the process of implementation, and finally, maintenance and evaluation.

If you noticed that the *pilot project* comes before the *business case*, rest assured it's not a mis-statement the editor didn't catch. Many intranets get built this way. Someone puts up a little pilot project—it can be done for very low cost—to have something to *show* to management: *This* is what we want to do. And then they ask for the money.

Planning

If your intranet begins as a grassroots effort, and you want to ensure its value to the organization, you need to consider where you stand on some design issues. On the other hand, if you're building an intranet by plotting and planning, then you have the opportunity to address these issues head on at the very beginning. Either way, most organizations can expect to redesign their intranet within twelve or eighteen months of the initial launch. Whether before or after the fact, at a minimum you should define:

- the purpose of your intranet
- its target audience or users
- its visual design
- the culture of the organization

and apply user-centered design principles,[1] before beginning the process of building (or re-building) it. This chapter will illuminate those design issues. The next chapter, "Launching a Pilot Project," will address beginning to build an intranet.

---

1. The shift in software design from application-centric to user-centric made it easier for users to use software to accomplish tasks by keeping their focus on *what* they wanted to do, rather than *how* they could use the software to do it. Microsoft uses the term document-centric reflecting the view that all tasks are document-based.

Overview

Designing an intranet starts with the same steps as designing a training video or a marketing campaign. You ask questions such as:

- What's the purpose of having it?
- How will we use it?
- Who will design it?
- Who will own and manage it?
- Who will provide and update the content?
- When will it be operational?
- How much will it cost?

The cost of an intranet depends on the design, scope, and the level of technology required

The answer to the last question is usually "That depends." In the early days of corporate video, first-time internal customers often asked video producers that same question: *I want a marketing video that I can use to train my sales people and build enthusiasm in the work force for the new product, but how much will it cost?* Like buying a car, the cost depends on the features and the scope. Video producers resist being backed into a corner with a premature *cost-per-finished-minute* quote before they have a chance to clearly identify the purpose, the audience, the creative concept to carry the freight, and a distribution plan. Was the customer envisioning a production on the order of *The Empire Strikes Back* or *Mom's Home Movies*? If you were going to replace all of your existing terminals and personal computers with Pentiums packing MMX technology[2] all around, the cost of an intranet would definitely be high. (See Chapter 11, "Building a Business Case.")

An intranet does not have to spring fully formed from the head of Zeus. It can be implemented in stages. It can be rolled out, division by division, across an organization, or

---

2. MMX is multimedia technology on a Pentium machine that can display film-quality moving images.

an enterprise-wide intranet can be launched with very simple features at first. The functionality can grow as people in the organization become comfortable using their intranet. One of the advantages of the Windows NT platform is easy scalability. This underlying flexibility makes it easier to launch small-scale experiments and then take them to the big time. (See Chapter 12, "Implementing Your Intranet.")

Design with modularity in mind

Determine the Purpose

Whether an intranet grows up from grassroots or is mandated from above, whether it's large-scale or small, the first answer at which you must arrive is *what is the purpose?* What can you do with it, that you can't do now?

Keep asking: what can we gain?

- Is it a communications device?
- Is it a medium for collaboration?
- Is it an accessible archive or quick dispenser for information?
- Is it a connection to (and for) external customers and suppliers?
- Is it all of the above?

Chapters 5 through 8 discussed how an intranet can be used for quick publishing, managing information, knowledge-working, and distance learning. The path to an intranet may or may not be a continuum, but the activities that take place across the intranet define its value to the organization.

What business problems can your intranet solve? To answer this question, of course you'll need to have a grip on what specific business problems could use solving. Intranets are particularly useful for solving problems that stem from lack of:

Advancing productivity through speed and teamwork

- Speed—of communication, decisions, cycle-time, and time to market
- Team work—hampered by distances or cumbersome methods of communication

Even planning for an
intranet can net
productivity gains

Often the process of developing an intranet ferrets out unproductive processes that have been accepted as *business as usual*. You may find routine processes that require extra (and really unnecessary) handling of either materials or decision points, such as a circuitous route for a work authorization or a purchasing process that seems more like an elaborate board game than a means to an end within a larger production cycle.

Planning for Productivity-Enhancing Changes

If you wish to use an intranet to save time and money for a certain department or division activity, gather a cross-functional team that includes at the least a software development specialist, one motivated person from each affected department or division, and a communicator to facilitate developing a new electronic process. Begin by identifying known problems or time-wasting weak points in your current situation. Pay particular attention to the verbs used to identify activities, as they may be clues to who can (or must) take charge of an activity. For instance, *authorizes* carries a different weight than *requests* or *initiates*.

Then it's a matter of *how else could we get there from here?* Establish clear and quantifiable outcomes for each responsibility area, identify any imperative approval points, then begin remapping which aspects of the situation could be handled electronically, and by whom. Don't shrink from challenging the verbs. However trite it sounds, you have to break some eggs to make an omelet. Use different colored sticky-notes on a whiteboard (or a wall) to map out the new process.

Look for opportunities to automate activities, to eliminate middle-man functions, and to shift responsibilities into the hands of the people who have the *need* and the *knowledge* to make decisions. For instance, the addition of a Frequently Asked Questions area on a departmental Web site might save specialists' time otherwise spent fielding routine questions. Putting customized supply catalogs (from approved vendors) on line with electronic order forms (including automatic routing for approval) could save time. Similar time and money savings can be uncovered in production or information processes.

There are additional issues to address if you wish to provide limited external access to your intranet, either by extending to partners via an extranet (see Chapter 3, "The Extranet Option") or by enabling remote access for members of your organization (see Chapter 4, "Risks and Mitigation Strategies"). In the same light, if you are going to allow users of your intranet to access the Internet, you will need to decide whether or not to allow unfettered surfing, or to restrict access to certain sites, or something in between. (See "Set Policies and Procedures," page 321.)

You can connect your intranet to the Internet and external partners

Define the Audience

Most likely there won't be a *typical* user of your intranet. Your user population will cover the spectrum from technically adept to technically challenged. Some will breeze confidently through your intranet (like an eleven-year old on a skateboard), finding what they need in a flash. Others will need training wheels. If possible, design the intranet with at least two levels of users in mind: a *fast-track* for the speed-racers to get what they need and get on with their work, and a *learner's lane* to help newbies build confidence and get up to speed.

Support the needs of both experienced and new Web-users

There will always be newbies. The success of your intranet depends on converting them to successful intranet users and searchers.[3] If you are unable to bring the inexperienced users into the fold, you run the risk of bifurcating your organization into the *haves* (Web-experienced) and the *have-nots*. Left unchecked, this situation can undermine not only your intranet, but the foundation of your organization.

Avoid a schism between the haves and the have-nots

Look at Web page designs from the point of view of a person new to a Web environment. Things that experienced

---

3. There's a distinct difference between searching and surfing. Surfing is exploring for curiosity's sake. Searching is targeted hunting for information or activities to fulfill a need.

Provide help for
new users, and
make sure the help
is easy to find

users take for granted, such as the meaning of icons, may not be apparent to new users. Adding a *New to this Site?* area on a Web site might provide a way to give newcomers extra assistance. In addition to an e-mail address for questions, where possible, provide a phone support hotline where users can reach a live person. New users will have an easier time finding what they need on a site if the navigation and page design make intuitive sense to them.

Consider Multicultural Aspects

If your organization is multicultural or has an international reach, you may wish to accommodate language preferences of intranet users. Obviously, to *localize* all the material on your intranet would add to the cost of development. However, you could provide certain areas or documents in multiple languages. For instance, a copy of a legal document or health plan information might be offered in native languages for the convenience of users, but your legal department may require that if individuals must electronically *sign* their acceptance of a legal document, they do so in the organization's primary language.

If you are providing text in alternate languages, include in your design team the person who will be managing the translation process (a *localizer*) or at least an interface designer with experience in multi-language visual design. They can prevent screen design problems before they start.

As a rule of thumb, if you are designing Web pages that will be localized, test how much text will comfortably fit on a screen by translating it into German. Words and phrases in the German language are generally longer than their equivalent in English (see Figures 9-1 and 9-2). Accommodating translations into Asian characters is more of a technical than a design challenge, as software code must be in double-byte character sets.

Microsoft Solution Provider page. **Figure 9-1**

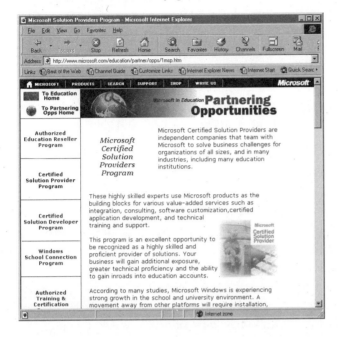

Microsoft Solution Provider page, text in German. **Figure 9-2**

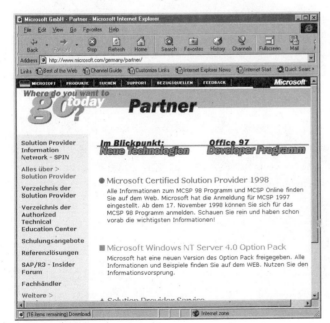

Whether or not you include language options, designing an intranet for a multicultural audience means being especially conscious of the cultural meanings associated with icons, numbers, and colors. For instance, in Southeast Asia, the color white is associated with death. So a white package would not be an appropriate image for a bonus or a surprise gift. In addition, as you undoubtedly already know, humor is hard to translate across language lines and can be unexpectedly offensive.

Icons are intended as a visual short cut. If you have to puzzle over their meaning, they are *stalling* rather than *speeding* communication. Icons that are instantly recognizable in North America, such as a light bulb image intended to communicate a *bright idea*, may not be intuitively understood in Singapore. On the other hand, an object inside a circle with a slash through it would be easily recognized as meaning *no*—for example, the no smoking icon showing a cigarette inside the circle. International icons are very useful.

Examine the User's Environment

Depending on the configuration of your organization, not all users might access the intranet from the comfort of the desktop computer in a cubicle. They might be using the intranet in a kiosk setting, perhaps in a lobby or a lunchroom. They might be dialing in from a remote location. Lighting at different times of day could make it hard to see a computer screen. The environment could also be noisy. Aural clues could be lost. Users might have little time on shared machines—they might need to find information very quickly. The visual and functional design should accommodate the differing environmental and time restrictions of intranet users.

The Westinghouse Savannah River Nuclear Facility learned this lesson the hard way. They installed computers with touch screens on the factory floor. But they did not consider that the fingers that touched the screens would be greasy from the factory environment. What the designers were aiming for was to avoid burdening inexperienced computer users with the frustration of fine mouse control movements. What they missed was a fundamental fact about the computing environment.

Even touch screens have their pros and cons

Include Options for Differently-Abled Individuals

In the United States, the American Disabilities Act (ADA) of 1990 made it illegal to discriminate against people on the basis of disability. Besides the fact that employers are required to make "reasonable accommodations," such as providing large print screen software so that people with (defined) disabilities can perform their jobs, it's both a good neighbor decision and a good business decision to create an inclusive environment.

ADA requires "reasonable accommodations"

In some cases, providing an easy way to change the screen display to large type can make the difference between ease of use and tiredness caused by eyestrain. A hypertext notice in 14-point type that reads *Click here to see text-only in large type* could be a solution.

Include a text-only large type option

About 80 percent of the male population in the United States has some degree of color-blindness. Depending on color fields alone to differentiate areas on an intranet site could miss the mark with a large percentage of your users.

Accommodate color-blindness

For some visually-impaired members of your organization, no amount of improvement to the intranet environment will assist them in seeing a computer screen. The solution is not as simple as a screen-reading program that goes left to right. The challenge is to grasp the structure as well as the content of the information. Whereas the original purpose of HTML was to define the structure of a document, the later emphasis on layout control excludes visually impaired individuals. Graphically complex pages with multiple frames or animated banners are difficult to translate into an aural medium.

Graphically complex Web pages are barriers for visually-impaired individuals

Hearing the Subject Headings

T. V. Raman, a blind research engineer in the Advanced Technology Group at Adobe Systems, has made great contributions towards barrier-free information access. In a special report published in *Scientific American*, March 1997, he points out that sighted people rely on many visual clues, such as the size of headings, the sidebars, and indexes, to form a context for the content and to select their pathways into the information. Non-sighted persons need other clues to content. For Raman and other visually impaired people, many *speak programs* provide the equivalent of a one-line, 40-character display, instead of a big 60-line monitor that sighted individuals take for granted. Raman has pioneered aural programs that make use of extensive audio clues to express the visual ones, such as increasing pitch for describing nested information.

Raman has developed *Emackspeak*, a speech output subsystem for Emacs[4] that enables a non-sighted person to work on UNIX systems. It has a voice-lock mode that presents different voice personalities to represent different content. While a heading shouts importance to a sighted person, hearing a heading read by a James Earl Jones voice could express its importance.

Adobe Access server converts files for screen-reading programs

To avoid disenfranchising sight-impaired individuals, you may wish to investigate the specialty programs available that translate screen contents into aural information.[5] For instance, Adobe, the makers of Portable Document Format software, has a free product to help sight-impaired people access information on their intranet. The Adobe Access server converts PDF files to HTML files that can be read by screen-reading programs.

---

4. Emacs is a text-based UNIX interface.

5. Web page accessibility is a world-wide concern. There is a growing concern that the Web become a medium for new assistive technologies and that it evolve towards a *universal design*, rather than a visual environment. The World Wide Web Consortium (W3C) announced in June, 1997, the formation of an International Program Office for accessibility research and development. W3C is also planning extensions to cascading style sheets (CSS) to support speech output for HTTP.

Chapter Nine

For other individuals with special needs, a Web page that offers more than one means to initiate computer commands (such as keystrokes, mouse actions, and voice commands[6]) can spell the difference between being on the intranet or on the outside.

Build Web pages that enable alternate ways to initiate computer commands

Set Expectations for Your Intranet

Part of the initial evaluation process should include setting expectations for the degree of acceptance for your intranet. Which populations within your organization do you expect will be frequent users of your intranet? What changes can you make to the design that would make it easier for other populations to get more out of the intranet? Are there functional changes, either in page design or the underlying architecture, that would boost productivity, such as providing remote access to production schedules for field representatives or telecommuters?

Plan to measure success

Use focus groups that include a wide range of users to uncover their attitudes, abilities, and preferences. What may seem like a logical design to software developers may leave users out in the cold. It can be a very humbling experience for a developer or interface designer to sit on the dark side of the viewing mirror and watch users fumble with an elegantly designed interface that they do not understand how to use.

Test your designs for usability

Design the Look and Feel

It is not axiomatic that conservative organizations always produce ironclad intranets and *quick-draw* groups invent laissez-faire ones; sometimes, the reverse proves true. An intranet can be an opportunity for people in a buttoned-down organization to let their hair down and enjoy a little creativity in their workplace. In this way, an intranet can

Intranets should suit the inhabitants

---

6. The *Naturally Speaking* program with *continuous speech* technology is a vast improvement over previous speech recognition programs.

function as a pressure relief valve or source of inventiveness. However, organizations that operate under some form of governmental scrutiny or a public/private hybrid cannot consider their intranet a private affair. Very few taxpayers are amused at humor invented on their dime.

It must feel right and be functional

Back to the car metaphor—it has to feel right *and* be functional, or they won't drive it. Once you've quantified the purpose, the audience, and the culture, the *look and feel* of the intranet will follow quite naturally. Recognize the expectations of your users.

Know your audience

In general, people expect to recognize that their intranet is a product of *their* organization—at least that it not clash with their perception of the organization. In this way, an intranet is no different from the architecture or accouterments of the building in which they work. The expectations of a team-based, jeans and hi-tops, converted warehouse culture would be far different from the cuff-linked, wing-tipped, Nordstrom-suited denizens of the sixty-first to sixty-fifth floors of the Columbia Tower. (But the *suits* might surprise you.)

Interface design begins with user aptitudes and needs

The *look and feel* refers not only to the physical appearance of the Web site(s), but also to its (their) functionality. Whether the *start* page is text-oriented or strongly graphical depends on the nature of your users as well as the circumstances under which they will be most likely to use the intranet. For example, the Georgia-Pacific West intranet *start page* offers an image map of the complex, as shown in Figure 9-3, as a graphical navigation device. A machine operator who needs to get to a safety sheet about a spindle on a paper machine clicks on the *building* where the paper machine is located. Once *inside* the building, the operator can choose a picture of the spindle. For an essentially non-computer-literate population, the visual interface is easier and quicker to navigate than a list of menu options.

Functionality—point-and-click and drag-and-drop

For experienced computer users, the usual mouse click functions are as natural as breathing, but they can be intimidating to new users. When to *double* click? When will a *single* click suffice? How do you know when to *right-mouse* click? In addition, unless you've paid your dues in a video arcade, it's going to take a fair amount of practice to guide a mouse with your *hand* to hit a small target on *screen*. (A 7-pixel square is about one-eighth of an inch—a very small

Point-and-click may not be as easy as it sounds

The start screen at Georgia-Pacific West is an image map.

Figure 9-3

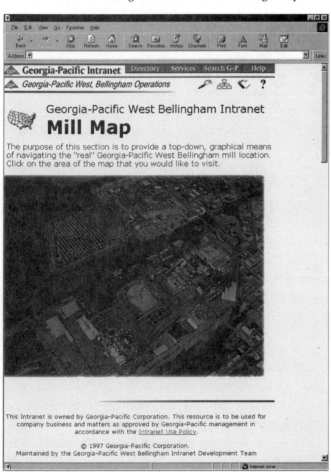

target.) To avoid alienating users who are relatively new to computers and Web environments, keep the navigation actions simple. These actions become the *language* of navigation. Consider making use of other pointing-device activities, such as drag-and-drop. The drag-and-drop action can be useful on a library Web site, or any site where ordering takes place. A visitor could make selections of articles or product items by dragging the item from a list into a basket or shopping cart. Another design option is the checkbox approach, but the action of selecting the items and *putting* (dragging) them into an image of a basket is consistent with *shopping*. Is it worth it? That depends on your users.

Drag-and-drop can be a more intuitive solution

Apply User-Centered Design Principles

Aim for designs that feel intuitive to the users

The key to actions—whether they are keystrokes or mouse clicks—is that they must feel intuitive. That is, the actions should be congruent with the context, and logical for the users. A counter-intuitive action or interface impedes learning and can cause extreme frustration for users as they have to stop, interpret the situation, and figure out what is expected of them. For instance, in Western cultures, we are acclimated to reading left to right, and top to bottom. To Westerners, this is a logical flow of information. Screen designers who set up a page so that users must make selections near the bottom of the screen and then return to the top of the screen to click the *OK* button are going against the flow. And the users will not thank them for it.

Extra bells and whistles are no substitute

The principles that Tandy Trowler set forth in his book on interface design, *The Windows Interface Guidelines for Software Design*, are an indispensable guide for realizing the promise of a user-friendly computing environment. These principles also apply to designing intranet environments. All the whiz-bang, spinning, twirling titles and adorable animations can never make up for the lack of a design approach that anticipates and serves the needs of the users.

User Control

In the military, the lead pilot of a helicopter or fixed wing aircraft is referred to as the pilot-in-command. In the same vein, users should feel in control of their intranet environment, rather than feel controlled by (or at the mercy of) the software applications that run it. Instead of viewing the intranet as a bunker-like, bricks-and-mortar establishment, users should feel empowered to direct their actions across its landscape.

Is *empowering the user* just a warm and fuzzy idea? No, not at all. An interface is the meeting point between the human and the computer. If users do not feel in control, they may feel defeated. It will affect their productivity.

Consistency

Changing rules in midstream can be an upsetting experience, but consistency is a tricky issue. If you control the look and feel and the functionality too tightly, you're liable to squeeze the life out of an intranet. Yet, users need to feel that they are operating in a logical and sane environment, where the same actions—such as a typing the first letter of a state in a drop-down list box to go to states that begin with that letter in the list—get the same results every time. Users want to trust that when they learn an action, it will yield the same results each time.

Users need consistency to feel in control

In addition, users expect consistency within metaphors. If the overall design metaphor for your intranet is an office building, with each floor representing a department, and the Maintenance Department decides to use a Pig Farm as their home page, it would be disturbing. And on an icon level, if you use an image of an *envelope* to indicate an e-mail address on the human resources Web site, that same icon should be used throughout the human resources site for the same purpose. On the other hand, each department could

Consistency in design and use of icons builds trust

have free rein to come up with their own metaphor (or no metaphor) for their site, if *that* were consistent across the intranet.

Feedback

Feedback options benefit users and designers

There are times when people feel compelled to register their opinions. Whether recording frustration or delight, users need to feel they are not locked out and that they have the ability to reach the owners of a site. Besides soothing the sensibilities of users, feedback is a crucial element in continuous improvement for intranet site designers. You cannot fix a problem unless you know it exists.

Looking Ahead

Once you've addressed these preliminary design issues, you can move to the real process of designing an intranet. You'll be able to approach the process with a better understanding of the productivity opportunities and challenges in front of you.

With a clear sense of the driving need behind your intranet —the needs of the people who will use it, the organization's attributes that it will reflect, and the look and feel that will brand it (and sell it)—you can roll up your sleeves and begin to build it. You can assemble the people to develop it, decide on the technology standards, and decide about setting policies and procedures. That's what you will see in Chapter 12, "Implementing Your Intranet." But first, the next chapter covers issues to consider when you're building a pilot project.

Chapter Ten

Launching a Pilot Project

You might be wondering why this chapter on building a pilot project appears ahead of the next chapter, "Building a Business Case." Am I building a cart before building the horse? This is not usual business procedure. But using an easy, one-for-all interface as a portal to colleagues, news, and data is not business as usual either.

For all the advantages of having an intranet (see chapters 5 through 8), it does not always follow that everyone will jump on the bandwagon to build it. Although the next chapter also addresses "Handling Resistance" (see page 288), this chapter shows you how to lay the groundwork for launching a successful pilot project that can serve as *proof of concept* that an intranet can be a means for accomplishing an organization's goals.

A pilot project is a trial balloon designed to provide value to the users and lessons learned for the originators. Pilot projects can range in size, scope, functionality, goals, and design—what may be a modest effort for one group is a major undertaking for another. And there's no consistency in who creates the pilot either, except that it's an innovative person or persons with the vision and energy to explore a better way of doing business.

Use a pilot to prove your concept

A pilot project is a test case for functionality and usability

In the early days of intranets (through 1995), pilots were usually seat-of-the-pants projects, often without the knowledge, much less the blessing, of the IT department that had charge of the network. Well, the ad hoc days are drawing to a close, now that more people know about this territory. There's more law and order, and more convenience tools too.

Addressing the Return on Investment Dilemma

Can on intranet add value to your company?

Because employing an intranet gives people in an organization greater opportunities for interacting efficiently, both with real-time data and with each other, the decision to build or not to build an intranet is more about *how* your organization can thrive than about *how much* the intranet will return on your investment over its lifetime.

Most companies do not do ROI analysis before launching an intranet pilot project

Most organizations that have approached an intranet recognize the difference between investing in a capital project—such as new laser-scanning sawmill equipment that will return more boards in less time, or cut with more accuracy to achieve a higher recovery—and building a strategic asset that will furnish faster communication and quicker, more accurate information. An intranet is a competitive tool that has moved beyond *nice to have*. An International Data Corporation (IDC) study[1] noted that many organizations in the study did not undertake a potential ROI before developing intranet applications. Instead, they went ahead and built an intranet application as a means to introduce new products and services or to revise their business processes. This has been the case for nearly all the organizations included in this book.

---

1. "European Intranet Application Return on Investment Study" (ROI Study). A market research study sponsored by Netscape Communications Corporation, Europe.

Focusing on Functional Business Requirements

If you aim your intranet pilot project at technology, you will surely miss your mark. Besides the fact that technology is a moving target, as mentioned in the last chapter, users want to *interact with data*, not fiddle with technology. Also, a pilot is an experiment, and if you have too many variables, you may lose your focus and end up confusing *and* underwhelming your test audience. Start simply and identify a pilot project that is both:

Focus on business solutions

- a solution to a business problem
- in alignment with your organization's strategic goals

Select a project that addresses an identified goal of your organization, such as *improving communications* or *reducing time-wasting activities*. Then your pilot project will have more value to your organization, and its success will have more weight in proving the worth of an intranet.

Address organizational goals

Pilot Process

The steps in developing an intranet pilot project are similar to those in developing other communications or process-improvement projects. However, most communicators and IT professionals agree that, unlike a video or a printed manual (which involve a physical end-product), an intranet is always a work in progress.

An intranet is always a work-in-progress

1. Determine your objectives. What problem will the project solve or what business goal will it support?

2. Identify the users and develop a marketing plan for selling the intranet to them.

3. Decide on measurement criteria and tools. How will you know if and when it's successful?

4. What resources—hardware, software, and personnel—will you need to build, test, and deploy the application?

5. Collect and analyze usability feedback.

6. Identify lessons learned, and revise as needed.

Limit pilot size and use existing resources

To keep the costs of a pilot down, control the scale of an initial project and use available hardware and free software as much as possible. Better to design and build a small, effective solution that is easy to maintain than a large-scale dirigible. And do *not* study it to death before you begin. You'll learn by doing.

Determine the Intranet Objectives

Identify the problem(s)

When choosing a business problem for the intranet to solve, start by defining the communication or content needs of the organization. What is slow, or unavailable, or frustrating? Does your organization need:

- A speedier way to disseminate information about sales leads?
- A faster way to get sales results?
- An easier way for individuals to search out expert advice or share best practices?
- An efficient way to reduce routine telephone traffic or improve scheduling?
- A better way to put up-to-date safety information where people can reach it?
- A reliable way to find a person's phone number and area of responsibility?

When you call a management consulting firm and ask to speak with a person who delivered an impressive presentation, it's a surprising experience to hear the receptionist first assert that person is not with the company and then mutter that the phone directory is *always* out of date, before finally locating the consultant's number in their branch office in another city. Not impressive. This is a candidate for an intranet pilot project—a company-wide employee directory, with searchable location, phone, fax, and e-mail listings on line with a browser—to solve the problem of a frequently out-of-date phone directory's slowing communication and giving a negative impression to customers. However, this may not be a suitable *starter* project for a fledgling intranet because of the need to build-in a means to keep the data up to date. (There are exceptions; see "Using Off the Shelf Tools to Build a Pilot Project," page 281.)

An initial pilot project need not span the entire organization or take on a large problem. Many intranets began within a division or department to solve communication or information-sharing needs that impeded progress.

As one director of communications for a business unit of a Fortune 100 company said, "Every person [in the business] has to have the information necessary for safely and productively supporting the company… You can't give it to them in a pill, you can't put a chip behind their ear. We can show them a videotape or give them a piece of print; but with the act of showing or printing, [the information] is old and static. We look at the Web technology—one hard drive, one file, one information source. How elegant. How simple. How cost effective. We started building."

London Underground Limited (a subsidiary of London Transport Ltd.) started their intranet to put up-to-date information, such as safety information, phone numbers, and procedures into the hands of employees (see Figure 10-1). The first project, in April 1996, was to post 13 volumes of the London Underground Railway Safety Case manuals online (see "What Goes On line?" page 141). In a year and half, the intranet has grown to include home pages from major lines (Piccadilly, Circle, and Baker) and many departments. For instance, the Automatic Fare Collection Depart-

An out-of-date phone list is bad for business, but it's a good pilot project

Identify an opportunity within a division, department, or team

The need for access to information drove development of an intranet pilot project

ment, as shown in Figure 10-1, posts information about Safety, Customers and Liaisons, and Projects.

Figure 10-1 *London Underground Intranet.*

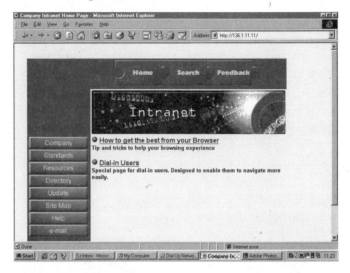

An intranet pilot can be a meeting "place" for a virtual team

An intranet pilot project can, even as it solves a temporary problem, lay the groundwork for expanded intranet applications. When two companies merge, they must work quickly to resolve any incompatibilities and align themselves towards

Norwich Union

Norwich Union, one of Britain's largest insurance and financial services companies, developed an intranet project to index and store property-user guides—about 200 Microsoft Word documents—that some employees refer to regularly. Through the *friendlier face* of the browser, users can get immediate access to the procedures for investing funds, buying and selling property, property management, and so on. It's quicker and easier than locating the right document either on a traditional client/server network or in a paperbound edition. The cost for the project was right, too. Microsoft Internet Information Server is a free add-on for Windows NT customers, and the Internet Explorer browser is also free. The in-house team that supports Microsoft Office built the Web page.

their common goals. In one case, a U.S. financial organization leading a merger activity used their intranet to create a virtual team Web site for the transition team. On that site, they could exchange information and they were able to resolve business issues. The transition team Web site also served also as a pilot for the acquired organization, which did not have an intranet before the merger.

Choosing the Project and Developing a Marketing Plan

To narrow the field of potential pilot projects, identify the group within the organization that is inclined to embrace an intranet (assuming that you are *choosing* the group, and they haven't already gone off and created a Web project by themselves). It could be a technically oriented department, with Internet-savvy individuals. It could be a division with a charismatic (and respected) evangelist who will lead the effort. It could be the group that stands to gain tremendously from the speed, ease-of-use, interactivity, and efficiency inherent in an intranet. They say that in filmmaking, more than half the director's job is choosing the right cast.

The key to a successful first project can be in selecting the group

ARAMARK Intranet Started on Campus

For ARAMARK, one of the United States' largest food service providers, the Campus Support Service division and Corporate Communications participated in the first pilot project at ARAMARK. Corporate had the highest need to disseminate information. Campus Support Service, a $700 million business, had the *most likely to succeed* population of potential users. Stationed on college campuses across the U.S., most members of ARAMARK's Campus division were already Internet users. They were comfortable with browser technology and with browsing, searching, posting, and downloading information off the Internet. As expected, they adapted easily to using *StarNet*, the ARAMARK intranet. "They are converting some documents to HTML and also some people

The Campus Support Service division at ARAMARK was already schooled on the Internet

are receiving training to use Microsoft FrontPage," said John Kallelis, Vice President of Information Technology. "We're making it an integral part of their job."

Results of the pilot led to expanding the project to a larger community of interest

The pilot project was modest; it involved a cross section of about 100 people in the Campus Division. From the pilot, "We concluded that we needed more *density*, a greater community of interest," said Kallelis. So for roll-out, they planned to expand to a region, "And the President of the Campus division said, 'Why one? Why not two?'" So the Southeast and Southwest regions went on line. There are three more regions, and that expansion is planned as well. As Kallelis sees it, "It's natural to expand to all regions, and have one business unit completely installed using their intranet. By that time, we'll have enough success stories, so another business unit..." and so on. Nothing succeeds like success.

Project launched as a rental unit and continues to grow on AT&T servers

The pilot project launched the ARAMARK intranet not on ARAMARK servers, but on rented space on the AT&T Web intranet hosting service. "They're hosting our content," said Kallelis. "We upload content every day and people are accessing it [over the Internet]. We don't own a [Web] server, both the production server and the staging server belong to AT&T. I don't have an investment in managing port contention or bandwidth...I've tried to get management to focus on the benefits, not the cost." There is an AT&T charge of $17.95 a month for dial-up to the Internet. "The cost of a firewall is the cost of doing business," said Kallelis. In the meantime, the number of intranet projects steadily grows.

Think of technology as a market strategy

The numerous food and related services divisions of the ARAMARK corporation serve about fifteen million customers a day in fifteen countries. Five thousand core managers potentially have information to share. When the decision was made to change the forums—which AT&T was hosting using DEC's AltaVista Forum—to Exchange, the migration process was an easy one. "The technology is there, it is so organic," said Kallelis. "If somebody doesn't like something, overnight it gets changed. Technology is not an issue, to me it's the *marketing* strategy." The strategy is working. The Culinary Standards Group put up a Web site on StarNet that covers information from how to prepare food (safety standards, health standards, carving standards, and recipes) to materials that managers can order on line and other "internal electronic commerce" projects, as Kallelis calls them (see Figure 10-2). The Uniform Services division is starting a pilot extranet project for its outside customers.

The Culinary Standards Group Web site on the ARAMARK intranet.

Figure 10-2

Kallelis plans to move the intranet *inside* when they become more involved with intranet database applications and material that has security implications. "You develop the concept, let *1000 flowers bloom,* in terms of content and number of users. Let it reach critical mass, and the justification will be there for bringing it in-house; then we're not *selling* the whole thing, it's an infrastructure change."

When it reaches critical mass, you can bring it in-house

While the ARAMARK intranet grows organically, project by project, division by division, there is no need to change the existing infrastructure to accommodate the scale of the intranet. They have the capacity within the LAN they put in three years ago. "Since AT&T was hosting it [the intranet], all we had to do was add a larger pipe between our LAN and the Internet. It started with 56 Kbps [kilobits per second], now it's up to 384 Kbps, and probably by the end of calendar year we'll be at T1 capacity. Adding capacity is not a big deal."

Marketing the Intranet to Intranet-Users

Granted, using a browser is easier than using any other tool except for a television remote control, but getting people to use an intranet—getting them to *change*—is not always automatic. In the words of the English poetess Stevie Smith, people can get very attached to the "painful and the familiar." The "painful and the familiar" may well describe software applications you have tried to learn.

People have accommodated dreadful software interfaces and relied on memory to find data they needed on their computers or in the piles on their desks, bookshelves, and credenzas. To wean them away, you may have to offer them an incentive. Some organizations have tried online contests such as *Name Our Web* and rewarded entrants with tee-shirts, gift certificates, or items from the company store. One organization planned a *Guess the Mystery Employee of the Week* contest for their home page. So each day when employees checked the site, they would find a few more pieces of information about the employee. Participants were rewarded. Competition may naturally develop between divisions or teams for the *best* Web site. It's a matter of careful timing as to when to make some information available *only* on the intranet.

Measuring for Success

Part of the design phase of an Intranet should include methods for measuring the success of the pilot project. Admittedly, not all organizations take this step. They build a project, and then adjust it as they go along according to informal feedback they get from their users. However, it is valuable to set up data-gathering and analysis procedures before beginning. Otherwise, how will you know if and when you've succeeded, and what needs remedial action? A good measurement of an intranet's performance should include an analysis of user acceptance, hardware performance, and software performance.

Evaluate user acceptance and intranet performance

For example, under the category of user acceptance, you should evaluate the following:

Finding information quickly How intuitive is the user interface design? How easy is the navigation scheme? Is it consistent?

Locating type of resource Can users identify chat groups and discussion groups and find an e-mail address? Can they locate specific information using the search tools?

Learning curve for using the application How long does it take for an employee to feel at home on the Web site? Can they take part in discussion forums? Where do they go to find help? If they have to spend a lot of time figuring out how to use this tool, it's not achieving its potential as an easy-access instrument.

In the area of hardware and software performance, consider:

Downtime problems How often have server(s) gone down, and for what reasons? How quickly were they back on line?

Interoperability problems Have all clients and servers been outfitted with TCP/IP? Are there proprietary products running that are causing conflicts?

Capacity problems What events precipitated network slowdowns? At what times of the day, week, or month have users been unable to log on to the network? Are there enough modem ports to handle remote access traffic?

Connection problems Track the number and timing of disconnections.

File sharing conflicts Problems with connections could lead to file-sharing problems.

Speed Evaluate speed of connecting and downloading.

Use varied measurement means and set benchmarks

Besides identifying *what* to measure, decide *how* to measure performance. For instance, to measure user acceptance (or usability) you can solicit feedback on a Web site by providing an e-mail link or offering a simple form for users to complete. (You may need to reward them for contributing.) Or, some organizations use focus groups to gather users' reactions. You will also need to set benchmarks. For instance, in terms of machine downtime, what level of performance is acceptable? If 99 percent performance is acceptable, what could the 1 percent cost the organization in terms of lost opportunity or lost productivity?

Assembling the Resources

Schedule a test run

Most pilot projects can almost be put together from materials at hand, plus application of some people's energies to paste it together. Remember that even the simplest site should be posted to an off-line staging area and tested—at least to make sure the links work—before you declare it ready for prime time. If you disappoint users once, it will be harder to win them over on the second try.

Part of selecting a project should include verification that your target users have access to client workstations with

TCP/IP installed.[2] Plus, if you plan any special features, such as posting audio files, make sure the machines have sound cards and speakers. Client machines should also have a version of a browser that can interpret the features that will be employed on the Web site. (For instance, Netscape 2.0 cannot interpret frames.) Either specify acceptable design elements, or specify a browser within the pilot group.

Make sure the client machines are Web-ready

Using Off-the-Shelf Tools to Build a Pilot Project

Chapter 12, "Implementing Your Intranet," addresses platform and software tool issues in more detail, but for launching a small pilot project, you may be able to use the tools you already have at hand. There are a number of Microsoft products you can use to create and deploy a modest-sized Web.

If possible, use tools at hand

If the information you wish to put on a site already exists, there is no reason to recreate it in HTML format for your Web. Documents that have been created in Microsoft Office 97 applications (such as Microsoft Excel 97, PowerPoint 97, and Word 97) can be saved in HTML format. This is a good choice for information that is not likely to change. If the information is liable to change, save the documents in their native format and *attach* them to a Web site with a hyperlink. Also, as mentioned in Chapter 6 (see "Building an Information Base," page 175), with Adobe Acrobat software you can convert any type of document to a PDF file and include it on a Web site. For users to view the files, the client machines must have the Acrobat Reader software, which is available free on the Adobe Internet Web site.

Microsoft Office 97 contains tools for building Web pages

And for putting it all together, Microsoft Word 97 includes a Web Page Wizard that makes it easy to create a Table of Contents and a Personal Home Page. You can add tables, scrolling marquees, background sounds, WordArt, lines,

---

2. Windows 95 and NT machines come equipped with the protocols.

bullets, hyperlinks to other areas in the document or to other Web pages, and other features to your Web pages.

Use Microsoft Front-Page for creating and managing a Web site

For creating a Web site, Microsoft FrontPage is a comprehensive Web development and management tool for any sized Web site. To run a site, the server must have the FrontPage Extensions software, which is included in the Microsoft Internet Information Server product.

Microsoft Personal Web Server can host a department-sized intranet

To go a step further, you can set up a small but sturdy intranet using older hardware (a 486, instead of a Pentium) with Personal Web Server (PWS) for Windows 95 with Microsoft Access 97. Microsoft Access 97 has an integrated menu command (that does the work of the old Internet Assistant and Internet Information System add-in) and an associated Publish to the Web Wizard. With the new command, you can publish static pages on a Web and share dynamic database content with browser clients. In addition, you can create hyperlinks with Microsoft Access 97.

PWS is also useful for site testing

The Microsoft Personal Web Server is a good solution for a light-traffic intranet such as a small business or a department within a larger organization. The PWS is also useful as a site to test HTML code before you upload to the server. Personal Web Server supports ISAPI extensions and CGI, but not Java. When your needs expand, you can convert the Web project from PWS to Internet Information Server running on Windows NT.

People Resources

Creating the content and launching the pilot project require different skill sets

How you divide up the tasks for creating an intranet pilot project depends, of course, on the people you have on hand. Ideally, either a department member or a communications specialist handles developing content, and an information technology specialist (or technically astute individual) handles the mechanics of getting the site up and running. As the Web expands, the people resources will, too.

Every pilot project needs a leader who believes emphatically in the benefits of the project and who can inspire others to work towards the same end. Very often this leader must also be a liaison between technologists and content creators. (Sometimes these groups may seem to present competing needs and visions for a project.) And the evangelist must often facilitate discussions and keep the group moving forward to their shared goal. Also, such a person carries a vision of what an intranet *could* be, and so drives it to become a better product.

A pilot project needs an evangelist

Another important addition to a pilot team is a usability specialist. As you will see in the next section, a usability specialist can help evaluate the effectiveness of your site and recommend specific improvements, based on studies of how users interact with the interface design and functionality of the Web site.

A usability specialist can make recommendations that will lead to increased productivity

Developing a Usability Analysis

It's standard on any communications project to research the users—such as their work processes, key tasks, capabilities and limitations—to identify what they need. As mentioned in the previous chapter, it's a good idea to involve at least one representative of the user community in the design of a project, and a usability specialist to set up usability tests for a pilot project. Usability is a very deep subject, and this section will only highlight some issues. Usability analysis can help the team focus on the business pay-off of the project in the design stage; it can also locate problems with the application that need fixing once it's running.

Focus on the customer

Usability begins with translating the business objectives into performance measurements. The tests should focus on the interface design as well as search and navigation strategies. Users must be tested on specific tasks with the pre-intranet system and then tested performing the same tasks on the intranet. Then compare the results.

Measure task performance

Avoid measuring meaningless outcomes, and focus on measurements that improve productivity and produce business results. For instance, counting *hits* to a Web page does not measure whether or not useful information was received. It only means someone walked in the door. On an Internet Web page you want users to linger on your site, but on an intranet, you want them to find what they need and complete their work—whether that is accomplishing a specific task or making a decision.

Usability studies yield valuable information for improving a project

Usability studies can lead to productivity improvements. For instance, a Web site that has users puzzling over where to go to find the information they need, and making false starts before finding it, will waste time and could increase congestion on the site. If they have to make six or seven jumps before they find what they need, they will both lose time and become frustrated. In time, such difficulties will discourage people from using the site. A simple change in navigation or the location of an icon could improve accessibility of information and leave the user feeling more empowered and productive too. Usage statistics can also be an important tool for planning.

Evaluation and adjustments should be a continuous process

The timing and frequency of usability testing for intranet projects differ from testing conventional software applications. In traditional applications, usability testing occurs during the development phase of the software life cycle. Changes are made, and the application is created along those lines, deployed, and used as is (until the upgrade). But the intranet life cycle is a more continuous roll than one big roll-out. Certainly, intranet applications are designed, tested, rolled out—but at this point, they diverge. With an intranet, an interface can be changed quickly, and even underlying functionality can be changed more easily than can conventional software applications. So, usability evolves into a more continuous monitoring and improvement cycle.

Identifying Lessons Learned

You can gather lessons learned from both user feedback and measurements. Look in particular for bottlenecks that slow performance of the system, and for areas that cause confusion (and therefore slow performance) for users. Analyzing logs of calls for help can help you identify major trouble spots. Review the measurement criteria you established before beginning the pilot—user acceptance, hardware performance, and software performance—and search for the root or underlying causes of any failures to meet expectations.

Naturally, de-briefing sessions to evaluate lessons learned, held in a blame-free environment, will gain the most. In the same vein, it's important to create an open environment so that users will feel free to supply useful feedback and not feel intimidated or inadequate if they voice honest opinions about frustrating experiences during the pilot stage. Statistics may help machine performance issues, but people-performance issues can be delicate. Simply talking to users can uncover valuable insights. These lessons are the foundations for improvements—and your next pilot project.

Selling the Intranet—Steering the Change

In the long run, what will *sell* your intranet is not the sizzle. It's content, content, content—and capabilities. Yes, early intranet projects can attract a lot of attention with *all that content!* But as your user base matures, they will want more accessibility *and* interactivity. Still, what will turn your intranet into a business-critical machine is very basic—it's convenience and confidence. If users find that it's quick and convenient to locate and use data, and that they can trust its accuracy, they will adopt it as their own. And like the answering machine and e-mail, they'll wonder how they ever got along with out it.

> Look for bottlenecks and areas of confusion

> Asking users about their experience can provide valuable feedback

> Sites that are quick, content-rich, and interactive will maintain interest

Looking Ahead

Every pilot project is a prototype for the next project. Building an intranet is an evolutionary process, partly because technology changes can be measured in the life of a May fly. (It was in the *olden days* that Internet years were equivalent to dog years.) Pilot projects can test the effectiveness of new technologies, such as new input devices (instead of a mouse) for hands-free computing, or test the effectiveness in meeting user requirements.

Keith Martin-Smith, PC Services Director at Dixons Mastercare, reports a high level of enthusiasm for developing information resources on their intranet. Now that people have seen what it can do, they're coming up with more ideas for what it can do. "Any one day, we probably have 20 or 30 mini-projects in the pilot stage. We'll run it [a pilot project] for a while, get feedback. The Webmaster is tough, and controls all of the postings to the site. It's a highly controlled environment. We do take a number of risks, but if you don't take risks, you don't get anywhere."

Some individuals see risks involved with building an intranet and will resist the change. The next chapter examines how to address the resistance and other issues related to building a business case for an intranet.

Chapter Eleven

Building a Business Case

As you saw in the last chapter, some organizations have started with a pilot project and have then gone on to expand their intranet, without ever stopping to prepare a formal business case. Information system improvements seem to defy traditional metrics. Unlike conventional capital outlay for a piece of production equipment, an intranet is an enabling tool that affects *how* people do business. How do you put a dollar value on improving communication? Or getting quicker results? Or transferring information?

As Ken Fenwick, Business Systems Analyst for SAFECO, said, "It used to be that if I developed *this* [change] and installed it in *this* department, this productivity improvement could replace 100 clerical people. You could count that as cost savings. Well, today we have very few clericals; we have all knowledge-workers. Now, the question is, how do I leverage knowledge? If it costs $100 to learn new technology, and 500 people need it, and I build an intranet that does not require them to learn new software, can I extrapolate that savings—$50,000—for an intranet?"

It is difficult, but not impossible to quantify intranet benefits

Cost savings are measured in leveraging knowledge, not in eliminating positions

In many organizations, preparing a business case is a required step in the annual *dash for cash* that determines how much money divisions and departments have to work with for the next fiscal year. So, this chapter offers insights on how to tackle that responsibility.[1] It offers some guidance for measuring intranet results and shows how some companies have quantified cost savings from their intranet and, in particular, reduced the total cost of computing ownership.

Transform any negativity about changing the organization's digital nervous system

But first, because not everyone who holds purse strings in an organization will leap at the chance to put money down on an intranet, this chapter begins by suggesting ways to handle any resistance you may encounter about having an intranet. Some executives may have already built a case *against* an intranet in their minds, based on what they've heard about people using the Internet, or they may simply not be aware of the advantages and may resist any change from the existing network. In either case, if you want to sell an intranet to your organization, this chapter offers ways to counter objections.

Handling Resistance

You may have to overcome fear of change before employing new technology

There are many reasons a person or group (including a group of executives) might resist attempts to build an intranet. Sometimes it's difficult to unwrap layers of resistance to get to the core concerns. People may express these concerns by F.U.D. (fear, uncertainty, and doubt). Of these, the greatest is fear of change.

---

1. It is beyond the scope of this book to advise on making creative budget requests. However, one respondent remarked that as part of a video department, they had eased around capital outlay ceilings by buying a video camera one piece at a time. They bought a lens. They bought a tripod. They bought a light stand. They bought a case of videotapes. They bought the camera body. All were separate expenditures, each of which stayed beneath the threshold that would trigger preparing a business case.

Fear of Change

Some people feel threatened by talk of a paperless office. They like paper; they like the feel of it. They trust paper. They can see it, feel it, hold on to it, carry it around, and read it wherever they want to without electricity. And for people who feel this way, no amount of raving about the speed of disseminating information or the ease of adding a hyperlink *pointer* to information will move them. As expressed in the first chapter, having an intranet is not likely to eliminate paper.

Not everyone yearns for a paperless office

You can easily offer a paper option by adding a Print button to a Web site or electronic document. Remind people that they can access the most current information available on line, and reassure them that they can print it out and peruse it at their own convenience.

Provide a page print option

For those who live by the creed of *knowledge is power,* knowledge hoarding is a way of remaining powerful. These people become fearful when the organization's culture changes to one that embraces information sharing. The problem here is really beyond the scope of the intranet, but the intranet often becomes the scapegoat because it encourages and enables such culture changes.

Many people fear loss of power when information is shared

Rebuilding incentives within the organization can help to combat this type of resistance. Reward group accomplishments, and reward individuals for their level of participation within a group. Then the intranet, which supports collaboration, becomes a constructive vehicle for change rather than a monster truck that will run you over.

Provide rewards and other incentives

Managers may worry whether people in the organization will accept an intranet as an information medium. Will they really seek out information on a Web page? Will productivity actually decline because people won't use it or will have trouble using it? The answer depends on the effectiveness of the design—is information easier to find than it was before?

Provide training and support to encourage people to use the intranet

Of course, if the intranet is the *only* place to find some information, that may encourage use. (This assumes everyone who needs it has access to online information.)

Usability testing and careful review of feedback provide a means for addressing those concerns. Test the logic and the intuitiveness of the design. Provide training and friendly support. Extend support hours beyond local business hours, especially if your organization spans time zones and you have remote users. Consider a peer network of individuals that users can go to for advice (and encouragement) without losing face.

Worry about Non-business Use and Abuse

Many managers worry that employees will waste time surfing the intranet, and if they have the connection, will waste even more time surfing the Internet on company time. Beth Beaty, Webmaster (and self-proclaimed change agent) of an international financial services association, relates a story about working in an ice cream shop when she was a teenager. Company policy was that all employees were permitted to eat as much ice cream as they wanted, which all the young employees did, for the first week, until the novelty wore off. Still, some managers worry that their employees will develop an insatiable craving for ice cream.

However, if you regard the intranet as a tool, like the telephone on an employee's desk, and expect (and allow) a couple of weeks of intranet (or Internet) exploration, employees will learn to use the tool. Mature people will use it as a tool; immature employees will misuse any tool—whether it's *The New York Times* or *The Wall Street Journal*. Specify in your online Intranet Policies Web site whether employees may use the Internet after business hours for their own interests.

Of course there is the possibility that if you allow employees to explore, they may venture to sites and bring back materials that

Test the design and provide user support

Many managers have concerns that an intranet will undermine their employees' productivity

Publish policies for intranet use

are totally unsuited to the workplace, such as pornographic, sexist, or racist materials. How can you control this behavior?

Some managers advise simply, *hire people you can trust.* Or, as Earnest Phillips, Communications Specialist for the Weyerhaeuser Company said, "If there is pornography on my screen, it's a sexual harassment issue – it's that simple." Whether an employee introduces offensive or illegal material into the workplace from the Internet or a magazine, it's a management issue. A Web administrator has the tools to monitor traffic, and to block access to certain sites.

> Web tools are available to monitor traffic and block access to specific sites

The Gas Dryer Incident—One Way to Ignite an Intranet

At the corporate headquarters of a restaurant chain, an executive secretary had a gas dryer to sell. So, she broadcast a message across the LAN e-mail system at headquarters. One of the responses came from an executive who was objecting to using the company's business resource to promote a private interest, and he also sent his message to the same distribution list. Then that message elicited a response from another person (same distribution list), temporizing and suggesting that this wasn't a bad thing, quite the contrary that people should communicate more with one another. And so it went. Opinions buzzed back and forth.

The incident sparked so much interest in improving communication that soon an ad hoc group took a stab at it and put up a small Web site. One year later, an intranet was launched reaching not only the people at corporate headquarters but also operations around the country.

And the moral of the gas dryer story is this: people in the company had an unmet need for a sense of community and a site where someone could post a notice about a gas dryer, or a school play, or a vanpool. While the business purpose of the intranet is not posting classified ads, a secondary purpose is to improve communication. And one way to do that, is to encourage a sense of community. This is one of those *intangibles* that is very hard to measure but very real in terms of energizing members of an organization, and that leads to better productivity.

Identifying Assumptions

Don't assume that the main issues are technical. There may be other reasons why an intranet will not work at your organization. Some of the issues that can lead to intranet failure include:

- Isolation and internecine quarrels between groups.
- Indifference or lack of motivation to get to know more about other departments.
- Unwillingness to share within or between groups.

For an intranet to be successful, you have to be able to assume cultural support for increasing communication and information sharing and for building a sense of community.

Specify performance assumptions and deliverables in the business case

As you prepare a project plan or business case, be sure to identify assumptions about which departments will shoulder which responsibilities (and costs) for development and maintenance of the intranet. Failure to identify these types of dependencies in planning will make it that much more difficult in practice. For instance, the IT department may supply the Webmaster, but who will furnish the content, and in what format and with what frequency? For instance, at Georgia-Pacific West, Inc. the content *owner* is designated for each departmental Web site, and responsibility for maintenance and approval rests outside the information resources group.

Assume the need for additional funds to support later development of Web applications

As an intranet goes beyond the publishing activities described in Chapter 5, "Using an Intranet for Quick Publishing," there will be additional costs for developing the kinds of Web applications that will improve access to data across the organization and that support decision-making. More and more software vendors are not only developing tools for professional software developers to use to build applications, they are also developing tools that a *layperson* can pick up and use to build intranet applications. You should build this expectation into your business case.

Examining the Cost

The previous chapter suggested that an intranet pilot project could be put together with materials at hand. If you have an adequate LAN or WAN, the network infrastructure is already in place. The following are the basic cost components, some of which you may already own, for building an intranet.

You may already own sufficient client and server hardware to operate an intranet

Hardware costs include:

- Client workstations with sufficient processing power to use intranet applications and an operating system that can run TCP/IP.
- Sandbox and development server. An isolated environment, physically separate from the rest of the network, using a stand-alone PC as a server.[2] A sandbox area is for testing new software applications. A development area is for developing Web sites and Web applications.
- Staging server to use as a pre-release site for testing.[3] It could also be used to mirror the production Web site.
- Production Web server to run the Web site. Size of the server depends on the size of the site.

Software costs include:

- Client software—a browser.
- Web development software, such as Microsoft FrontPage, Visual InterDev, Microsoft Visual Basic, Microsoft Visual J++, Java, Symantec Visual Café, Rogue Wave, Adobe Acrobat, and Adobe PhotoShop.[4]

---

2. On a stand-alone server, you cannot test network performance by performance simulations, you can only test specific applications.

3. The staging server can be smaller than the production server (less RAM and less hard disk space), but it must run Web server software.

4. Visual J++ is Microsoft's Java scripting language. Rogue Wave is a Java development environment. Any development languages or editors will also be used for page maintenance.

- Web server software, such as Internet Information Server (which includes FrontPage Server Extensions) or Netscape Communicator.
- Site licenses. Servers require purchase of licenses, a sliding scale based on the number of connections. Some database programs require either a license or purchase of a driver like JDBC (if not supplied) from a third party vendor in order for the database to be connected to the Web server.[5]

Support costs include:

- Basic user training. Users should receive basic instruction in browser capabilities and Web navigation. They may need training to learn a specific Web application.
- Help Desk. Provide 24-hour support, to serve geographically dispersed users.

Document sharing costs less on an intranet than on a traditional client/ server

Compare the cost of document-sharing using Microsoft Internet Information Server (IIS) on an intranet with that of using Lotus Notes on a traditional client/server network. Microsoft IIS is free with an NT 4.0 server. Microsoft's Web client software (Internet Explorer) is free to anyone. So the cost of Web client and server software is zero. By comparison, Lotus Notes' client costs $69 per desktop, and that doesn't include the cost for the server software.[6] It also takes less time to set up an intranet server. And a Web server can be assembled by a novice Webmaster, whereas installing a Notes server requires several days of hard labor by a highly trained technician.

"There is no big upfront cost," said Aaron Bathum, Mill Technical Analyst, at Georgia-Pacific West, a pulp and

---

5. The trend is towards license fees, rather than purchased drivers. A license for a driver could also entail an ongoing maintenance cost.

6. According to a report by Forrester, a Lotus Notes 5,000-user, 50-server system would cost more than $200,000.

paper subsidiary of Georgia-Pacific. Their main cost has been $10.50 per hour for a few months for a computer science intern from Western Washington University to develop the Web site. They also bought a $700 scanner, and about $1,000 worth of software, including Help desk software. They purchased a copy of NT, which comes with Internet Information Server, and use the Internet Explorer browser on the workstations. "But the time will come when we will need two or three dedicated people," said Bathum of the growth he anticipates.

Cost is rarely a barrier to starting an intranet

Reducing Total Cost of Ownership

The total cost of computer ownership, commonly referred to as TCO (total cost of ownership), has been an issue since 1995.[7] An intranet can drive down the TCO by providing a computing environment (including the network infrastructure, servers, and clients) that is more scalable, more interoperable, and easier to use than a traditional LAN or WAN.

An intranet can lower the TCO

Checklist for Evaluating an Intranet Proposal

- What business problem does the project address?
- How is this solution better than what we have now?
- What is the ultimate cost? Over what time period?
- What is the cost of not making the change?
- Besides hardware and software, does the cost estimate include retraining? (or will they be slipped into another department's budget?)
- Is the new technology compatible with our old technology?
- Bottom line: how will this new thing help us be a more profitable (*fill in your company's business objective here*) _____-producing company?

---

7. Study completed by Gartner Group (see research note titled "Windows NT 3.6: Projected to Be a TCO Winner," Policy K-230-1233, Personal Computing (PC), 18 October 1995, by W. Kirwin) and others.

Scalable—saves cost and effort to add new users	Intranets are scalable. There are no finite restrictions on the number of users that an application can support. The only limitation is the capacity of the particular server or section of the network. Capacity can be upgraded segment by segment.
Interoperable— saves time spent solving hardware or software conflicts	An intranet—a network built on TCP/IP and HTTP protocols—has a better shot at achieving interoperability than a traditional network made up of a mix of different computers.[8] The same Web application can run on any TCP/IP client machine, whether it's a Macintosh, an IBM-compatible personal computer, or a UNIX machine. This means that only one standard application needs to be created, instead of separate applications written for each operating system. Intranets provide high capability for exchanging information across heterogeneous computing environments.
Easy to use— saves time for IT staff and users	Where an intranet wins hands-down is in ease of use. Intranets increase productivity because they are simpler for both administrators and users. There are many, many ways that ease of use can contribute to achieving cost savings and reducing TCO. In fact, you could trace almost every benefit of an intranet to the fact that it is easier to use—for users and IT staff—than traditional LANs or WANs. Easy saves time; saving time saves money and sometimes spells the difference between a great success and an also-ran.
Intranets keep users free from technical hassles, free to do their work	An intranet offers simplified installation—starting with the initial server installation, through software upgrades—and this saves time for IT staff and for users. Web applications do not require installation, or upgrades, on a user's computer. Web applications and database access are managed by applications running on one or more servers. The savings keep multiplying, since each new revision of an intranet application does not translate to lost productivity while

---

8. Although, with so many instances of rival standards nowadays, such as remote objects management, interoperability between rival vendors' products is not entirely assured.

employees take time first to install the application then to learn how to use it. Plus, less user support is needed.

Reducing Costs of Deployment and Support

HarperCollins has documented ways in which their intranet has simplified many computing activities and thus reduced TCO. Their computing environment consists of both Personal Computer and Macintosh systems. "Traditionally, desktop deployment cost us $500 per workstation, but now, through the Intranet, we can deliver a solution with equivalent or superior functionality, including training, for about $100 per workstation," said Chief Information Officer Lyle Anderson.

Desktop deployment was more expensive

The SAFECO Insurance Companies IT department looks for opportunities to leverage knowledge as a way to cut costs. Ken Fenwick, Senior Business Systems Analyst, cited a Gartner Group study that reported fifty percent of the TCO was spent in supporting users. What he saw was a "very large target" for cost savings.

User support represents fifty percent of the total cost of computer ownership

The SAFECO PC Support group routinely received a couple of hundred calls a day, but a study of their logs found that they were spending eighty percent of their time answering the same questions. Their solution was a network—not of computers—but of about 400 representatives, individuals working within each department in the company who, in addition to their regular responsibilities, assist their co-workers with computer problems. PC Support built a knowledge repository on their Web site that provides these representatives (and anyone else) with solutions to common problems, software to download, and connections to other resources, such as configuration guides.

Leveraging knowledge is a way to cut costs

"We train [PC Reps] to look to the PC knowledge repository first," said Fenwick. "If they are unable to help, we have a means to escalate the issue up the food chain… [PC Support]

Use an escalating support process

can focus on the twenty percent and get our business customers back to work quickly. Ka-ching, ka-ching!" (See Figure 11-1 and Figure 11-2)

Figure 11-1   *The SAFECO PC knowledge repository is an easy-to-use online resource for computer support information.*

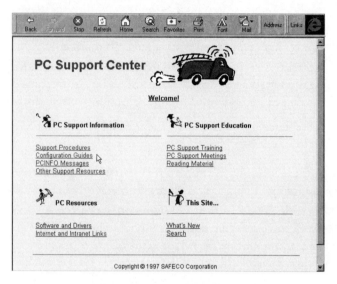

Figure 11-2   *On the Configuration page PC Reps can find step by step instructions to guide them.*

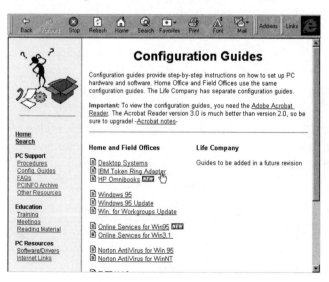

"We recognize that knowledge is an asset that's worth a lot of money," explained Fenwick. "If a [PC Rep] in Seattle takes an hour to learn something, and that's $50 worth of internal expense, and if we can leverage that piece of knowledge across the organization and prevent a hundred other people from having to spend the time to learn what he already knows, that's pretty powerful metrics."

Teaching one person to help a hundred extends the investment

Georgia-Pacific West achieves cost savings on their intranet with a similar program. As they add personal computers around the mill (replacing terminals), they're drawing people who have had some experience with computers at home into a User Liaison program. "If they're interested, we're giving them training in basic PC support, so they can take care of users in their area," said Mill Technical Analyst Aaron Bathum.

Georgia-Pacific West also engages workers as a first line computer support team

Measuring Intranet Productivity

You probably already have several tools in hand that you can use to measure how productivity has been affected through the building of an intranet. You can use existing audit forms, feedback forms, and user interviews to gather data. Usability data from pilot projects is also helpful. Of course, when you launched your pilot projects, you identified objectives and established measurement criteria.

For instance, if a business objective is to improve communications, you can use existing communication audits and add the intranet as an alternative mode of communication. If the business objective is to improve access to information, the scenarios in Chapter 1 about the two lab technicians checking for Human Resource benefits information are examples of a comparison of the time it takes to find the information necessary to complete a task (see pages 20-22). Perhaps one main impetus for starting an intranet is to supply information in a timely manner. Measure how frequently customer

Compare performance against objectives with the old network and an intranet profiles, sales reports, and price lists are updated before an intranet is installed. Use that as a base-line to measure improvement.

Soliciting user feedback is crucial in building a case and planning the next improvements

If you are measuring productivity, use survey forms and interviews to ask employees directly if they are getting the information they need when they need it. Be sure to go the next step—if they are not completely satisfied, ask *why not?* to solicit information you can use in the next cycle of projects and improvements.

Saving Paper and Gaining Efficiencies

When Microsoft instituted a Web-based purchasing project to achieve a corporate goal of eliminating paperwork, they gained many other efficiencies and cost savings as well. According to figures by the market-research firm Killen & Associates, the cost of processing a paper-based purchase

Setting up Measurements

It's not always easy to take an accurate measurement of progress towards a goal. In real life, unexpected developments may skew the results. Charles Wang draws an example from the automotive industry.[9] Responding to consumer demand, auto makers spent billions of dollars making cars more efficient. Yes, today many cars are made of lighter materials, and the new technology of combustion and gearing has made them more efficient. But if you measure gas mileage alone, the numbers would not prove this is so—there are no cars on the market that can get 100 mpg. What they saved with lighter materials, they have turned around and *spent* on air pollution control devices. So, the results show that yes, they are more efficient, and yes, we have cleaner air; and yet there has been no net gain in miles per gallon. However, cleaner air was not an expected outcome of the original mission. So measurements alone are an unreliable method of determining value.

9.   Wang, *Techno Vision*, p. 108

order is $144, most of which is related to correcting purchase order documents. They further estimate that an electronic purchase order costs between $7 to $40. For requisitions greater than $1000, Microsoft built a Web front end, called MS Market, to the SAP R/3 accounting system; they wrote their own code for purchases under $1,000.

Considering that the system handled 250,000 transactions last year, the savings amounted to nearly $35 million from processing alone. But the savings ripple out from there. From the employees' point of view, they now have a one-stop, online shopping location. As shown in Figure 11-3, they can order business cards, software, and catering; they can use direct links to vendors and purchasing. No more searching and asking others where to order envelopes or whom to call to arrange catering for a lunch meeting. It takes less time to get the job done.

An intranet purchasing system saves money and is easier for the user

On the MS Market site, employees can order office supplies and catering and use links to vendors and Purchasing.

Figure 11-3

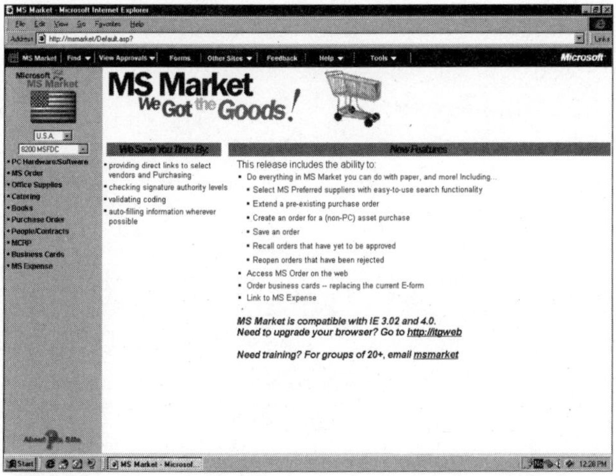

From the accounting point of view, when employees order from a Web purchasing site, they are ordering from preferred suppliers, and this accounts for additional savings

because it reduces maverick buying.[10] Maverick buying is a large concern for purchasing departments because it can cause the company to lose out on volume discounts. Also, centralized electronic purchasing gathers valuable data about consumption patterns and buying preferences throughout the organization. This information can be used in many ways, such as to negotiate vendor discounts and to find new ways to increase the automation of the buying process. As with many intranet cost savings projects, the value ripples and extends through the organization. The MS Market system is easier for the user, increases cost-savings through greater volume discounts, and provides a valuable data stream as well.

Questioning the Cost of Not Adopting

Time spent building bridges between incompatible legacy systems

Another approach to a business case is identifying the cost of not proceeding with an intranet. It is easy to enumerate the problems that will arise in trying to manage an ever-expanding, increasingly complex traditional network computing environment. More and more of the IT staffers' time must be devoted to managing this complexity, and to do so, they will haveto create extra applications to draw together systems which were not intended to work together.

Confusion caused by multiple interfaces

In addition, employees are still saddled with a cumbersome technology-oriented system for accessing information, rather than a simple interface for all their computing needs.

The first chapter of this book outlined the benefits of an intranet to each population—IT professionals, communicators, users, partners, and managers. Chapters 5, 6, 7, and 8 depicted ways in which an intranet could be used to overcome inefficiencies and improve productivity within the

---

10. Maverick buying refers to employees' purchasing products from any vendor they choose because they do not know what sources the company prefers to use for purchasing.

organization. Can you imagine getting a *no* answer to these questions?

- Can our organization benefit from improved communication?
- Can our organization benefit from making information easier to access and maintain?
- Can we consolidate our current and legacy information sources in a single place, that could hold all the manuals, databases, templates, policies, contracts, procedures, directories, sales performance, product descriptions, and price lists that our organization owns?
- Can we benefit from a technically empowered work force?
- Can we provide improved partnership opportunities through an extranet?
- Can we build a more well-informed, tighter community within our organization?

Looking Ahead

"We're making a decision to go down this road, and at least investigate it," said Ken Fenwick of their intranet projects. "You can't afford not to investigate these technologies. Because if we ignored it, and we get three or four years down the road, and realized this was the greatest thing since sliced bread, starting from scratch doesn't mean you can leapfrog to where everyone else is. Even if you could learn to understand the tools, it's the supporting infrastructure that you gather and groom, and the knowledge you create— those experiences will differentiate those that are successful, and those…"

In the final analysis, perhaps you can't afford not to build an intranet

The next chapter explores implementing an intranet: building a development team, setting standards for technologies and policies, and technical design issues.

Implementing Your Intranet

This is it. It's been a long time coming. After digesting the lessons learned from pilot projects, giving stirring presentations, and justifying the costs, you know it's time to start implementing your intranet. This is where you get to show the world—well, at least the people on your intranet—the tremendous benefits Internet technology can bring to an organization. You're ready. After all, if we can land a Sojourner on Mars, you ought to be able to launch an intranet.

At this point, you've identified goals and desired outcomes for your intranet (short-term ones, at the least). You've profiled your user audience so you have an idea what they want, and what they are able to use (see "Determine the Purpose," page 255, and "Define the Audience," page 257). You've decided how much of this implementation effort is focused toward publishing content and how much toward providing applications that offer improved ways of getting business done. You've reminded yourself (and anyone within earshot) that an intranet is a work in progress.

Intranet implementation will be built on goals, user capabilities, and needs

This chapter will illuminate the decision layers (some may already be hard-wired) that stand between you and implementing an intranet—from building the intranet team, to choosing platforms and technology standards (hardware and software), to policies and guidelines, and finally, to going from a *nice to have* to business-critical. As you fasten your seat belt, this is a good time to remind you that this is not the *How to Build an Intranet Fortress in 14 Days or Your Money Back* book. This book raises the issues that your organization will need to address, and this chapter charts an approach to dealing with them within your organization.

An intranet represents different opportunities to developers, communicators, and administrators

Building an intranet means different things to different people. If you're a network or systems administrator, this could be your chance to reduce some of the complexities that have evolved as the network and the organization have grown. If you're a developer (or a developer at heart), this might be your chance to show how information technology can save time. If you're a communicator, this might be your chance to move information quickly and easily. If you're a manager, this could be the solution to cut cycle time down to size and still raise morale. And if all these parties work together, and listen to each other's needs for the intranet, that's an implementation project made in heaven.

Decide Who Is In Charge

Web development is shared jointly between content providers and technologists

Who's in charge here? While the answer may depend on who started the intranet, most likely it will depend on the structure (and culture) of your organization. Typically, an intranet is a shared endeavor between technology providers and content providers. For this reason, the lines of communication and areas of authority must be crystal clear.

- Will the intranet be centrally managed, or will each business unit have authority for technical and content aspects of their Web domain?

- Will Web developers and Web authors be guided by Best Practices, or have to stay within firm limits— and who will develop either?
- Who can green-light development of a new breed of Web application?
- Who has the final word over what material may go on line?
- Will corporate IT or Communications departments— or both—develop a Web Services bureau to assist with the development of intranet or Internet Web sites?

Some of these questions will be relevant not only at the top levels of an organization, but also within a division or department.

Create the Team

The best intranets are developed with a cross-functional team who can apply a wide range of skills to the project. An intranet deployment of any substantial size will need technical people: programmers, system administrators, database experts, and application developers. But it will also need people experienced in creating graphical user interfaces and in writing and editing written content. Others will be called in too, depending on the size and scope of the project— security experts, users, lawyers, testers, translators, and representatives of the main departments on line (or those whom you would like to be on line).

Not all team members will work full time on the intranet at the beginning

Webmaster Role

The Webmaster is responsible for making sure the site is functioning properly, that problems get resolved quickly, and that updates are made seamlessly. During the initial phases of an intranet, someone may step into the Webmaster role part time. But, for a serious roll-out, you need to allot full-time resources. Some prefer the title WebManager to

Webmaster is a full-time position

Webmaster, because it sounds less like the leader of a cadre of teenage gamers settled in for a weekend of Dungeons and Dragons.[1] It's a profession now, and a growing number of educational institutions are offering Webmaster courses or certificate programs.[2]

Webmasters need a blend of HTML and customer service skills

The skills required of a Webmaster will vary depending on the site. Certainly a sound understanding of HTML is essential, as is a firm commitment to customer service. He or she should be very detail-oriented, since even minor misspellings, broken links, and misplaced graphics can quickly ruin a Web site's reputation.

Other required skills will depend on the nature of the site

Other required skills will probably depend on the character of the site. For example, an online procurement site, which is entirely database-driven, will do well with a Webmaster skilled in database management. On the other hand, some sites consist mostly of linked documents and graphics, in which case a person with an editorial background may be more appropriate.

InfoMasters

InfoMasters are responsible for content

Someone has to furnish the content. Some organizations that use the publishing industry as their model create a Web Editor or Web Content Editor position, or contract with one from the outside. According to Bill Monroe, Skills Trainer at Harris Corporation, they've used the term InfoMaster to refer to the content providers. While a Webmaster assures technical operation of the site, the InfoMaster assures that content is accurate and timely. One advantage in this title is that it

---

1. Dungeons and Dragons was a popular and very elaborate role-playing adventure game in the 1980s. The DragonMaster spun the story and ruled on the play.

2. Two notable ones are Bellevue Community College, Bellevue, Washington, and Santa Cruz Community College, Santa Cruz, California. One is in the Silicon forest and other is in the Silicon valley.

seems to put the content providers on a more equal footing with the technology providers or Webmasters.

These roles, InfoMaster and Webmaster, may refer to managing the entire intranet or to one of the sites, such as the Human Resources site. So an organization can have many Webmasters and InfoMasters.

An intranet can have multiple masters

Advisory Groups

Some organizations establish large Web advisory groups, including representatives from legal and public affairs. Whether or not they are actively involved, it's a good idea to educate people in these departments—and encourage them to learn from their peers in other organizations. Then, if you need their advice, they are up to speed and not still struggling at the intranet versus Internet level. One organization reported that their legal department was "clueless" about online issues, such as copyright and rights to privacy.

Part of the intranet leader's role will be to educate others

Other organizations get along with informal get-togethers every couple of months among the active players. At the Baltimore Gas and Electric Company, they have an informal *Route 96* working group. Kim Ethridge, Communications Manager reports, "We have occasional meetings of the content providers throughout the company, designers, and information systems people—for one or two hours over lunch. We talk about any problems, ideas they have, new applications they need to pursue."

A Web advisory group can raise issues and establish policy

For a working group of communicators, online departments, and IT people, one important reason to get together is to establish priorities jointly. All the players have their own department priorities (and associated budgets), as well as their aims for the intranet. Without open communication, it is easy for frustrations to develop about who is holding up the game.

Open communication is essential

Different Priorities

Even when there are no territorial conflicts over who can or must do what with regard to the intranet, there still might be the challenge of mismatched priorities among the players. For example, suppose that in September a Web Editor in the Communications department learns that the Human Resources department is planning a company-wide benefits re-enrollment choice period in December.

The Web Editor and the Webmaster see it as a great opportunity. "Great! We can build you this little form," says the Webmaster, "so an employee can enter in some variables, and see which plan suits best. They could put in their Zip Code and get a list of doctors in their area that are covered by the plan. And then we could…" The Web Editor, chiming in, adds "We can put a new article on the Web site every two weeks explaining each of the plans, to build momentum."

Everyone but the Human Resource representative is ready to run with it. The Human Resource department swamped with new hires coming in, hasn't planned to allocate resources to do anything but put up an announcement that a change is coming in three months. To the Webmaster, this will be missed opportunity to build a prototype for the main event (a form for online registration). To the Web Editor, just announcing a future change will only raise employees' concerns, not supply information for better decision-making. Three different agendas, one Web site.

Supporting Players

A high level sponsor needs to champion the intranet

While an intranet may start from grassroots—like regional theater, full of enthusiasm and exciting possibilities—at some point it has to develop *legs*. What usually makes the difference is funding.

Funding an intranet is invariably a creative exercise. Often IT departments have absorbed the early costs, confident that once managers in other departments experience the benefits, they will sponsor further development. This is the approach that Webmaster Ted Wagner has taken at Air Products and Chemicals, Inc. One intranet project in particular, putting a surplus equipment database on a Web site, represented a solid opportunity for the company to reduce costs. The Web site vastly increased visibility for the items the company wanted to liquidate (see Figure 12-1). Wagner used the project, as he explained it, "to kickstart this technology."

Figure 12-1

In Air Products and Chemicals Inc., a group charged with liquidating surplus equipment put up a Web site on the intranet.

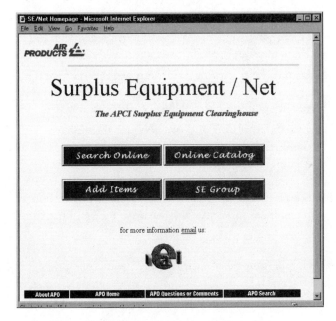

"The purchasing department has a MIS person who is a database developer, and he was leading the [surplus equipment] project. So I loaned him my Web developer. We're spreading knowledge within the company... We're soaking up a lot of overhead, but we're planting seeds. They are starting to grow." Later Wagner said "The CEO didn't come down and say, 'You will do intranet.' He still hasn't done that, but he knows what we're doing and he's behind it."

An intranet that is under-funded will under-perform. It will not achieve its goals. Another approach is to seek out senior management sponsors for your intranet. Give them a copy of this book.

You need funding and support

Set Technology Standards

The content needs a framework. There are important decisions on what hardware and software will become the foundation of your intranet.

Open standards enable product interoperability

Throughout this book, the subject of standards and open standards has come up repeatedly. You know by now that standards are agreed-upon industry specifications to guide developers in creating new products that will interoperate. Products that interoperate work together on more than one platform. The term platform has meaning in context, as you can see from these platforms and some examples of each.

- Hardware platform: Mac, UNIX, or IBM compatible
- Software platform: Windows, Win32, BackOffice
- Development platform: ActiveX environment or a Java language environment[3]

You also know that unlike oak trees, standards are not long-lived. They behave more like inhabitants of a petri dish; they colonize and evolve.

If Internet years were measured in dog years, intranet years are measured in flea years

Every time a vendor (or industry group) proposes a new standard, the situation is again in flux. In the light of these uncertainties (and the fear of buying Betamax), how do you decide what operating platform, what developing platform, what authoring tools, what client software will be allowed on your intranet?

---

3. Vendor A develops technology, a software product to "sell," and proposes standards, hoping 3rd party companies will use those standards to develop other products that use Vendor A's primary product. But products with proposed standards (because of unique features) may not play completely (or well, or at all) with competitor, Vendor B's, software product. This situation (born from enterprise competition) starts divergence from universal interoperability, and instead now "standards" means, *you can trust that these products work together in this platform environment.*

Most likely you already have at the least a network infra-structure in place, with workstations. You may also have accumulated a particularly eclectic collection of computing equipment, because responsibility for purchasing computing equipment has been divided up by division or operating area. Most likely your system has enough types of comput-ing languages to start your own United Nations. (Which is, of course, what your intranet will do.)

Take stock of what's at hand

You can't stop evolution, but you can standardize your intranet operating environment. By standardizing, you will ensure better integration of applications, which in turn will mean less time spent solving interoperability problems for the Web administrators, Web developers, users, and, last but not least, the Help Desk. You can also create more manage-able administrative and development environments.

You can't standardize the world, but you can set technology standards for your intranet

The Route to Standardizing your Intranet

So where do you start? Start with what you have and evalu-ate your IT staff, hardware, and software. Here are some of the questions you might address:

What are the skills of my technical people? For example, are the technical resources on your intranet team skilled in Visual Basic, Java, C++ or COBOL? Do they know scripting languages such as Perl, Visual Basic Script, or JavaScript? Do they have experience in designing modern user interfaces? While there are a lot of fascinating new technologies avail-able for developing dynamic Web sites, the reality is that your choices may be constrained by the skills of the people who have been assigned to support the organization. For example, if your chief technical person is a long-time UNIX guru, the best approach might be to start with a UNIX Web server, and create interactive forms via CGI scripts written in the Bourne Shell or Perl scripting languages. On the other hand, if you have a bunch of Visual Basic programmers at

Begin by assessing the skills and strengths of your intranet developers

your disposal, a Windows NT Web server that makes use of Visual Basic Script and Microsoft Component Object Model (COM) technology might be a better choice.

Assess training needs and budget

Do I have the time and budget to train staff in new technologies like Java? Some companies decide that they want to standardize on a specific technology. In this case, make sure there is money in the budget and time in the schedule to train developers or outsource development (and possibly maintenance) of the intranet.

Web servers differ in features, ease of use, and appropriateness for large or small intranets

Will my Web server have to run on a specific operating system? Sometimes a decision has already been made about what operating system will host the new Web server. In this case, your choice of Web server and the supporting technologies will be more limited. However, you'll still have a choice among a number of Web servers and development tools, no matter which operating system you have.

Both UNIX and NT operating systems scale well enough to support large intranets

What are my scalability needs? An important issue concerning the operating system that supports the intranet is scalability. Scalability refers to the capability of a system to expand or *scale up* to support either more users or more transactions. It applies to hardware and software. An NT-based network should scale up as well as a UNIX-based network, and for a lower cost, too. Intel machines can now accommodate more than 32 processors, and so can compete with UNIX machines. Tandem Computers is preparing an NT clustering configuration that supports 64 processors. Using a combination of NT Server 4.0, Transaction Server 1.0 and SQL Server 6.5, 1.8 billion automated teller machine transactions have been processed in a 24-hour period.[4] Organizations such as NASDAQ, General Motors, and Lockheed Martin bet their business on NT operating systems.

---

4. The ATM example was offered at the Microsoft NT Scalability Day event, May 22, 1997. The purpose of the event was to demonstrate the robustness of NT and Back Office.

Will I have to use a specific Web server? Again, for reasons that are often mysterious, management will sometimes predetermine that a specific Web server needs to be used. This certainly makes technology choices easier, but it may not be the best solution. If the Web server that has been chosen does not support the other tools you feel you need to make your Web site successful, prepare some justification and fight it. Or do the best with what you have, impress your managers, and then artfully describe how you could make your site ten times better if you only had complete freedom to choose the operating system, Web server, and development tools. (Bear in mind that *better* to a manager is lower total cost of ownership and higher contribution to productivity.)

Some tools are more compatible with one server than another

How do I choose a Web server? The choice of a Web server is the most important one you will make, for it establishes the basic capabilities for performance, administration, security, content development, and site management. This is the engine that sets the pace for the rest of your intranet. Some leading choices for Web servers today are Apache, NCSA HTTPd 1.5.2a, Microsoft Internet Information Server, Netscape Enterprise Server, O'Reilly's WebSite Pro, and WebStar (for Macintosh). For overall performance and site management, Enterprise Server and Internet Information Server are very competitive. WebSite Pro is a good start-up server for less experienced developers. Apache and HTTPd are for UNIX devotees; Apache has the largest market share of all Web servers. (See "Comparison of Web Server Features" table on the next page.) These are by no means the only Web servers on the market. Two others are Novell's Intra-netware and Sun's new Solaris for Intranets for personal computer intranets.

Web servers have different capabilities, but they all operate with Internet protocols

Comparison of Web server features[5]

Web Server	Performance Monitor	Authoring Tools	Security features	Development Tools	Database Connectivity
Apache (for UNIX)	yes	no	password, domain/ IP access	CGI	no
HTTPd1.5.2a	yes	no	password, domain/ IP access	CGI	no
Enterprise	no	yes	password, domain/ IP access, SSL	CGI, server-side JavaScript and LiveWire, Java; Visigenic CORBA tools, LiveConnect	ODBC to NT, native to Informix, Oracle, Sybase, IBM DB2
IIS	yes	yes	NT challenge/ response, single logon, SSL, digital certificates	use any language and any script to create ASP applications	ODBC, OLE-DB
WebSite Pro	yes	yes	password, domain/ IP access, SSL	CGI	ODBC/SQL with iHTML Professional
WebStar	no	yes	SSL, Reams, access control	CGI, server-side Java	no

Establish minimum standards for client machines

What are the client platforms I have to support? Is it a heterogeneous environment (UNIX, Macintosh, 32-bit Windows, 16-bit Windows)? Or are the end-user systems fairly consistent (all running Windows 95 and Windows NT)? Are there any plans in place to upgrade existing workstations or to add personal computers? Are there plans to install kiosks to ensure that all employees have intranet access? Decide on a minimum hardware configuration, so that Web designers can plan applications that can run on all machines. To avoid disenfranchising some users, Web developers must design to include the lowest common

5. This table was drawn from "Look Who's Serving the Web," a review of Web servers published in *ZD Internet Magazine*, October, 1997.

Microsoft Internet Information Server (IIS)

The Microsoft Internet Information Server (IIS) provides the back-end tools to create content and build server-based Web applications for an intranet. It has six server components: Active Server pages (ASP), Microsoft Index Server, NetShow, FrontPage 97 extensions, Crystal Reports, and ISAPI.

- Active Server Pages, an open compile-free application environment
- Microsoft Index Server, an integrated search engine for full-text indexing and querying of all formats (HTML, text, and all Office documents)
- Microsoft NetShow, for streaming audio and video
- Microsoft FrontPage 97 Server Extensions, which integrates with FrontPage for publishing and managing web sites
- Crystal Reports, a visual tool for creating reports and integrating them into database applications
- ISAPI, for integrating dynamic databases

The Microsoft Internet Information Server runs on an NT server, as a free add-on.

denominator. When you're ready to implement an intranet, it's also a good time to determine if hardware needs are being met in your organization and to decide whether upgrades should be part of the plan.

Do my users need special support? Make sure your solution includes support for users of differing abilities. In particular, heavy dependence on graphics or elaborate layouts can be difficult for those with visual impairment. Think about providing a text-based alternative that can be used in conjunction with text-to-speech software. Since some people with mobility difficulties are unable to use a mouse, select a browser that has keyboard alternatives.

Plan to support users who have visual or motor impairments

Creating an IP Address
Every computer connected to the intranet must have an identifying IP address. The Internet Protocol (IP) requires a

An IP address
identifies each
computer on the
intranet

four-part numerical address (such as 251.51.51.123). Computers like numbers, but people prefer words. So they find it easier to remember IP addresses that are expressed as *friendly names* for the location of their network share (portion of a server reserved for their work group).

WINS is a dynamic
naming service for
an NT Server-based
network

The Windows Internet Naming Service (WINS) dynamically maps IP addresses to the friendly names for network resources in a Windows NT Server-based network. So one workgroup may be given space on the *Rosebud* file server, and another may frequent *RickCafe*. When they click on *RickCafe*, WINS automatically connects them with 153.43.122.123. Users of the network only have to remember movie memorabilia, rather than numbers like 153.42.122.123 (or was it 153.43.122.123?) to get to their files. And, because the system is dynamic, network administrators don't have to map the connection between the friendly name and the IP address manually .

DNS is a naming
service for UNIX

The Domain Name System is another service, like WINS, that maps friendly names to IP addresses. But DNS is used on most UNIX systems and it is static.

Connecting Everyone with TCP/IP

Creating IP addresses doesn't have to be done all at once. You can phase in connectivity by division, or by department, or even by project. There are alternatives to the tedious and time-consuming task of assigning an IP address for each and every workstation by hand.

A gateway program like Firefox's Novix software can give the IT people time to learn about managing TCP/IP before they deploy a wide scale intranet.

Use DHCP to
assign IP addresses
automatically

Another solution is to rely on DHCP (Dynamic Host Configuration Protocol) to manage frequently changing desktops and to deploy TCP/IP across the organization. Whenever a user plugs a machine into the network, the machine is

A Block of Bogus IP Addresses

Every computer on a TCP/IP network must have a unique IP address to identify it. If two computers had the same address on the Internet, there would be no way to tell which messages should go to which one. Three blocks of IP addresses have been reserved for use on private IP networks that are not connected to the Internet. Different organizations can assign any of these same addresses to individual computers on their respective intranets, as long as they do not link their network to the Internet. Routers on the Internet ignore any packets that reference addresses within these ranges.

10.0.0.0 through **10.255.255.255**, inclusive (16,777,216 available addresses)

172.16.0.0 through **172.31.255.255**, inclusive (1,048,576 available addresses)

192.168.0.0 through **192.168.255.255**, inclusive (65,536 available addresses)

These reserved addresses are convenient for use in documentation, since, like the unreal 555 telephone exchange used in movies, no computer on the Internet will ever use them.

automatically assigned an IP address on the fly. Because the process is handled dynamically, this frees network administrators from having to set IP addresses for different machines manually. DHCP is included in Windows NT and in Novell's NetWare servers.

Choosing the Development Tools

Development tools are used to create special functionality for a Web site, such as retrieving data from a database or displaying a chart. Knowing the target client platforms, and particularly the browsers currently in use (or that you will specify), can go a long way in guiding your choice of development tools. Naturally, if client upgrades are already in the works, this affects your options. Choosing development tools affects the type of content—static HTML, or enhancements via ActiveX Controls, Java applets, Visual Basic,

Develop for the lowest common denominator to ensure compatibility

JavaScript, or Dynamic HTML—that you can use on your intranet. If the users all have 32-bit Windows and Internet Explorer, all the technologies listed above can be used. However, other browsers and other operating systems may limit what will run on all platforms, as will the current skills and capabilities of your Web developers. On the server side, you can be comfortable using CGI, Active Server Pages or JavaScript, since all of them send straight HTML output to the browser.

In spite of W3C and IETF standards, browser makers have veered repeatedly from the standards to offer special features to their customers. Each new step forward leaves some people behind. If you permit people to choose their browser, it might be better to stick to straight HTML, and perhaps some animated GIF files to liven up the graphics. (But keep them small or you'll deaden performance.) You may be able to use Java applets as well. It is important to test your Web pages on all the target platforms, particularly because the Java interpreters differ among operating systems and browser brands.

Standardizing the Browser

Specifying a browser simplifies the developer's tasks at the beginning of a Web application project, and reduces support needs at the other end. In the meantime, it ties the organization together through a common interface. Both Web developers and HTML authors are spared the extra steps and time for design, creation, and testing to make sure that the content displays as well (or almost as well) in different browser environments.[6]

People might have developed strong preferences for a particular browser. If you permit choice, at least specify

---

6. In addition to browsers from different vendors supporting different features, earlier versions of a vendor's browser may not display certain tags.

which browsers will be supported (by the Help Desk and on Web pages), and provide would-be Web developers with instructions on how to get along in a multiple-browser world.

Limit browser support

Air Products and Chemicals, Inc. has allowed users to choose between using a Microsoft or a Netscape browser. Their Web Authors Standards and Guidelines specifies, under "Technical issues," that developers using ActiveX or VB Script should provide alternate pages for Netscape users. "Our external Web site supports both browsers. Internally, we run Windows 95, and Netscape is being phased out. It's just simpler to manage that way," reports Steve Cameron, Manager of Communication Programs.

Set Policies and Procedures

Besides setting the technical standards, someone will need to define policies and procedures about how people will use and participate in the intranet. Consider the following questions; there are no right or wrong answers.

Most intranets begin with chaos as their model, but standards bring control

- Who can create Web pages? Just the IT department, or any division, department, group or individual?
- Are personal pages allowed, or only business pages?
- Do the Web sites have to look the same? What type of information, if any, must be included on all Web pages?
- What tools may be used?
- What training, if any, will be provided for users or would-be Web developers?

Assuming the IT department has the infrastructure firmly in hand (by setting technical standards), the issue is *how much control does IT want or need over development of Web sites?* The answer will be a blend of purpose and culture.

Who Can Publish?

Anyone who wants to. Most companies allow any division or department or group to put up a Web site. At the Baltimore Gas and Electric Company, departments can go to creative services for writing and design. "Not many have taken advantage of that, they want to do it themselves," said Kim Ethridge, Communications Manager, BGE. "It's not like a brochure that needs to be printed, typeset—people are attracted to the technology. Our HR department has completely designed [their site], done the graphics, the whole nine yards on their own. Why? I think because they can."

Using Best Practices and Standards

Most organizations allow anyone who is capable to create a Web site, within limits

Many organizations that rely on *best practices* to leverage knowledge have created Best Practices Web guides for all aspects of Web development, from tools and pre-design planning (layout principles, navigation, formatting, and file types) to content management. Guides might include recommendations on how to optimize pages—such as using 'alt' tags that give a graphic a text name, and setting the height and width, so the server doesn't have to go back and ask for pixel dimensions. With these guides, nearly anyone can succeed at becoming a Web author.

A pre-development checklist can get new Web authors started down the right path and steer them to decisions, such as using version-control software, that will avoid known pitfalls to Web development and site maintenance.

But to be published, pages must meet certain content standards

A pre-publishing checklist can inform Web authors and Web developers of the technical requirements their Web pages must meet before they are added to the organization's intranet. For instance, a checklist might specify *meta* content— different meta tags that must be included in the header to comply with the needs of the search engine. Other items on a checklist might include requirements for displaying copyright and legal notices, as well as the name(s) of the content owner, the person responsible for receiving feedback about the site, and who is in charge of maintaining it. This last criterion—show me your maintenance plan—has become a firm requirement in most organizations (see "Updating Web Pages and Controlling Change," page 337) before permission to publish is granted.

Publishing Web Authors Standards and Guidelines—Air Products and Chemicals, Inc.

On the Air Products and Chemicals, Inc. intranet, the Web Authors Standards and Guidelines contains a wealth of information. It explains that the current Standards, Guidelines, and Best Work Practices are a baseline for developing materials for the intranet or Internet. As shown in Figure 12-2, one document, *Design Point for HTML*, includes sections on Page Content, Technical Issues, Page Style, Hypertext Links and URLs, File Naming Conventions, Inline Images and Graphics, Best Practices for HTML Authoring, Servers, and Appropriate Use.

Guidelines can include both requirements and recommendations

Standards, Guidelines, and Best Work Practices are posted on the Air Products and Chemicals Inc. intranet.

Figure 12-2

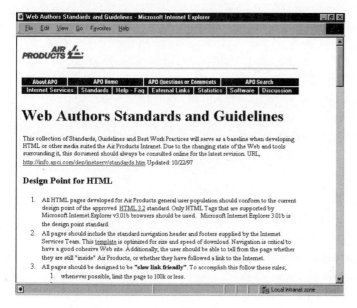

Requirements are intermixed with recommendations, but
the Design Point document is clear and simple to follow,
with embedded links to other documents and specifications.
For instance, rather than define page style, the guide points
to two links: one link is to the World Wide Web Consortium's
style guide with a notation that it is "considered prerequisite
reading for the Web Author," and the second link is to an
internal style guide.

The "Appropriate Use" section is also very direct. The first
point reminds everyone that Web servers and resources are
intended for valid business purposes. The second point
acknowledges that, "Currently individual user pages are
hosted on company Web servers. These pages are a privilege. Personalized information and creativity is encouraged
as a way to stimulate interest and develop skills. Owners of
the pages should consider other's opinions and feelings
before publishing any material that might offend someone."

Air Products and Chemicals, Inc. changed their Web server
standard from O'Reilly & Associates WebSite 1.1 to Microsoft NT 4.0 running Microsoft IIS Web server and Perl v5.
Special purpose UNIX Web servers run either Netscape
Enterprise Server or Apache Server. On the "Internet Services Team Support" Web page, there is a wealth of self-help
links, from browser settings to TCP/IP DNS Lookup (for
finding your Hostname and IP address), remote access
instructions, Cold Fusion documentation, and a list of other
documentation and tutorials—such as Adding a Web Access
Counter to a Web Page and Help with Tables.

Training Web Authors and Web Users
The need for training and support, both for authors and
users, depends on the organization's commitment to doing
business on an intranet and on the level of knowledge
within the organization. Many organizations started up
intranet training classes for users as soon as their intranet

went prime time. The Harris Corporation developed a Harris Intranet Training module[7] that also included awareness training in Internet usage.

But, as an intranet becomes part of the landscape, or as pressures of other responsibilities rise, intranet training may fall off. Putting the information on line is another way to provide the support, without the cost of classroom sessions. The previous chapter described SAFECO's *PC Rep* program as in-the-field support for users (see "Reducing Costs of Deployment and Support," page 297). For some organizations, intranet training is part of their orientation for new hires. Some people learn how to develop Web pages because they want to, not because an organization provides formal training. Online discussion lists can serve as a place to ask for help on a specific issue or to offer new information.

> Create a Web site to post information about how to use the intranet

At Air Products and Chemicals, Inc., the Webauthors' Group meets about once a month. They review tools and provide tips. At one meeting two Internet Services team summer interns gave presentations on using Microsoft FrontPage and FormMail, a generic mail script that can handle HTML forms. APCI also offers on line "A Beginner's Guide to HTML" on the Webauthors' Group Web site.

> A Web authors group can transfer knowledge about Web development

Northrop Grumman created a Web Developer's Kit (WDK) for the fledgling Web adventurer. The WDK is a set of tools and instructions, based on FrontPage, on one Web site. It provides answers to questions such as *how do I create a Web site?* and *what tools do I use?* and *whom do I contact about hosting a site?* "The release of the Web Developer's Kit was a turning point. We went from managed chaos to a managed environment," said Natalie Stone, Chief Architect for Internal Information Systems at Northrop Grumman.

> Northrop Grumman created their own developer's kit

---

7. Harris has also developed World Wide Web Usage—Guidelines for ESS (Electronic Systems Sector) training structured along the lines of Benefits, Awareness, and Do's and Dont's. This educational guide alerts employees to assumptions that could create vulnerabilities, and points as well to opportunities of WWW usage.

Move from "Nice to Have" to "Business-Critical"

Change on an intranet is gradual, application by application

With each new application, Web developers and users gain new skills and insights about how to use the intranet to solve problems and improve productivity. Consider these four criteria as benchmarks for taking your intranet to the next level:

- How will the application scale to handle hundreds or thousands of users?
- Do you have sound systems management and monitoring support in place?
- Do you need transaction support, not just for financial transactions, but for in-house ordering as well?
- What new levels of security do you need to employ?

"At Air Products, our intranet has grown—I wouldn't like to call it chaotically—it's growing in a less controlled manner than our Internet [Web] site," said Steve Cameron, Manager of Communications Programs at APCI. "There are many department home pages, and some of the larger groups have either hired someone or assigned someone within their department to take the responsibility. At first, it's fun. Then, when it's 'Let's keep this thing updated,' it becomes a job." At APCI each of the main groups—Gas and Equipment, Chemicals, Corporate—have a professional Web developer in the group.

Web responsibilities become part of the job, not an on-the-side activity

Part of the step from *nice to have* to *business-critical* involves having adequate funds not only to make network, hardware and software upgrades, but also to staff Web developer and Web editor positions. As long as Web contributors are squeezing Web work around their *real work*, the intranet is a second class citizen. Until job descriptions reflect Web duties, the intranet is nice, but not really necessary.

Consider the Costs

As your intranet matures, and attracts more users who make more creative demands of Web developers, costs can escalate. Long-range planning should take into consideration the following cost categories:

Growth means increased costs

- Personnel
- Training (developers and users)
- Hardware (network equipment, servers, clients)
- Software (including Web server, development tools, database, graphics tools)

Developing any custom application can be a costly proposition, depending on the expectations of internal customers and the ambitiousness of the undertaking. Using object technology and templates speeds development, but still, the cycle of development, testing, and deployment is long and, with new technologies, sometimes hard to predict.

Custom applications can be costly

One of the best defenses in keeping costs controlled is to control the development process. And this begins with planning—with a customer-developer team jointly developing specifications that identify the need and the functionality and a solution that will work for the customer, for the developers, for the users, and the Help Desk who has to support it. Just like constructing a building, making changes mid-stream is expensive. Kimberly Tripp, a consulting database architect, used to post a sign on her door when starting a new project, "The sooner we start [to write code], the longer it will take."

Mid-stream changes are expensive

Address Performance Issues

If performance slows, users will become frustrated and the intranet will draw down productivity instead of enabling it. Some portions of the network may experience more slowness than others.

Speed and reliability are important

Bandwidth

Create a profile of network performance before deploying the intranet, and keep track of any ongoing major changes outside the intranet that might affect performance, such as a division's granting Internet access to all their employees. That way, you should have a baseline from which to compare how the new intranet is affecting the network.

Isolate and solve local problems

Factors that will affect the bandwidth include the network topology (number of bridges, routers, subnets, and so forth), number of simultaneous users, amount of data contained within pages, type of multimedia, and protocols in use. You can solve local slow-downs with local solutions. For instance, if one group is engaging in video conferencing, that portion of the network can be upgraded, or a separate pipe can be installed to provide the capacity for video, and to keep the rest of the data rolling.

Take slow remote connections into account

Does the network consist of all 10 Mb/s Ethernet connections or are there dial-in connections too? A slow Web site will quickly lose its audience, especially on an intranet where things are expected to be fast. Be sure to think about all your users, not just those at the office or production area. Over a remote connection, Web pages will take longer to appear than they will over a direct LAN connection.

Use graphics sparingly and with care

A common mistake for the beginning Web designer is to use too many graphics or pictures that are too large. The result is pages that take forever to appear, especially if it's a high traffic site. Certainly there is much to be said for a visually appealing Web site, but often this can be accomplished more easily and efficiently through the use of a few small, consistently-implemented design elements.

Security Overhead

Of course it's important to make sure only authorized people have access to each Web site. Users also need to feel confident that data is protected. A unified security environment such as that provided by Windows NT can make this easier. Webmasters can allow or prohibit people access to their site, or parts of their site, based on a Windows user or group ID, with little or no effect on performance.

Select a security level to avoid crushing performance

The right amount of security is a good thing, but overzealous use of security technology can also affect performance. Encrypting data slows things down on the sending side; decrypting slows things down on the receiving side. In addition, the information needed to decrypt can often add to the size of the information being sent. Use the appropriate amount of security for the data.

Encryption and decryption slow the process

For special cases, such as the transmission of very confidential information (corporate financial data or customer transactions and such), you may wish to use SSL encryption. SSL encrypts and then decrypts every packet. With any protection measure, evaluate the cost of the loss of data (including time and effort to restore it and potential competitive disadvantage) in relation to the effect of the security measure on the network. You have to find the proper balance between speed of access and security.

Weigh the need for speed against the cost of loss

Looking Ahead

Intranets are susceptible to the dynamics of a life cycle. There is the first rush of enthusiasm; it blooms. Everyone wants to get on line and be part of the new world. The tide of enthusiasm overrides the difficulties—time constraints and tools-learning—and pages wondrously appear. A buzz circulates about new pages or new innovations.

The beginning is always exciting

But before long, other duties and responsibilities flood back in—and updates may be a little slower in coming. The advisory group's meetings might become irregular because of the pressure of other assigned priorities. These conditions signal an adjustment phase.

Then the novelty wears off

Focus on the benefits and look forward to your intranet's evolution

An intranet cannot sustain itself on hopes and enthusiasm. Unless there is a plan for maintenance and sufficient resources are allocated—both funding and job time—the intranet will not thrive. Remember that an intranet is a work-in-progress. Look to the business value of your intranet—what has it enabled, and what does evaluation data reveal? The next chapter, "Maintenance and Evaluation," addresses handling site maintenance issues, infrastructure needs, the change-management process, and ways to keep alert to new and useful technologies.

Chapter Thirteen

Maintenance and Evaluation

In the olden days, information technology used to serve systems—the accounting system, the production system, and so on. Today, technology tries to serve its users, especially with an intranet. But users are not as orderly or as easy to manage as systems.

The chief challenge of an intranet is not maintaining the momentum—most behave like a cartoon snowball rolling downhill—but maintaining the light touch of control, while guiding it towards ever increasing productivity. To maintain the intranet, you will need administrative tools, enforceable policies, a commitment to upgrade skills and knowledge on a continuing basis, and the vigilance to keep your efforts aligned with the business value of the intranet. The commitment to keeping current is crucial.

Maintenance doesn't mean standing still

Whether you consider your intranet an exercise in democracy or anarchy, you can count on it's being more challenging to manage than a traditional client/server network. In the olden days, the IT people were in charge of data. As keepers of the technology, these specialists managed the network and the applications. Now, you have *non-professionals* careening around data on the intranet, like conventioneers in bumper cars.

Today, everyone is a player on an intranet

331

IT staff, Web managers, and content developers face different challenges

In this free-for-all environment, there will be new challenges to maintain service and security, which are as ideologically different as can be. As your intranet grows, the ability to get on line will quickly shift from being a privilege to a business requirement. As more and more critical data is accessible from a browser, controls must be in place to limit access. The IT staff will be challenged anew with load balancing and network security. Those responsible for the Web and its contents will wrestle with document version control and access to information. Organizations want to be able to engage in e-mail, discussion groups, workflow, decision support, and document management, and to run the bandwidth-intensive graphical user interfaces that speed user performance.

Monitor for shifts in intranet load

This means more people will affect network load in some unpredictable ways. In some cases, load may shift. For instance, one company reported that before they developed an intranet, department newsletters used to be distributed as e-mail attachments, often bogging down mail servers at the end of the month. Now that newsletters are posted on department Web sites, the load has shifted away from mail servers to Web servers. The fact that changes will occur, not only in volume of use, but in needed resources, makes it all the more important to monitor the network, keep security patches up to date, and to exhort users to take an active role in maintaining a secure computing environment.

Intranet maintenance must be a collaborative effort

It will take the combined efforts of network administrators, Web developers, content developers, and rank and file intranet users working together to maintain a secure and productive information environment.

Outsourcing and Out-tasking

One way to maintain your intranet is to hand over the keys to a professional intranet management company. Many organizations in the public and private sectors have found that outsourcing IT functions is cost effective, and that it enables them to concentrate on their core business functions.[1] Outsourcing management of an intranet is consistent with this trend.

Outsourcing Web Management

There are many ways to use outsourcing as a management solution for maintaining your intranet. The arrangements and the costs depend on the size and complexity of your intranet.

Outsourcing solutions vary

If your goal for your intranet is to publish non-confidential company information for employees, one of the easiest solutions is to contract with an outside agency to host your site. You would supply Web-ready content and that agency would manage the server and network connections. Typically, the outside management firm would maintain your servers (or rent space to you on theirs) on their site. To access your intranet, you would either use a direct connection (T1 or 56 Kb line) to their site or dial in through an Internet Service Provider.

Create content in-house, then use an off-site host

An outside management firm can also furnish monitoring reports. These reports should include overall usage, and at least the number of hits per page. This data will help you to determine what your employees are interested in and to set priorities for keeping pages current or making changes.

The host agency provides monitoring reports

Some organizations that use their intranet for information management and knowledge-working prefer to keep company data on company premises. As mentioned in Chapter 10 (see "ARAMARK Intranet Started on Campus", page 275), John Kallelis, Vice President of Information Technology for ARAMARK, got their intranet started by taking advantage of

You can always move your intranet back on-site

---

1. In some cases, organizations have chosen to outsource support for remote users, as configuring and supporting mobile users typically absorbs disproportionate amounts of IT staff time.

AT&T's Web hosting program. Their long-range plan has been to move the intranet inside, not for reasons of cost but for better control as they move beyond publishing to Web applications accessing databases on LANs.

Before You Sign up for Outsourcing

Specify service level agreements and security plans

Before even interviewing applicants to manage your intranet, you need to do your planning homework—long-term planning as well as short-term. In particular, you should be clear about security and service quality standards. Before proceeding, your organization needs to decide if you're going to have secure areas, and what will be your strategy for access control, such as the use of the Secure HyperText Transfer Protocol or digital signatures. You should receive in writing from applicants a detailed plan about how they will guard the intellectual assets on your intranet. What measures, and backup measures, would they put in place? And when it comes to cost, is the value of their service commensurate with the full cost—in terms of people, hardware, and hassle—of maintaining the intranet yourself? Finally, the contract itself should include service level agreements, plus a process for a graceful termination, because it's not a perfect world.

Still, you must supervise

Before the final handshake, be aware that outsourcing an intranet requires ongoing monitoring and supervision of the vendor, plus perpetual evaluation that the service levels are acceptable.

Consider Out-tasking

Outsource specific tasks instead of the whole project

In network parlance, out-tasking means buying unbundled network services, instead of a vendor's full outsourcing package. Another solution to the problem of maintaining the staff to run an intranet is to out-task specific roles such as Web Editor, Webmaster, application developers, and graphic artists. On the other hand, outside vendors may not appreciate the nuances of how a customized application enables your business. You should evaluate the roles carefully and assign some tasks to internal staff—making it part of their official job descriptions—where it makes good business sense.

Organizations that must maintain absolute confidentiality for their clients' data, such as financial institutions, may be more comfortable with out-tasking performance monitoring, while shouldering full responsibility for managing their network themselves. Out-tasking vendors configure and install the equipment they need (both hardware and software) to collect performance data and produce reports. Performance monitoring is an important aspect of intranet management (see "Monitoring Performance," page 342).

Consider confidentiality requirements

Creating Service Level Agreements

Whether your intranet is being managed on the outside or the inside, there is a real benefit to creating service level agreements. These agreements should spell out all expectations between interested parties, and can be an important element in long-range planning. Each participant in an intranet may have a different set of priorities and opinions about resolution. A service level agreement should get them all out on the table.

SLAs clarify expectations

"When we first delivered," said Alex Bruty, consultant for the London Underground intranet, "it was pretty lucky if we had a couple of pictures—it was mostly text…Now we have people whose expectations have gone up, and they're asking 'Why hasn't the content provider updated it?… A company has to tighten up its production processes, and in effect, we need to have service level agreements between IT and content providers." For the London Underground, (see Figure 13-1 on the next page), service level agreements work both ways. For instance, the technical side agrees to keep the links working and to post changes within a certain

Clear procedures make it easier for technical staff and content providers to work together number of days. And if content providers want new material to go on line every Monday morning, then, according to their SLA, they have to deliver it by Thursday afternoon.

Figure 13-1   ***London Underground intranet page.***

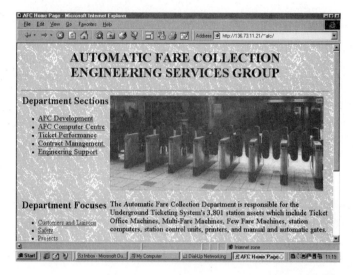

Gather monitoring data as a baseline of performance

Service level agreements may start with analyzing performance data and enumerating technical requirements. Users will have opinions about what constitutes adequate support and time frames for high use. IT staff will have their concerns about bandwidth, response times, scheduling backups, and system maintenance. Together, IT and users should develop a priority system for service, based on business needs. Operating under an SLA also helps support personnel to avoid being flagged down and dragged into someone's office to fix a problem, instead of having users go through channels to log the problem. Openly discussing needs for service and limitations will improve relations.

Provide a means for users to contribute feedback

Devising a method for exchanging feedback is an important part of maintaining an intranet. Feedback should be part of the SLA, as well as an item on each and every Web site on the intranet.

Updating Web Pages
and Controlling Change

You start your intranet talking about hyperlinks, but before long, you'll be talking about its *hypergrowth*. Managing links and keeping content updated in an expanding universe is a larger and larger job. If Web site owners don't keep the sites updated, they'll drift like space junk. If the only person authorized to change a Web file is the Webmaster, your changes might be implemented sometime after colonizing the Sun. As you already know, an intranet that offers out-of-date information is not doing its job.

Ted Wagner, Air Products and Chemical, Inc. Webmaster, believes in getting out of the way. "I knew it was going to be absolutely impossible for MIS to be gatekeeper or service provider. The whole thing was to connect users with their own publishing media—whether databases or HTML files, give every user in the company a means to publish. If you stick MIS in the middle, you drastically reduce value, or create a bottleneck. The thing is so big, it's the only strategy that works."

Specify Responsibilities of Site Owners

"Show me the maintenance plan," said the Webmaster of a financial services organization, "then, we'll talk about the procedures for posting your Web site on line." Many organizations outline very specific responsibilities of a Web site owner. It's good policy to insist that each page include the Web site owner's name, the person responsible for changes, and the date of the last update. It's also a good idea to specify the length of time that a site may remain dormant—no changes—before it is removed from the server.

As shown in Figure 13-2, on the next page, the first page of the BC Hydro Web Intranet Content Creation Policies and Procedures spells out what's expected for Web site owners. The third point specifies that all sites will have an identified

Maintaining content and managing links is an ever-expanding job

Don't create an MIS bottleneck

Require site owners to have a maintenance plan

BC Hydro enforces their requirement for updating content

owner. The fourth point declares: "All web content owners will be responsible for the currency of ownership information and will ensure that web content is regularly reviewed and updated or deleted as necessary. *This will be strictly enforced.* Note that, eventually, Intranet page related services (e.g., disk space) will be charged to the owner." The BC Hydro guide also specifies:

- "Information that is more than 6 months old will be considered 'stale' and the owner will be contacted to verify the validity of the application or information.

- Information that is found to be out of date or inaccurate will be removed from the Web until it is updated. 'No information is better than wrong information.' The content provider is responsible for guaranteeing the currency and accuracy of the information."

Figure 13-2   ***BC Hydro Web Intranet Content Creation Policies and Procedures.***

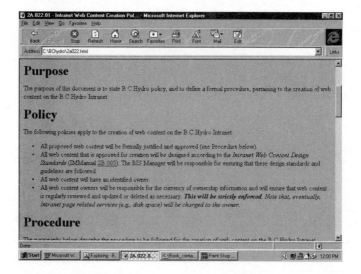

Automate Web Content Updates

Naturally, the more content owners can use automation to update their sites, the more frequently the sites will be updated. At Baltimore Gas and Electric, Kim Ethridge aims to get the day's news on line by noon. "Some days, it's not ready until 12:15. We tried contacting the [Information Systems department] as needed, but they'd be at lunch or maybe in a meeting, so the solution was to automate it." Information Systems developed a routine that automatically checks a folder for new information for the JUST NEWS section of Route 96, BGE's intranet. Between 7 a.m. and 7 p.m., the program checks each hour. Between 11 a.m. and 1 p.m., it checks every quarter hour. "If I have the day's news ready at 11:30, it checks, takes it right out of the development server folder, and pops it onto the Web."

Where possible, use automation to maintain sites

Institute a Change-Management Process

If you are hearing comments such as "Somebody moved the Web site to a different server location, and the links don't work!" or "We were both editing copies of the same file at the same time; I finished first, but then her changes over-wrote mine!" or "Who made *that* change?" it's time to put in place a *change-management process*. Change-management processes have been de rigueur in the software industry for years.

Implementing a change-management process for your intranet is imperative

Version control A version-control product sets up strict procedures for who may have access to and control of files under development—HTML or any other type of file. The process of checking a file out and in controls the sequences in which changes will be recorded.

Version control manages access and alteration

Software developers were the first to rely on Microsoft Visual SourceSafe (VSS). You may already have a copy if you own Microsoft FrontPage, Microsoft Visual InterDev, Microsoft Visual Basic Pro, or Microsoft NT 4.0 Enterprise Edition. Now Web developers (professionals and user-

VSS is well-suited to
intranet development

developers) can employ it to control HTML documents and
Java code. Visual SourceSafe has several features that suit it
to Web site content control from development through to
launch. As shown in Figure 13-3, VSS maintains a log on
each file to track who checked the file out and when the file
was checked back in. It also has a note area for comments
during check-in. VSS also assures that links are in good
working order. After development, testing, and code freeze,
VSS manages branching and implementing[2] the site.

Figure 13-3   *Visual SourceSafe keeps a log of who checked files out and in.*

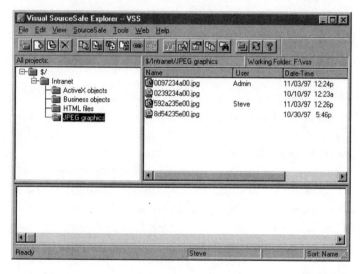

Using relative path
names for links
reduces potential
housekeeping chores

Site Housekeeping Another important aspect of site maintenance is assuring that all links are working and that the site
is in good health. There are some steps you can take when
creating HTML files to ease the complexity of maintaining a
site. For instance, assigning relative path names, rather than
absolute path names, makes it easier to move Web page
files and have them maintain the same relationship to each

---

2. VSS can be used to branch or replicate that code. The release branch is
    posted online and the development branch is ready for a new cycle of
    changes.

Updating Files

Having two copies of a file for a Web page may seem like a safety precaution, but duplicate documents eventually will diverge. To avoid this problem, put your trust in one copy. Actually, it's not blind faith; your intranet should have a mirror or backup site that will still contain the old file. Here are three steps you can take to manage Web page updates:

- Use dynamic updating; create scripts that update pages automatically.
- Use version control software, such as Visual SourceSafe, which acts like the reserve section of the public library. Anyone (who has permission) has to check the file out to work on it, then check it back in.
- Use push technology to create an internal channel for updating a Web site.[3]

However you manage it, institute a uniform plan to control change. Procedures for changing content on a Web site are important additions to a Web policy manual.

other. But as a site grows, *orphans* (files without links pointing to them) and duplicates take up space on the Web server, and can contribute to degraded performance. The most common reason individual file links become broken is that the name of the target file has been changed. The fact that link references are case-sensitive makes file management even more difficult.

Web site creation and management tools have special features that make housekeeping easier on Web sites. For instance, the All Files View in FrontPage 98 Explorer gives a single flat view to all the files on a Web site. There are also several specialty software programs that will check links and do other site housekeeping chores as well. Tetranet's Linkbot can be scheduled to find and fix broken links and to identify slow pages and old pages that need updating. Imagiware's

Some Web programs will check links and perform housekeeping functions for you

---

3. A Web server can act as a client to receive data pushed from another server. The Web server's administrator would request that this "client" (aka Web server) receive updates through the channel.

Doctor HTML is another Web analysis tool that checks spelling, verifies links, and checks document structure.

Monitoring Performance

Now that you have an intranet, the way people do their jobs has changed. E-mail replaces phone calls; e-mail with file attachments replaces overnight packages. Where they used to receive a fax, they download a document from a file server on the network or from the Internet. And, unless you tell them not to, they'll be downloading multimegabytes of video and audio files. And somebody (who has read Chapter 8, Distance Learning) is waving the flag for online training.

An intranet will, in most circumstances, increase network traffic

With the onslaught of intranet and Internet users, plus an increase in Web applications, the concern is that bandwidth constraints will hamper productivity. An increase in the total volume of traffic over your network may have already slowed down your production transactions, and customers may be starting to complain about the reduced level of service. Slowdowns are caused by an increase in the number of transactions that are taking place on the network. For example, the new personnel questionnaires on the intranet, which reduce the need for phone calls requesting information, increase the total number of transactions, which in turn leads to an overall increase in network load. Web pages have varying effects on network performance. Pages with large graphics, audio, or video files will have a dramatic impact on the total speed of the network. These types of files will slow the total number of transactions that occur over your entire network. This problem may worsen when mission-critical applications are ported to the intranet. Declining performance increases user frustration and can be reflected in declining user productivity.

The wonderful flexibility that an intranet supplies also plays havoc with planning for progressive network expansion. One of the challenges for network administrators in maintaining an intranet is to define *average use*. When IT controlled the client/server network and applications, usage levels were fairly predictable, but not any more. Some experts advise that a network manager should use any change as an opportunity to increase capacity. They contend that it is no longer safe to design a network for average use (being unable to define it), and like electric utilities, they must design to serve peak demand. In one view, this is over-building; in another view, it's building-in needed flexibility.

Experts disagree about whether to build for average use or peak use

As network administrators wrestle with the changes an intranet is introducing to their orderly network, the questions that they will want to address include:

Evaluate your situation

- How can we guarantee users there will be enough bandwidth?
- How close are we to capacity?
- Can we adjust network allocations, temporarily?
- How can we improve efficiency?
- How do we validate quality of service (and service levels) of an ISP?
- How do we allocate charge-back?

One part of the solution is a way to monitor traffic and then manage network resources on a real-time basis. Another part of the solution is to maintain some control of a growing intranet by placing some controls on what can be posted on the intranet. At BC Hydro, potential Web site owners fill out a checklist that estimates the size of a typical page, whether the content requires connection to a database, if special search capabilities are needed, and expectations for growth ("Will the site double in size in the next 6 to 12 months?") This information is useful for network planning.

Solutions include a mixture of control through advance planning and real-time monitoring of resources

"We have many remote offices on shared 28.8 lines that have to get to the same information as users on our WAN in Vancouver," Steve Whan, BC Hydro Webmaster wrote in e-

Consider setting size limitations

mail. Because of this limitation, Web content providers are given size limitations. "Essentially, pages must be less than 30 [Kb] with no more than 7 calls [per page] to the server."

Monitoring—Alert the Bandwidth Police

Monitor trans-
actions size as
well as volume

Monitoring enables early decision-making. A good monitoring plan should monitor not only traffic and total transactions, but also the size of each transaction as it moves across your Intranet. A monitoring program should also identify problem areas and bottlenecks. Having a good monitoring program in place should reduce intranet cost as well as build justification for new investments and upgrades or measures to control bandwidth usage.

Allocate bandwidth
to accommodate
special needs

To accommodate both bandwidth constraints and users' needs, network administrators can allocate bandwidth usage based on policy. Ideally, they need the flexibility to allocate it on a temporary or permanent basis, for a specific time frame or for certain hours in response to business needs. For example, if a videoconference is planned, an administrator should be able to temporarily allocate sufficient bandwidth to handle this need, and then return to the default network settings.

Use software tools
to monitor real-
time performance

There are numerous monitoring packages available. A hybrid hardware/software device by Aponet Inc., the Bandwidth Policy Monitor, can monitor real-time intranet and Internet bandwidth usage and display the results in a graph (see Figure 13-4). By attaching the hardware component to routers or other devices, it can monitor traffic from specific IP addresses, groups of addresses, or TCP-based applications (FTP, HTTP, Telnet, and SMTP). Usage data can be ported to a spreadsheet or database application for analysis or charge-back (Aponet's SmartAudit software product adds the capability to generate the accounting information required for charging different business units their fair share of network costs.)

Aponet's Bandwidth Policy Monitor displays results in a graph.   *Figure 13-4*

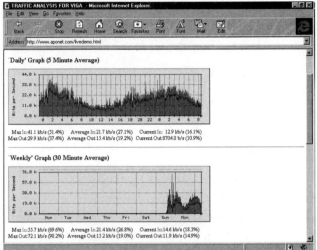

Reports on network performance serve several purposes. Report data is often used to validate users' experiences. The data can also be used to verify whether an SLA is being met. And perhaps most importantly, these reports can provide useful benchmark data from which to plan and build improvements. For example, if response time for user support showed signs of increasing steadily, then the situation might warrant hiring additional staff or providing additional training.

Ongoing performance data collection serves long-range planning

Network Evaluation—Testing the Waters

Before deploying a Web application, developers and network administrators can use tools to evaluate the effect of the new intranet product on the network. Traffic simulation programs help administrators decide the most efficient way to configure and deliver new services or applications. Web application developers can test applications or networks with the various traffic volumes and patterns that occur on their network. For instance, administrators can test *what if?* scenarios by changing bandwidth or the number of users who engage in receiving Webcasts. Programs like these let network administrators find problems before their users do.

Stress tests or simulations can determine the effect of a change on a network

Software tools can assist you in making predictions	A software product named Chariot by Ganymede, a builder of performance management products for multi-protocol networks, evaluates performance and capacity of network devices (such as routers, switches, adapters) and network software. Chariot also includes scripts that will aid administrators in predicting the effect of push tools such as Castanet, by Marimba Inc., and PointCast.

Enhancing Performance

Evaluate your server as well as your database management system	If you determine that your intranet is straining your bandwidth and slowing operations, you have several options to explore.[4] Sometimes performance is determined more by the hardware and physical database configuration on the backend server than by the network equipment. Depending on the type of database transactions that occur and the total number of hits, you will need to decide if your existing database management system and the physical server are adequate. Also, there may be improvements you can make to the physical database model. For instance, using integers instead of text or concatenated primary keys can increase the speed of database access.

Consider creating a data warehouse	Another good idea for improving performance is to create a data warehouse, on a server separate from your production machines, that contains extracts of information needed by your intranet applications. You can update the warehouse as often as needed. However, depending upon the amount of data that is liable to be requested, it's a good idea to run tests to determine the best time to execute the update jobs. Usually cyclical down times like lunch time or after business hours will have less impact on production systems.

Upgrades Other areas for possible change or upgrade include your database software, servers, subnets, and bandwidth.

---

4. A slowdown could occur during any phase of a transaction: client communication over the network to the server, the server processing, or server communicating over the network to the client.

Upgrade your database software when new versions offer significant changes. Some upgrades offer neat front-end gadgets and widgets, without a real effect on the actual performance of the database engine. Any changes to your database management system that affects overall performance with regard to SQL (Structured Query Language) transaction speeds, index improvements, or direct database engine enhancements should be incorporated into your software maintenance schedules.

Database software upgrades often bring speedier access

Upgrade your servers. The decision to upgrade servers will depend upon the total load your system is carrying. It is a standard rule that you should have one Mb of RAM for every existing or new user.[5]

An increase in users requires an increase in RAM

Put your intranet on a different subnet, not connected to your production environment. Production databases can be accessed through the Active Server Pages (ASP), CGI script, or a direct database call; page access can be routed around the production environment. This may be the best solution. It usually entails adding a gateway to your existing network, adding the appropriate wire, and making sure your employees use the correct proxy server from their browser for any internal pages. The separate subnet option could be the easiest way to ensure the integrity of your production environment.

Use subnets to separate your production environment from your intranet

Upgrade your network to a higher bandwidth. This, however, will be the most expensive option. For example,

Increase bandwidth

---

5. It's also important to make sure you have adequate backup and mirrors on your site. Depending upon the importance of the information, an additional server can be used as both a backup and a mirror. However, to be open 7 by 24, you may need to include an additional server as a secondary mirror. Each of the servers should be on a separate uninterrupted power supply (UPS), and have an entirely separate power supply coming from a different power station or power company. Oftentimes you can use a testing server as your mirror or backup. However, you need to make sure your mirror server contains the updated production pages and the page links are set up correctly. Depending upon the importance of the information, you may want to run daily tests should you need to switch to your mirrored server.

moving from 10baseT to 100baseT may not cost much at all, other than upgrading your hubs, routers and network interface cards on your servers and clients, assuming your network line is category 5 wire and can handle 100baseT throughput. However, if you are running on old category 3 wire that only supports ten megabytes per second (10baseT), the cost of upgrading to a higher category (category 5 or fiber optics may be cost prohibitive.[6])

Clustering can distribute load across servers

Clusters As an intranet grows, servers and communication links may buckle under the strain of additional users, and the end result is a distributed infrastructure. This works for information, but makes it hard to maintain access control and application add-ons. One way to distribute network load across several servers and maintain computing availability to end users is by clustering.

Clustering involves three functions: fault tolerance (also called failover), load balancing, and centralized administration and monitoring.

- Fault tolerance ensures there is a backup to carry the load for a failed resource (a server, router, or network). In a client/server network, the solution entails additional servers, disk mirroring or replication, or redundancy of network connections to reduce communications failure.

---

6. Category 3, 5, or fiber optics refers to the type of wire used to transfer data across your intranet. Category 3 is analogous to a two-lane road with potholes. Because it's unshielded, interference from electrical, microwave, or radio sources can cause data loss within the line. This type of wire can only support 10 megabytes per second transfer rates. Category 5 would be like a four-lane freeway. It is shielded wire (so data losses will not occur due to electrical, microwave, or radio sources) and has a data-tranfer rate of 100 megabytes per second. The final type is fiber optics. This type of wire is like a four-lane divided freeway. With fiber optics, the data transfer rate is limited only by the types of hubs, routers, network interface cards, and workstation bus speeds. Because light is used to transfer data, interference does not occur.

- Load balancing is the process of detecting overload of one resource and distributing the load to other resources, without dropping load.
- Centralized management of clustered servers means managing the servers from one workstation, whether the task is troubleshooting or routine maintenance.

There are several products on the market that offer one, two, or all of these capabilities. At this point, NT 4.0 can cluster two servers with Wolfpack technology.

Maintaining Security

Because control of data may become more decentralized with the introduction of an intranet, it's imperative that an organization establishes and promulgates policies on security. A good policy would detail access rights and responsibilities. Section 3.0 Policy of the ARAMARK Corporate Intranet Policy Manual details the security responsibilities of the business unit that sponsors a Web site. The section addresses managing authentication and encryption, passwords, firewall software, and virus software updates. It also places the highest priority on requiring immediate notification to the MIS Administrator or Web Administrator when an employee's permission to access the intranet is withdrawn.

A well-defined security policy underscores responsibility

Nevertheless, yesterday's security policies and products will not protect you from tomorrow's attacks. It is very important to be vigilant about installing software patches to firewalls and servers. You might inquire in advance what constitutes a free patch, and what determines an upgrade you must buy to fix a security hole. Regardless, like a seat belt, a patch or virus detection only works if you use it.

Install service patches immediately to plug leaks

Every major server and browser vendor posts on their Internet sites antidotes to known weaknesses in their products. The official NT security source is www.microsoft.com/security

Find new virus antidotes on line

Using the Internet to Keep Up with Hackers

Ironically, one of the best ways to keep up to date about hacks is on the Internet. The fact that, in 1997, NT servers gained the attention of hackers is a back-handed compliment from the hacking community about the market gains of NT servers. The L0pht, a band of Boston-based *white hat* hackers, worked over UNIX, Novell Netware, and IBM's Lotus Domino before turning their attention to NT.

The Nomad Mobile Research Center maintains the Unofficial NT Hack FAQ on its Web site (http://www.nmrc.org). This well-organized guide contains information about how one might break into an NT system, and what actions will prevent it. The guide explains *the ping of death,*[7] numerous *denial of service*[8] (DOS) attacks, Samba,[9] and certain quirks of the NT file system (NTFS) and access controls. Some particularly surprising reading can be found under 07-1: "How do I bypass the screen saver?" The most reassuring FAQ on the Nomad Mobile Research Center site is 11-1: "How do I secure my server?" The list suggests using auditing heavily if connected to the Internet, reading logs daily, loading the latest service packs, and "Re-read this FAQ and note every time you see 'this attack won't work if the Sys Admin did...' and actually do it."

Another interesting source of current information is http://www.ntsecurity.net, which offers as its motto the words spoken by Wednesday Addams, "Be afraid. Be very afraid," to set the tone. This site posts reports, organized chronologically, of specific hacks and solutions. It details the systems affected (specific browsers and servers), specific explanations of the hack (including the code), and steps to prevent invasion.

---

7. Ping is a program normally used to test network connectivity between machines. It uses ICMP protocol's ECHO_REQUEST to elicit an ICMP ECHO_RESPONSE from the target. The "ping of death" overwhelms the target. Because of the large size of the packet, the buffer bogs down when it tries to reassemble the ping and overflows, causing unpredictable results, such as reboots or hangs.

8. A "denial of service" attack effectively closes down a Web site. It is caused by the bombardment of a site with such a high volume of requests that the servers become overloaded and have to *deny service* to would-be site visitors. This type of attack is often directed at a target with whom the attacker has a strong philosophical difference.

9. Samba is a freeware tool developed by Andy Tridgell for helping integrate UNIX into Microsoft Windows and LAN Manager environments. With Samba you can allow a UNIX machine to access file and directories and, as with most UNIX freeware, you get the source code.

for Service Packs and Hot Fixes. Hot Fixes are triage, but because they are so quickly issued, they are released with disclaimers about unanticipated interactions.

Maintaining security requires human resources

To maintain security on an intranet, network staff must maintain firewalls, take steps to ensure server security, protect network administration functions (such as passwords and network configurations) from discovery, and make sure users keep their virus protection software up to date. On a daily basis, staff must analyze logs to spot attempts to invade secure areas. In addition, staff needs time and resources to keep informed about potential new threats and solutions.

To ensure that users have in hand the latest virus protection software, rather than trusting that they will seek it out and download it, consider using push technology to deliver it. It's easy for people to procrastinate or even completely forget about upgrading their protection software, but when it's sent *special delivery*, it also sends a message about the importance of keeping up to date.

Use push technology to deliver virus protection updates

NCSA Surveys About Firewalls and Security

The National Computer Security Association (NCSA) occasionally surveys network managers to see how they are dealing with threats from viruses and other assaults on the security of their networks. In 1997, NCSA found that only 61 percent of the more than 125 managers surveyed had installed firewalls. That's bad. And they found that *all* of them had reported problems in managing their firewalls. That's really bad. More than 60 percent reported that firewall installation was a problem.

NCSA found that the main types of attacks sustained by companies with firewalls were *denial of service*, sendmail attacks, port scanning, IP spoofing, and mail bombs. The survey also showed that many firms were outsourcing firewall security because of the complexity. NCSA concluded that network managers can secure their networks, as long as they have adequate financial and human resources.

VSAT may provide
an inexpensive,
secure alternative to
WAN connections

Besides dealing with the day-to-day details of maintaining a secure environment, network and Web administrators also need time and resources to explore more secure ways of doing business. For instance, what are the implications of using wireless technology to connect remote locations? What would be the effect on the network of deploying a VSAT (very small aperture terminal) satellite network, instead of landlines? It might reduce monthly access fees for dial-in lines and also provide a more secure intranet environment. Data is encrypted, and satellites only recognize IP addresses assigned to stations on the network, so there is no need for a firewall. VSAT is packet technology similar to X.25: it uses Time Division—Multiple Access (TDMA) wireless technology.

Security vendors
must offer support as
well as protection

Security vendors are under the gun to keep pace with the new intranet products and technologies, too. This means not only creating bulletproof protection, but also accommodating new services. For instance, in mid-year 1997, Trusted Information Systems Inc., maker of the Guardian firewall system, announced support for Microsoft NetShow 2.0. This means that an organization can deliver live presentations (or stored files) to extranet partners or remote access intranet users.

Looking Ahead

The final chapter, "Looking Further Ahead," explores horizon technologies and trends that may expand the capabilities of intranets. Some of these technologies are here now, but they are not yet mature enough to have made significant contributions to productivity.

Chapter Fourteen

Looking Further Ahead

New developments in data distribution, retrieval, and display technologies that are not yet mainstream may provide opportunities for organizations that are using intranets to achieve their business goals. In addition, the types of applications in use, plus the resolution of cultural and access issues will also continue to influence the effectiveness of intranets.

In mid-1997, just four years after the invention of the first Internet browser, the META Group Consulting firm completed the study "Intranet Business Value: Return on Investment Analysis." This study found that intranets achieved an average annualized return on investment of 38%. The breakdown was particularly interesting. The study found that:

META Group Consulting prepared a vendor-neutral report for IBM, Microsoft, and Novell

- static Web pages returned 22%,
- collaborative applications yielded 40%,
- dynamic applications gave back 68%.

According to the META Group study results, the size of the intranet application does not correlate to the size of the return on investment. Department or division-sized intranets

Mission-critical solutions achieved the highest ROIs

can produce very impressive ROIs. What does matter is the degree to which a Web application is aligned with supporting mission-critical, value-adding, line-of-business endeavors.

New E-Business Applications

Vendors are converting client/server applications to run on intranets

Software vendors are rewriting existing client/server applications to work on client machines across the Web, but as you already know, an intranet application is much easier to update. An administrator can update the application running on the server and avoid updating all the clients. When an application serves 100, 1000, or 10,000 individuals spread across many states or countries, the savings can be significant. "Applications! Intranets started as static publishing forums. More and more applications are being built to run on the intranet," according to Rob Bilson, Senior Webmaster, Amkor Electronics.

"E-business" is the process of doing business on line

On October 7, 1997, IBM took out an eight-page spread in the business section of major daily newspapers across the United States. The advertorial heralded the bandwagon of *e-business*, a term that includes the use of the Internet, intranets, and extranets in doing business. The copy explained, "You *become* an e-business by connecting your traditional IT systems to the Web. You *do* e-business by taking the information in those systems and deploying it in new ways over the Web." IBM's purchase of an eight-page section sends a message about the economic importance of the opportunities for today and tomorrow.

The focus is component-based and transaction-oriented

Building and maintaining intranets will become easier as software components and transaction-oriented intranet applications become increasingly available from software vendors. Developers can purchase little servlets, Java applets, and ActiveX controls to create special features for their Web applications. While organizations will continue to commission custom-built applications, the availability of off-the-shelf intranet software products will expand their options for

Expense Reports Contain Useful Data:
The Xpense Management Solution

The expense report is a gold mine of data about vendor purchasing volumes, budget variations, and adherence to travel policies—information that fuels decisions and that can lead to improved financial control. Management can use this information to negotiate better rates, adjust budget projections, and redirect employee spending habits.

Portable Software's flagship product, Xpense Management Solution (XMS), began as a client/server application for recording and managing Travel and Entertainment (T&E) expenditures. With the next generation XMS product, travelers, managers, and financial personnel obtained the option to use XMS as a client/server application, a disconnected Windows application, or as an intranet application. The checkbook-style interface looks the same in each environment, so there is no time wasted retraining employees who migrate from one type of application to another. The intranet application is open architectured, so it can run on all platforms. It is built in HTML with Active Server Pages and, where it does not slow performance, some use of Java language. On the back-end, the application provides the same transaction processing, workflow management, status reporting, and analysis capabilities for all applications.

For ease of deployment and updating, the XMS intranet application wins out over the other two versions. To change a T&E policy that is accessible through a hyperlink, or add a field to gather different data, such as a checkbox to specify domestic or international travel, it's simple to modify the T&E policy document or rewrite a small amount of server code. Then, the update is complete. The intranet user sees a new field to fill in. To make changes on client/server or Windows versions, an executable file and instructions are mailed (or e-mailed) to each user who must then install the update or call for support.

using in-house talent. Some new intranet application products may be hybrids that, for example, combine workflow and data-mining. Expect to see more configurable supply-chain Web products, in particular. "One thing I'm sure of...is that this environment will become easier to use," wrote

Web applications
will become both
more comprehensive
and easier to use

Diana Jones, Manager, Systems Analysis, Data-Tronics
Corporation, in e-mail about new directions for intranets.
"I believe it will eventually be as stable and 'user friendly'
as the telephone. The average user will no longer have to
be concerned with connections, phone lines, servers, routers, and all the infrastructure mess so many of us worry
about today. It will be accomplished behind the scenes,
and it will work."

Enhanced Data Displays

Intranet users will
benefit from ad-
vances in ways to
display data

You saw in Chapter 6 that an intranet provides tools to
capture and update data dynamically. Executives, in particular, will benefit from emerging 3-D technologies that provide new ways to display complex data relationships to help
decision-making. In addition, engineers, designers, and
customers can make productive use of virtual reality technologies in an intranet environment to *show*, as well as
describe, new products to anyone with a VR-capable browser.

VRML and Virtual Reality Displays

As VRML matures,
it will come closer
to realizing it's
potential for
expressing data

Virtual Reality Modeling Language (VRML) is a language
akin to HTML for describing virtual three-dimensional
interactive environments.[1] When you link a VRML file to a
Web page, VRML-enabled browsers can display such environments on the Web. The VRML Consortium is working to
create common standards for multi-user worlds and avatars,
textures and data libraries, and VRML networking protocols.
The fact that both Microsoft Internet Explorer 4.0 and Netscape Communicator 4.0 support VRML has alleviated the

---

1. VRML is a derivative of SGML. The basic building blocks of VRML are
nodes that describe how 3-D objects are lit, textured, and animated.
The VRML Consortium is reviewing proposed VRML 2.0 standards.

problem of users' needing to find and download proprietary browser plug-ins to view different VRML applications.[2]

The next big hurdle for all 3-D and virtual technologies is bandwidth—a problem more manageable on closed-circuit intranets than on the Internet. Virtual technologies typically have a Tyrannosaurus-size appetite for bandwidth. Intel MMX hardware, affordable 3-D accelerator chips, and larger data throughput over bigger network pipes will shrink this barrier. The solution at Northrop Grumman, which uses virtual-photographic reality for simulations, is to build heavy-duty subnets that won't break under intense traffic.

Bandwidth is the next big hurdle

Convergence: More Data, More Access

"In a few years, with huge advances in compression algorithms, such as the evolving MPEG standards,[3] we will distinguish voice and data simply by the device it comes to us through, rather than by the network and transport technologies," e-mailed Ryan Christian, Web intern, Georgia-Pacific West, Inc., about the future for intranets.

The term *convergence* is already shop-worn. Exactly *what* is converging depends on which technical specialists are discussing it. In the mid-1990's, convergence meant the *digital domain*—a catch-all for any media (sound, images, data) that could be converted to a digital format. Now it may mean the convergence of telephony and computing, or computing and television, or an amalgam of cable, satellite, and wireless broadcasting converging with Web-based computing—or all of the above. What is clear is that a host of converging technologies are applicable to intranets.

Convergence means the merger of hithertofore separate technologies

---

2. The virtual-world builders have been experiencing the same problem as other software developers regarding shifting standards, when one competitor's technical advances scoot beyond existing specifications.

3. MPEG, an acronym for Moving Pictures Experts Group, is a set of standards for audio and video compression established by the Joint ISO/IEC Technical Committee on Information Technology.

Digital TV—Broadcasting Data

Digital TV opens a new opportunity for pushing high volumes of data

"The Federal Communications Commission (FCC) laid out a plan for broadcasters to replace 80% of the analog TV with digital TV by 2006, and set in place a wide new avenue for pushing data," said Sheryl Olguin, Manager of DTV Software and Data Technology for the Harris Corporation. "Digital television specifications and protocols are flexible, multiple standards that govern simultaneously broadcasting a mix of data (audio, video, data). For example, a broadcaster could send a standard definition TV signal combined with a data signal, or send a single high definition TV signal."

Delivery mechanisms include cable service and digital satellite

This means that a network such as NBC, for example, could broadcast the regularly scheduled morning news program, while simultaneously fulfilling their scheduled feed of a training video on Web security or a software update to every desktop and laptop on your intranet. Stay tuned. Details at…whenever the organization schedules its next delivery. The broadcaster could also be like an ISP, a *broadcast delivery service provider* offering channel services. Content (data, video, and audio) could be pushed through channels, either to the public through regularly scheduled programming or to intranet subscribers. Delivery mechanisms for carrying one or more of these channels ultimately will include cable service, digital satellite, and, down the road, MMDS (microwave multipoint distribution system), and LLDS (local loop distribution system).

Greater capacity will enable delivery of a wider variety of data

This trend has already begun. The Public Broadcasting Service (PBS) is now delivering instructional video programming over The Business Channel (TBC) via satellite on a "pay-per-view" basis, so a company can subscribe and pay to receive a certain scheduled program, such as a Tom Peters seminar. The difference is that with the greater capacity that will be available through the digital pipeline, organizations will be able to schedule delivery of software upgrades, their company video newsletter, sales data, a weekly address by the CEO, and more.

What is so attractive about data-casting by way of digital TV for intranets is the generous and encryptable bandwidth that is deliverable to any workstation that has the hardware and software to receive the signal, without building an expensive infrastructure. Also, digital TV can enable a blended experience, allowing users to click on Web-based content that shares the screen with images. The first digital TV applications being explored, of course, are a blend of the sitcom and home shopping experience. Where entertainment goes, though, business is sure to follow. Digital TV signals can be encoded at the point of delivery and decoded at the desktop.

Digital TV and intranets: wider reach, faster and cheaper than hard-wired connections

Outfitting computers with a TV tuner card[4] and either a cable connection or an antenna enables employees to tune in and receive the signal. The Windows operating system upgrade being released in 1998 will include viewer software (by WavePhore, Inc.) that can decode data embedded in broadcasts. Adding encryption technology can create the broadcast equivalent of a VPN tunnel to deliver programming securely to intranet desktops. Smartcards (see "Sophisticated Access Control" on the next page) could be used to identify eligible viewers.

Windows 98 will be able to decode data embedded in broadcasts

What could you send to your employees over a private pipe that's larger than New Hampshire? The maximum data delivery rate for digital TV is 19 Mbps (6 MHz).[5] This is G-force compared to the remote user crawling in over a 28.8 Kbps modem or the small branch office with a 56 Kbps or an ISDN line. Even a T1 is in the slow lane by comparison.

Compare digital TV data delivery at 19 Mbps with an ISDN line at 128 Kbps

---

4. New television will come equipped with a tuner card. Or you will be able to purchase a TV tuner card as a plug-in. like a sound card. Signals could be received from satelitte, cable, radio-frequency, and microwave delivery channels.

5. The full signal is 19.39 Mbps, but there is a low overhead that renders a usable signal up to 19 Mbps for data transfer.

Better Retrieval Technology

Image recognition systems and intelligent agents will ease the problem of finding useful information

With the potential for so much information coming to you over an intranet, improvements in information-retrieval technology to filter the flow are becoming more important. Advances in image recognition will make it possible in the near future to archive and retrieve images, not just by using keywords but by discerning the difference between a black cat on a white bedspread and a black gas grill on a white cement patio. Information retrieval technology experts are also wrestling with intelligent agents and natural language queries to sift, sort, and find the information you need. Then, if you type in a query to find the *most powerful computer chip* you won't get information about a hulking potato chip. However, even with highly intuitive search tools, some members of your organization may still be left on the outside of the Web community.

Sophisticated Access Control

Start with digital identification numbers

As more and more of an organization's vital data migrates to the open reaches of an intranet environment, managers will demand more assurance that only those with permission can gain access. A password is a flimsy protective device. Giving every member of your organization a digital ID is a first step to more advanced access control and document protection. If the organization becomes a certifying authority, you can even hand out encryption keys.

Smart cards and fingerprint systems are digital identification systems

Smart cards and fingerprint recognition systems are two new ways to prove identity for secure private and commercial transactions. The first product from Veridicom, a joint venture for Lucent Technologies and U.S. Venture Partners, is a fingerprint sensor the size of a postage stamp. The Veridicom product has four components: a silicon sensor, analysis software that reconstructs the fingerprint in digital form, matching software that matches the sample from the *enrollment* sample first given by the user, and data protection software to prevent tampering. Until new computers are outfitted with the sensor devices, add-on products can be plugged into a computer.

Vendors need standards to ensure compatibility between identification software and hardware products

Smart cards that store a digital certificate could be used as an on-the-go hardware token to identify an individual's right to intranet, dial-up, and building access. The good news is that both Netscape Communicator 4.0 and Microsoft Internet Explorer 4.0 support smart card authentication. The bad news is that they support different standards. Internet Explorer 4.0 relies on SSL encryption and Microsoft CrytoAPIs. Microsoft is also co-developing PC/SC, a smart card/personal computer protocol. Communicator 4.0 supports a security protocol from RSA Data Security for Public Key Cryptography Standards or PKCS-11. A growing number of network security firms and smart card vendors have declared support for PKCS-11.

Sensory Enhancements

Ironically, as organizations open the doors to publishing information on an intranet, they may be closing the doors to people with vision loss and other impairments. "[The problem is] a lot of adaptive technology today is predicated on yesterday's solutions," said T.V. Raman, a researcher with Adobe Systems who is blind.[6] For example, screen rendering technology was developed in the 1980s, when visual interfaces were simple—just 24 lines and 80 characters across a page. "But screen readers haven't kept pace," said Raman. New technologies create new problems. "To a screen reader, a Java applet is a black hole," said Raman. Feature wars between browser makers add to the difficulty.

Web interfaces confound traditional screen reading programs for blind users

---

6. T.V. Raman is the author of *Auditory User Interfaces*, a book about using sounds in Web environments.

Interface designers should consider aural interfaces

The solution may not be to control creativity, but to take a look at the needs of different populations in Web environments, such as remote users dialing in with 28.8 modems, those using palm-top computing appliances, and people with physical disabilities. For many populations, simple works best. Although Windows CE can be a low-vision environment, it's easy to see that just enlarging characters does not make information on the screen more accessible. (You might get three or four letters for a level one heading.) A new emphasis on the "sound and feel" would benefit many Web computing audiences.

Avoid lawsuits, keep informed about Web access issues

If employees feel locked out of participating in their organization's intranet, expect an increase in legal actions. Now, few intranet software designers, either inside or outside the corporation, are well-informed about the need for equal access. A suit settled in 1997 in the state of California over access to the Internet from a university library may set a trend, if not a direct precedent. Many private and public organizations are addressing *augmentative communication* solutions.[7] Adaptive products are available, but because of the small market, they tend to be expensive. The W3C is also addressing accessibility.

Web Access Initiative

The W3C Web Access Initiative (WAI) is a consortium that works to assure that Web standards reflect the need for universal access. T.V. Raman, a member of the W3C WAI, wrote the Oral Cascaded Style Sheet Spec. "It's not specific to the blind," says Raman, "if somebody wanted to access the Web over a cell phone, they'd better have an aural [interface]." Although the results of the WAI efforts will not come to a Web environment before the next millenium, momentum is growing—in listservs, newsgroups, and Internet Web sites—to avoid designing-in barriers to intranet and Internet communications.

---

7. The Trace Center, formed in 1971 at the University of Wisconsin, was designated as a research center on "Access to Computers and Information Systems," by the National Institute on Disability and Rehabilitation Research, U.S. Department of Education.

Dealing with Evolving Standards

While intranets trace their roots to the open standard Internet protocols that have enabled a revolution in cross-platform computing, natural competition and market opportunism exert an equal pressure against uniform standards for Web products. The IT administrators, Webmasters, Web developers, user-developers who engage in light rather than professional-level development, and even users are caught in the middle. The situation is not likely to improve. It's worrisome enough for organizations to invest in technologies that seem wet behind the ears, but more so to feel at risk with moving-target standards. However, unlike the wide-open Internet, an intranet can be easily standardized.

Short of naming a Vice President In Charge Of Keeping Track Of Proposed Standards, the best defense is to use open technologies as much as possible, and also to choose a platform that will support the types of development endeavors your organization needs to do business. In this manner, you can take advantage of native platform performance and functionality. Carefully select listservs and newsgroups to keep you informed, but also to keep you from becoming overwhelmed by the play-by-play of controversy over new developments.

BC Hydro instituted a *Web Technology Watch*. "Part of my job is always to be on the lookout for ways existing Internet technology can be tailored for a corporate intranet environment, so it's very possible that VRML, MUDs, MOOs, and others could find use as part of a business solution. You never know." said Steve Whan, Corporate Webmaster, Network Consulting Services, BC Hydro.

> Internet changes are rapid, but you have more control over your own intranet

> Use open-standard technologies whenever possible

> Emerging opportunities for intranets may originate from environments that are not standard business issue

Going Forward

After the year 2000 problem is history—one way or another—many more organizations will focus resources and attention on developing the potential of an intranet or extranet.

"What's needed is a fully funded workgroup with the responsibilities of information systems, Web design and marketing, and intranet/Internet business development" Bill Monroe, Harris Corporation, Electronic Systems wrote in e-mail. Although this is absolutely essential, it's not enough.

It takes time, money, open-mindedness, and leadership

In addition to adequately allocating time and monetary resources, it also takes a quality of open-mindedness to reap the real benefits of interactive Web technologies. It takes leadership that can inspire others to remain open to new and different ways. There is a part of Karate training that reminds us that, "In the mind of the beginner, there are many possibilities. In an experienced mind, there are very few." You must strive to keep the mind of a beginner.

Northrop Grumman has been doing business on an intranet since 1994. According to Natalie Stone, Chief Architect for Internal Information Systems at Northrop Grumman, their focus has changed. "We're steering more towards cultural issues, as opposed to technical ones. In the first stages, the focus is heavy on technology. Now that it's in place (and we're looking at how we can leverage that), we're turning more and more to the cultural aspects [of intranet development]. How can we truly facilitate and package these technologies to people, rather than throwing technology over the wall, and letting the users fend for themselves." In the final analysis, intranets are not about technology, they are about people—giving people the support and the tools to work and collaborate more effectively.

Are you looking at a sea of opportunities, imagining what an intranet could enable in your organization? If you're still holding on to the edge of the dock, the only way to get your crew to the other side is to let go, and start paddling. Trust me, the earth is not flat.

Index

A

A/UX 44
ABF Freight Systems, Inc. 87
Access Control Database 112
access-based computing 165
Active Data Objects 180
Active Server Pages
    61, 158, 181, 188, 317, 320
Active Streaming Format 245
ActiveX 10, 28, 61, 65, 152, 158, 180,
    181, 187, 192, 312, 319
Adleman, Len 118
Adobe Systems 135, 262
  Acrobat 145, 175
  Acrobat Reader 281
  Capture 175
  Catalog 195
  PDF files 176
  Photoshop 49
ADSL. *See* Asymmetrical Digital Subscriber
    Line
agents 10, 200
Air Products and Chemicals, Inc. 86,
    177, 205, 310
alias 57, 112
AltaVista 156
  Firewall 121
  Live Topics 198
  OnSite 156
  Personal Extensions 9, 195
Amdahl Corporation 1
American Disabilities Act 261
Amkor Electronics Inc. 158
Anderson, Lyle 297
anti-virus programs 97
Apache 315

API. *See* application programming interface
Aponet, Inc. 344
applets 8, 9
application programming interface 42, 186
applications
  distributed 64
ARAMARK Corporation 174, 215, 275, 333
ARCnet 50
Arkansas Best Corporation 87
ASP. *See* Active Server Pages
Association for Information and Image
    Management I 168
asymmetric encryption 118
asymmetrical digital subscriber line 83
asynchronous transfer mode 83
AT&T 78
  Bell Labs 43
Atkinson, Richard 223, 229
ATM. *See* Asynchronous Transfer Mode
authentication 95, 104, 110
auto industry 72
Aylsworth, Wendy 79

B

back-end machines. *See* servers
Baltimore Gas and Electric
    30, 144, 309, 339
bandwidth 165, 222, 241, 328
bandwidth policy monitor 344
Bank of Hawaii 147
baseband 59
Bathum, Aaron 294
BC Hydro 145, 171
BEA Systems 186
Beaty, Beth 290
Bemis Company 146

Berkeley System UNIX 44
best practices 322
Beth Israel Hospital 192
Bilson, Rob 158
Boeing 231
Border Services 76
Boyer, Tom 193, 201
bridges 51
British Aero Space 82, 89
broadband 59
Brown, Anthony 60
browser-based software 14
browsers
    applications for 14
    defined 9
    functions of 65
    monitoring tools for 23
    plug-ins 10
    tracking tools for 23
Bruty, Alec 146, 335

C

C++ 313
Cameron, Steve 205
Campbell, Heather 231
Castanet 346
CB Connector 190
CBT. *See* computer-based training
CD-ROM 239
CDF. *See* Channel Definition Format
central file server 49
centralized administration and monitoring
    348
CERN 63
certificate authority 116
certificate revocation list 116
certificate servers 116
certificates
    digital 115
    issuing 116
    revoking 116
certifying authority 115
CGI 320. *See* Common Gateway Interface
change-management processes 339
Channel Definition Format 28, 75

Chariot 346
Chart FX control 159
charts 160
chat areas 173
chemical industry 72
Christian, Ryan 357
CIBC Architecture and Consulting Services
    231
client/server 5, 15, 180, 186, 187
    architecture 49
    environment, advantages of 49
    networks 48
clients 5
    software 8
clustering 348
CNNfn 28
COBOL 191, 313
collaborating 7, 18, 89, 212. *See also*
    knowledge-working
collaborative learning 246
command and control organizational model
    39
common denominator protocol 12
Common Gateway Interface 158, 180
Common Object Request Broker Architecture
    186
Component Broker Connector 190
component object technology 64
Computer Fraud and Abuse Act 102
computer-based training 239
Concentric Network Corporation 83
conferencing 216, 238
content. *See* information
content-management tools 61
Continuum software server 76
convergence 357
cookies 188
Coors Brewing Company 146, 176, 205
CORBA. *See* Common Object Request Broker
    Architecture
corporate-wide Web 2
cost of ownership 27
costs
    controlling 327
    hardware 293
    long-range 327
    reducing 295

software 293
Crossware initiative 75
Crypt encryption utility 117
Cryptographic Service Provider 121
Crystal Reports 317
CSP. *See* Cryptographic Service Provider
CUseeMe 221

D

dark-siders 101
data. *See* information: types of
data binding 182
data conferencing 217
Data Encryption Standard 105, 117
Data-Tronics 87
databases 189
    intranet applications 191
    Web enhanced 189
    Web front end for 180
    Web front ends for 191
DataPage 191
DCE. *See* Distributed Computing Environment
DCOM. *See* Distributed Component Object
        Model
Deaconess Hospital 192
denial of service attacks 350
DES. *See* Data Encryption Standard
DHCP. *See* Dynamic Host Configuration
        Protocol
dial-up connections 77
digital certificates 106, 115
digital IDs 360
digital signatures 119
digital TV 359
directories 5
directory services 56, 57
discussion forums 173
    categories for 174
    membership in 174
discussion threads 16
distance learning 19, 235–252, 238
    advantages of 240
    applications 242
    benefits of 250
    cost savings of 249

course materials repurposed for 251
defined 238
disadvantages of 241
instructor-led 247
models of 247
student-centered 247
team-centered 247
distributed applications 64
Distributed Component Object Model 186
Distributed Computing Environment 186
Dixons Mastercare 88, 166, 193, 231
DMZ 71
Doctor HTML 342
Document Object Model Working Group 161
documents
    life expectancy of 168
    management, cost of 168
    sharing 15, 54
Domino 214
Dow Jones 176
drag-and-drop 265
Drucker, Peter 18
DTV Software and Data Technology 358
dual key encryption 118
dumb terminals 6
Dynamic Host Configuration Protocol 318
Dynamic HTML 66, 75, 161, 188, 320
dynamic validation 191
dynamic Web pages. *See* Web pages:
        dynamic
dynamically updating information 177

E

e-business 354
e-forms 189. *See also* forms
e-mail 5, 15, 54, 171, 173
    effects on communication 173
    privacy of 172
    standardizing 172
EDI. *See* electronic data interchange
editing 15
education 235
electronic brochure-ware 132
electronic commerce 73
Electronic Communications and Privacy Act

102
electronic data interchange 73
electronic document distribution 145
Electronic Performance Support System 246
electronic whiteboard 15
Emacs 65, 262
Emery WorldWide 227
encryption 95, 104, 116, 329
   assymetric 118
   dual-key 118
ENIAC 39
Envoy 195
Ethernet 50
Ethridge, Kim 31, 144, 309, 322, 339
evaluation 331
Excite 198
Extra-Link 83
extranets 4, 69–91, 354
   anatomy of 74
   benefits of 25, 70
   challenges of 73
   compatibility with 76
   contractors on 89
   customer support with 88
   defined 70
   dial-up 77
   focus of 70
   hub 70
   joint venture partners on 89
   key customers 85
   managing 83
   planning 90
   private lines for 78
   sales representatives 86
   server software for 76
   suppliers on 89
   uses for 84

F

failover 348
fault tolerance 348
favored partner status 4
Fenwick, Ken 194, 231, 249, 287
Fernihough, Bill 145, 171
Fiber Distributed Data Interface 50

file sharing 5
File Transfer Protocol 52, 62
filtering 228
firewalls 53, 95, 104, 351
   defined 106
FocalPt 69
Ford Motor Company 69
forms 158, 178, 181
   developing interactive 181
frame relay technology 83
freeware 8
Fremuth, Mary-Ellen 178
front-end devices. *See* clients
FrontPad 66
FTP 62. *See* File Transfer Protocol
Fujitsu 176

G

Ganymede 346
Gates, Bill 14
gateways 52, 318
General InterORB Protocol 186
Georgia-Pacific West, Inc. 135, 264
Gordon, Jack 249
graphical user interface 65
groupware 15, 214, 220, 225
Guardian 352
GUI. *See* graphical user interface

H

HarperCollins 144
Harris Corporation 308, 325, 358
Harris Electronic Systems Company 144
Hewlett Packard SharedX 224
Hitachi Corporation 131
HomeSite 9
HTML 9, 62, 151
   authoring 151–156
   code 153
   HTML 4.0 64
   tables 159
HTTP 10
HyperText Markup Language. *See* HTML
HyperText Transfer Protocol 62. *See* HTTP

I

IBM AIX 44
IDEA. *See* International Data Encryption
    Algorithm
IEEE 63
IIOP. *See* Internet InterORB Protocol
image maps 265
Imagiware 341
information 176
    acquiring 169, 171
    bases 175
    customers for 164
    customized search interfaces for 201
    duplication 167
    dynamically updating 178
    filtering 228
    indexing 195
    integrating 189
    management 163–209, 185
    multimedia 169
    multiple views into 183
    objects 185
    online archives of 176
    organizing 182
    providers 165
    requesting 205
    searches 196
        hierarchical category 197
        keyword 196
        parametric 197
        smart 196
    searching for spiders 198
    structured 169
    types of 169
    unstructured 170
    Web front ends to 191
information management 18, 185
    compatibility standards for 189
    cost of 168
information parts store 133
information technology 37
Intel iNDX 59
Intel VideoPhone 221
intellectual property rights 94
Inter Relay Chat 175
interactive videodisks 239

International Data Corporation 270
International Data Encryption Algorithm 119
International Engineering Task Force 219
International Standards Organization 63
Internet
    protocols 10
    service provider 3
    TCP/IP protocol 52
    vs. intranets 3
Internet Explorer. *See* Microsoft Internet
    Explorer 4.0
Internet Information Server 317. *See also*
    Microsoft: Internet Information Server
Internet InterORB Protocol 186
Internet Protocol 53, 317
Internet Relay Chat 62
Internet Server Application Programming
    Interface 180
Internetwork Packet exchange 53
interoperability 186, 296, 312
InterSystems 192
intranets
    abuse of 290
    authority for 306
    bandwidth of 328
    benefits of 20–27
    business cases for 287–304
    capacity planning for 343
    charts on 160
    collaborating on 212–233
    compared to corporate networks 2
    conferencing 216
    content for 169
    controlling growth of 337
    converting from networks to 167
    cross-functional team for developing 307
    definition of 2
    dependencies of 292
    derivation of term 1
    designing 266
    determining purpose of 255
    development tools for 319
    disabilities and 261
    distance learning on 235–252
    document distribution with 144
    dynamically updated 158
    employee directories on 144

evaluating 331–352
five functions of 5
functional business requirements of 271
funding 310
hardware costs of 293
HR uses for 141
implementing 305
information on. *See* information
interface guidelines for 267
issues relating to failure of 292
job openings on 141
knowledge-working 211–233
large-scale 6
long-range costs of 327
look and feel of 264
maintaining 331–352
maintenance plans for 322
manuals on 145
measuring productivity 299
monitoring performance of 342
monitoring programs for 344
multicultural aspects of 258
pages from databases 158
pilot projects for 269
planning 253
policies and procedures for 321
pre-publishing checklists for 322
product information on 147
publishing on 131
    advantages 136
purpose of 2
reducing cost of ownership 295
ROI of 353
scalability of 24, 314
security on 329
servers for 315
setting expectations for 263
simple 6
software costs 293
standardizing 313
strategic benefits 37
support services on 146
tracking expenses on 355
training on 235–252
usability 283
using for information management 163–
    209

Web design for 157
Webmasters for 307
Iona Technologies 187
IP 317. *See* Internet Protocol
    bogus addresses 319
IP Multicast Initiative 206
IP spoofing 351
IPSec 105
IPX and SPX 53
IPX protocol 12
IRC 62. *See* Inter Relay Chat
ISAPI. *See* Internet Server Application
        Programming Interface
ISDN 83
ISO. *See* International Standards Organization

J

Java 28, 158, 180, 186, 187, 293,
    312, 319
    scripts 10, 61, 152
JavaScript 313, 320
Javascript 28
Jennings, Phil 208
John Deere 184
Jones, Diana 87, 356
just-in-time information 147

K

Kallelis, John 215, 276, 333
Knight-Ridder 176
knowledge bases 231
knowledge networks 212
knowledge workers
    needs of 165
knowledge-ware 15
knowledge-working 7, 18, 211–233

L

Lang, Ilene 156
LANs 11. *See* local area networks
    limitations of 12
    linking 50

learning. *See* distance learning
leased lines 78
Leeper, Kirby 80
legacy systems 13
Lexis-Nexis 176
libraries 8, 15
Linkbot 341
Linux 44
listserv 173
LLDS. *See* local loop distribution system
load balancing 348
local area networks 48
local loop distribution system 358
logic bomb 97
login 57
logout 57
London Underground 145, 189, 273
Lotus Notes 12, 54, 213
Lucent Technologies 233, 360

M

Macintosh Operating System 6
Macrae, Scott 148, 156
mail bombs 351
mail programs 8
mail servers 6
mainframes 39
  disadvantages of 45
maintenance 331
  housekeeping 340
  outsourcing 333
  service level agreements 335
  updating 341
Majowicz, Bob 86
managers
  needs of 165
Marimba Inc 346
Marimba Inc. 28
Martin-Smith, Keith 88
Mayles, Bernard 93
McAfee VirusScan 97
McDonnell Douglas 82, 89
MCI 78
MeetingPoint 221
Mentys 237

Merck & Company 93
metadata 209
Metcalfe, Bob 81
metropolitan area networks 11
Microsoft
  Access 146, 178
  Active Streaming Format 245
  ActiveX 187
  Authenticode 107
  Certificate Server 107, 116
  CryptoAPI 107, 121
  DCOM 187
  Exchange 54, 172, 178, 214
  Exchange Server 64
  FoxPro 183
  FrontPage 9, 61, 282
  Index Server 189
  Internet Explorer 154
  Internet Explorer 4.0 28, 66
  Internet Information Server
    65, 146, 192, 317
  Internet Locator Server 221
  Internet Security Framework 107
  NetMeeting 15, 217
  NetShow 245
  NT 5.0 60
  Office 64, 154
  Office 97 281
  Personal Web Server 282
  PowerPoint 9
  Publisher 9
  SQL Server 146
  Visual Basic 192
  Visual InterDev 61, 161
  Visual SourceSafe 339
  Wallet 107
  Windows 6
  Windows 95 107
  Windows for Workgroups 59
  Windows NT 107
  Word 9, 49, 154
  Word 97 155
microwave multipoint distribution system 358
Midas 65
MIT 43
MMDS. *See* microwave multipoint distribution system

monitoring 344
Monroe, Bill 308
Mosaic 65
MPEG 357
MS Market 301
multicasting 203
MULTICS 43
multimedia 16
multitasking 56
mutant virus 97

N

National Computer Crimes Squad 127
National Computer Security Association
    125, 351
NCSA HTTPd 1.5.2a 315
Netiva Software 191
NetMeeting 66
Netscape 75, 181, 214
    Communicator 221
    Enterprise Server 315
    Netcaster 4.0 28
NetShow 66, 87, 317
NetWare 12
network architectures 50
Network Computer 191
network computing 48
    advantages of 54
network file system 53
network management 5
network operating systems 48, 56
networks
    architecture of 13
    baseband 59
    broadband 59
    communication protocols 52
    components of 51
    converting to intranets 167
    Ethernet 50, 59
    limitations of 59
    managing 23
    metropolitan area 11
    peer 11, 48
    scaling 13
    sneaker 11

Token Ring 50
Token-Ring 59
types of 11
WANs 11
News Network Transfer Protocol 62
NFS. See Network File System
NNTP 62
Northrop Grumman 81, 89, 141, 223, 325
Norwich Union 274
NOS. See Network operating systems
Novell 76
    NetWare 53, 319
    Sharenet 59
NSAPI 181

O

Object Management Group 186
objects 10. See information: objects
ODBC. See Open Database Connectivity
ODMA. See Open Document Management
    API
Olguin, Sheryl 358
on line performance support 246
online learning 19
Open Database Connectivity 190
Open Document Management API 189
Open Software Foundation 187
open standards 155
open systems 63
Open Vista 191
OpenConnect Systems 190
Oracle 183, 190
Orange Book 127
O'Reilly WebSite Pro 315
out-tasking 334
outsourcing 333

P

packet filtering 53
packet networks 78
passwords 57, 113
    how not to create 114
PDF 145, 175, 195, 262, 281

peer networks 11
Penzias, Arno 233
Perl 154, 313
permanent virtual circuit connections 78
permission 57, 112
Personal Communications Technology 107
Personal Information Exchange 107
Personal Web Server 66
PGP. *See* Pretty Good Privacy
Phillips, Earnest 135, 138, 291
PhoneDisc 193
pilot projects 269
  cost of 272
  evaluating 279
  example of 274
  marking 278
  people resources for 282
  process 271
  resources for 280
  tools for developing 281
  usability analysis 283
ping of death attack 350
plug-ins 10
point-and-click 265
point-to-point lines 78
point-to-point tunneling 79
PointCast 28, 202, 346
policies 321
port scanning 351
Portable Software 355
Potomac Electric 30
prank virus 97
Pretty Good Privacy 105, 106, 119
privacy 172
private IP network 71
private key 118
private network. *See* intranets: purpose of
processes
  standard 14
  unstructured 14
productivity 299
  groups 15
  individual 14
  intranet tools for 16
  organization 16
  tools 14
program management 229

project management 15, 228
protocols 203
  common denominator 12
  conferencing 217, 219
  DHCP 318
  FTP 52
  HyperText Transfer Protocol 62
  Internet 53, 62
  Internet InterORB 186
  IPX 12
  IPX and SPX 53
  multicasting 203
  News Network Transfer Protocol 62
  Personal Communications Technology 107
  Remote Call Procedures 53
  Secure Sockets Layer 77
  SNA 12
  T.120 217, 221
  TCP/IP 12
  Transmission Control 53
  unicasting 204
  User Datagram 53
proxy servers 108–109
public folders 15, 16
public key 118
public packet networks 78
publishing. *See also* quick publishing
publishing for networks 76
push technology 28, 66, 201
  PointCast 202

Q

quick publishing 17, 131–162
  administrative 142
  advantages of 134
  compared to paper publishing 151
  corporate 142
  defined 132
  departmental 143
  HR info 143
  process 148–157
  types of information 142

R

Raman, T.V. 262
RAS. *See* Remote Access Server
RCP. *See* Remote Call Procedures
real estate industry 72
RealAudio 217
remote access 206
Remote Access Server 77
Remote Call Procedures 53
Remote Method Invocation 186, 227
REXX 87
risks. *See also* security
    awareness of 98
    checklist 122
    cost of reducing 125
    education about 98
    hackers 100
    internal 98
    policies and procedures for managing 123
    recognizing 96
    risk groups 99
    sabotage 99
    solutions for managing 103
Rivest, Ron 118
RMI. *See* Remote Method Invocation
robots 99, 199
Rogue Wave 293
ROI 270, 353
routers, screening 107
RSA Data Security, Inc. 105, 106
Ryan, Bill 250

S

S-HTTP. *See* Secure HTTP
S/MIME. *See* Secure MIME
S/WAN. *See* Secure Wide Area Network
sabotage 99
sacrificial lambs 110
SAFECO Insurance Corporation
    194, 231, 297
sandbox 293
scalability 314
scaling 13
Schering-Plough 93
screening router 107

scripts 8, 9
search engines 9, 197
    features of 197
searches 5
    customized interfaces for 201
    hierarchical category 197
    keyword 196
    parametric 197
    smart 196
Seattle Times 192
Secure Electronics Transaction standard 105
Secure HTTP 105
Secure HyperText Transfer Protocol 106
Secure MIME 105, 106
Secure Server Network 105
Secure Sockets Layer 77, 105, 192
Secure Wide Area Network 105
Secure Wide Area Networks 106
security 93–129, 329
    Access Control Database 112
    authentication 110
    checklist for designing 122
    costs of maintaining 125
    dark-siders 101
    goals of 95
    hackers 100
    Microsoft Internet Security Framework 107
    packet filtering 107
    protocols 105
    proxy servers 108
    remote access 113
    sacrificial lamb 110
    services 56
    solutions 103
    strategies 120
    strategy for 95
    sub-networks 110
    tracking computer crimes 127
    viruses 98
    viruses and bugs 96
    zones 126
SemioMap 198
sendmail attacks 351
Sequenced Packet exchange 53
servers 5. *See also* Web servers
    applications 8
    software 8
    upgrades 347

service level agreements 335
SET. *See* Secure Electronics Transaction
    standard
Shamir, Adi 118
sharing 54
Simple Mail Transfer Protocol 62
Simple Network Management Protocol 53
smart cards 360
smart clients 7
SmartAudit 344
SMTP 62
SNA protocol 12
sneaker networks 11
SNMP 62. *See* Simple Network Management
    Protocol
software
    browsers 9
    intranet 64
    proprietary 12, 14
    search 9
    server 8
    speciality 9
Software FX 159
spiders 198
    blocking 200
    indexing with 199
Sprint 78
SQL 166, 183
SSL. *See* Secure Sockets Layer
SSN. *See* Secure Server Network
staging server 293
standards 63
statelessness 187
stock tickers 10
Stone, Natalie 325
streaming audio and video 16, 217, 245
sub-networks 110
Sun Microsystems 81, 187
support 27
symmetric encryption 103

TCP. *See* Transmission Control Protocol
TCP/IP 8, 12, 62, 186, 296
    stack 52
TDMA. *See* Time Division—Multiple Access
technical support 166, 231
telecommuters 206
Teleres 24, 71, 80, 208
Telnet 62
Tetranet 341
The Open Group 187
thin clients 6
three-dimensional space 64
tiger team16 126
Time Division/Multiple Access 352
token ring 50
training 19, 235–252, 324
Transmission Control Protocol 53
Tridgell, Andy 350
Tripp, Kimberly 327
Trojan Horse 97
Trusted Information Systems Inc. 352
Tumbleweed Software Corporation 195
tunnels 77, 79
Tuxedo 186

U

U.S. Venture Partners 360
UDP. *See* User Datagram Protocol
unicasting 204
Uniform Resource Locator 62, 157
UNIX 6, 8, 12, 42, 43, 76, 117, 224, 262,
    313, 314, 350
URL. *See* Uniform Resource Locator
usability 283
Usenet 62, 195
User Datagram Protocol 53
username 57
UUNet 83

T

Tapscott, Don 18, 38, 213
task workers 165
task-based authorization 129
task-working 7

V

value-added networks 73
Vancouver 148
VANs. *See* value-added networks
Veridicom 360

VeriSign 116
version control 339
vertical industry networks 71
video 222
videoconferencing 217, 222, 344. *See also* conferencing
virtual communities 71
virtual environments 213
virtual private networks 77, 83, 207
virtual reality 356
Virtual Reality Markup Language 64
Virtual Reality Modeling Language 356
virtual teaching. *See* distance learning
viruses 96
    logic bomb 97
    mutant 97
    prank 97
    Trojan Horse 97
Visual Basic 154, 319
Visual Basic Script 313
Visual J++ 293
Visual M 192
voting 15
VRML. *See* Virtual Reality Markup Language; Virtual Reality Modeling Language
VRML Consortium 356
VSAT 352

W

W3C. *See* World Wide Web Consortium
Wagner, Ted 310
Walt Disney 82
Wang, Charles 37, 163
WANs. *See* wide area networks
    limitations of 12
    outsourcing 83
Warner Brothers Animation Studio 79, 144
Warnock, John 135
WatchGuard's Security Management System 121
WavePhore, Inc. 359
Web applications 61
Web authoring. *See* HTML: authoring
Web content-management 61
Web design 157

Web pages 9
    designs for 257
    dynamic 158
    static 158
Web Publishing Wizard 66
Web servers 315
    Apache 315
    features compared 315
    Microsoft Internet Information Server 315
    NCSA HTTPd 1.5.2a 315
    Netscape Enterprise Server 315
    O'Reilly WebSite Pro 315
    WebStar, for Macintosh 315
Web-based training. *See* distance learning
Webcasting 18, 28, 66, 201
WebConnect Pro 190
WebEdit 9
Webmasters 307. *See also* InfoMasters
WebStar 315
Webtop 28
WebTV 189
Westinghouse Savannah River Nuclear Facility 260
Weyerhaeuser Company 135, 138, 291
Whan, Steve 343
White Pine Software Inc 221
White, Richard 117
whiteboard, electronic 15, 216
wide area networks 11, 50
Windows NT 8, 76, 314, 319
Windows NT Server 65
Windows NT Server 4.0 195
workflow 15
    applications 225
World Wide Web 62, 63
World Wide Web Consortium 63, 152
WWW. *See* World Wide Web

X

XML 28, 64
Xpense Management Solution 355

Z

Zimmerman, Phil 119

Tyson Greer

Tyson Greer's eclectic body of writing, which includes feature articles, books, documentaries, corporate television programs, and interactive communications, explores expanded opportunities for productivity and efficiency in new technologies.

While Greer was Environmental/Energy Analyst for Simpson Paper Company, she led industry efforts to develop business applications of cogeneration, a highly efficient energy production technology. The award-winning video she co-produced and wrote, "Cogeneration…Once is Not Enough," helped launch a revival of cogeneration investments, and redirected Greer into producing media and writing. She took with her an understanding of how business leaders make decisions, especially during periods marked by great change. Greer has also produced, written, and directed numerous videos about total quality.

Since the 1990's, Greer has focused on the evolution of computer and new media technologies. She has been a featured speaker at media conferences, and teaches a scriptwriting course for the University of Washington Film-Video Certificate Program. Greer was a key member of the original design and production team for "Mastering Visual FoxPro," the first in the Microsoft Press "Mastering" series of CD-ROMs for self-directed learning. Greer's company, Tyson Greer….Writes, can be reached at tyson.greer@usa.net.

The manuscript for this book was prepared and submitted to Microsoft Press in electronic form. Text files were prepared using Microsoft Word for Windows. Pages were composed by Studioserv (www. studioserv.com) using Adobe PageMaker 6.5 for Windows, with text in Optima and display type in Optima Bold. Composed pages were delivered to the printer as electronic prepress files.

Cover Graphic
Designer and Illustrator
Becker Design

Interior Graphic Designer
Kim Eggleston

Interior Graphic Artist
Travis Beaven

Manuscript Editor
Gail Taylor

Principal Compositor
Steve Sagman

Project Coordinator
and Technical Editor
Devra Hall

Proofreader
Jill McManus

Indexer
Audrey Marr

You work with Microsoft® Office.

Now you want to build a great intranet.

Congratulations, you're nearly done.

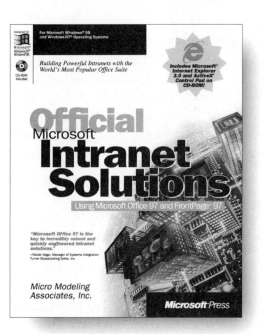

You don't need to start from scratch. In fact, once you upgrade to Microsoft Office 97, all you add is Microsoft FrontPage® 97, Microsoft Internet Explorer, and this book. Here technical managers and developers can discover how to use these popular programs to quickly create awesome, full-featured intranets that are easy for everyone to use—administrators and users alike. So build on the foundation you've already put in place. To find out how, get OFFICIAL MICROSOFT INTRANET SOLUTIONS.

U.S.A.	$39.99
U.K.	£37.49 [V.A.T. included]
Canada	$54.99
ISBN	1-57231-509-1

Microsoft®Press

Profitable strategies for a business revolution.

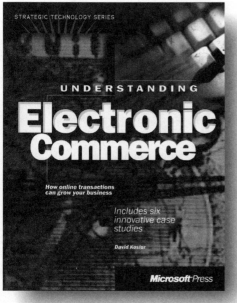

STRATEGIC TECHNOLOGY SERIES

UNDERSTANDING

Electronic Commerce

How online transactions can grow your business

Includes six innovative case studies

David Kosiur

***Microsoft* Press**

U.S.A.	**$19.99**
U.K.	£18.49
Canada	$26.99
ISBN	1-57231-560-1

In five years or less, analysts say, sales transactions on the Internet will total $100 billion annually. In short, online commerce is big and it's growing fast—and here's the book that shows you how to understand and profit from it. This invaluable overview includes:

- **Basics**—how electronic commerce works in the real world
- **Strategies**—the mind-set of companies that will get the most from electronic commerce
- **Consumer applications**—credit cards, digital money, and more
- **Business applications**—purchase orders, invoices, and other large transactions
- **Security**—its paramount importance and the five things it requires
- **The Future**—from electronic agents to microcash and microtransactions
- **Case studies**—insightful snapshots of electronic commerce innovatively applied

The *Strategic Technology* series is for executives, business planners, software designers, and technical managers who need a quick, comprehensive introduction to important technologies and their implications for business.

Microsoft Press® products are available worldwide wherever quality computer books are sold. For more information, contact your book or computer retailer, software reseller, or local Microsoft Sales Office, or visit our Web site at mspress.microsoft.com. To locate your nearest source for Microsoft Press products, or to order directly, call 1-800-MSPRESS in the U.S. (in Canada, call 1-800-268-2222).

Prices and availability dates are subject to change.

***Microsoft*® Press**

Register Today!

Return this
Understanding Intranets
registration card for
a Microsoft Press® catalog

U.S. and Canada addresses only. Fill in information below and mail postage-free.
Please mail only the bottom half of this page.

1-57231-702-7   *UNDERSTANDING*   *Owner Registration Card*
                      INTRANETS

_____

NAME

_____

INSTITUTION OR COMPANY NAME

_____

ADDRESS

_____

CITY   STATE   ZIP

Microsoft®Press
Quality Computer Books

For a free catalog of
Microsoft Press® products, call
1-800-MSPRESS